DELEGATING RIGHTS PROTECTION

Delegating Rights Protection

*The Rise of Bills of Rights in the
Westminster World*

DAVID ERDOS

OXFORD
UNIVERSITY PRESS

OXFORD
UNIVERSITY PRESS

Great Clarendon Street, Oxford OX2 6DP

Oxford University Press is a department of the University of Oxford.
It furthers the University's objective of excellence in research, scholarship,
and education by publishing worldwide in

Oxford New York

Auckland Cape Town Dar es Salaam Hong Kong Karachi
Kuala Lumpur Madrid Melbourne Mexico City Nairobi
New Delhi Shanghai Taipei Toronto

With offices in

Argentina Austria Brazil Chile Czech Republic France Greece
Guatemala Hungary Italy Japan Poland Portugal Singapore
South Korea Switzerland Thailand Turkey Ukraine Vietnam

Oxford is a registered trade mark of Oxford University Press
in the UK and in certain other countries

Published in the United States
by Oxford University Press Inc., New York

British Library Cataloguing in Publication Data

Data available

Library of Congress Cataloging in Publication Data

Data available

Typeset by SPI Publisher Services, Pondicherry, India
Printed in Great Britain
on acid-free paper by
MPG Books Group, Bodmin and King's Lynn

ISBN 978–0–19–955776–9

3 5 7 9 10 8 6 4 2

To the memory of my grandparents

Contents

Preface

Since early adolescence, I have been fascinated by the issue of constitutional reform and, in particular, how this relates to broader political, social, and cultural developments. As a teenager growing up in London in the early 1990s – before the days of the mass use of the Internet – I vividly remember writing off for information from the various British constitutional reform pressure groups, notably Charter 88, and devouring the literature which returned. At roughly the same period, I visited my relatives in New Zealand for the first time and, being interested in such matters, was introduced to current themes in law and politics in that country. Two factors immediately struck me. Firstly, similarly to the situation in Britain, many of the critical social and political issues confronting the public – a possible reform of the electoral system (then the subject of the first indicative referendum), the evolving relationship between Māori and Pakeha New Zealanders, and changes in the meaning of, and mechanisms for protecting, human rights – were, at root, deeply constitutional questions. Secondly, that, given the reality of a largely common 'Westminster' institutional heritage, there was a strong case for work examining Britain and New Zealand side by side. Travels to both Canada and Australia in the late 1990s led me not only to interest in both of those countries but also to an intellectual appreciation that this case for systematic comparison was also shared with this wider subset of countries.

This project on the socio-political origins of bills of rights has provided me with a wonderful opportunity, albeit somewhat circumscribed, to systematically test those hunches which I developed as a much younger student. Its concrete roots date from the doctorate which I completed at Princeton University in 2006. I, therefore, would particularly like to thank my dissertation supervisor at Princeton, Keith Whittington. Keith's wide knowledge and scholarship encouraged me to link my detailed study of the four Westminster cases to theoretical debates and controversies within a much broader literature. Beyond one's doctoral adviser, a project of so many years duration inevitably entails many other debts of gratitude. At a personal level, I would particularly like to thank the following individuals for their constructive help and/or advice at various points: Simon Baptist, Alfonso Donoso, Matthew Flinders, Denis Galligan, Elizabeth McLeay, Alan Renwick, and, most especially, Lisa Hilbink. I would also like to express my appreciation to my research assistants, namely, Ryan Goss (who helped on a great variety of matters), Tal Ofek and Yael Peled (who both worked on the Israeli case study touched on in the conclusion to this book), and Mila Versteeg (who proved invaluable in relation to the quantitative aspects of this study). I must, more generally, thank my colleagues at both the University of Oxford's Centre for Socio-Legal Studies and Balliol College for providing me with such a friendly and supportive atmosphere within which I could complete my analysis and writing. I also express my appreciation to both Victoria University of Wellington and the University of York (UK) for providing me with a much-needed academic base during various points in the last few years. In addition, I am most grateful to the various archives and archivists who provided such ready access to valuable documentary material, as well as the many individuals who agreed graciously to be interviewed. Oxford University Press has been immensely supportive of me throughout this project and I thank Dominic Byatt and Lizzy Suffling for all their help and guidance.

Both this and related academic work depended on funding support from a wide variety of sources. I particularly thank Oxford University (including Americans for Oxford), Princeton University, and the United Kingdom's Economic and Social Research Council (for a Postdoctoral Fellowship in 2007 (PTA-026-27-1514)). I also acknowledge the reproduction (in a modified and updated form) of material which has been published elsewhere, namely, on Australia ('Elite Supply "Blockages" and the Future of National Bill of Rights Initiatives in Australia: A Comparative Westminster Analysis', *Commonwealth & Comparative Politics* (Vol. 46) (2008) (http://www.informaworld.com)) and on the United Kingdom ('Ideology, Power Orientation and Policy Drag: Explaining the Elite Politics of Britain's Bill of Rights Debate', *Government and Opposition* (Vol. 44) (2009)).

Last, but certainly not least, I thank my family whose support has been a great source of strength to me over many years. My aunt and uncle, Mary and Trevor, have not only taken a keen interest in this work from its inception but also provided a home away from home in Wellington from which to base my New Zealand research. My family in Melbourne, especially my cousins Colin and Eric, did likewise during my trips to Australia. Finally, and most importantly, I thank my parents, and also my sister, without whose nurturing this project would have been impossible.

Note on Book Structure

This book forms an organic and logical whole. It develops from the broad theoretical and comparative material presented in Part I, through the detailed Westminster case studies of Part II, and finally ends in the integrative conclusions of Part III. Ideally, therefore, it should be read sequentially and as a whole. Despite this, I am conscious that many readers may principally be interested in just one country (e.g. the United Kingdom) or even just one case (e.g. the origins of the Canadian *Charter* 1982). To accommodate this likelihood, the book has been designed so that, so long as the reader reads the very short introductory first chapter in Part I, each of the case study chapters in Part II can be read separately and are largely self-standing. In the few instances where one of the case study chapters specifically refers back to material covered in a previous chapter, the index should provide the reader with the appropriate reference.

List of Charts

List of Tables

List of Abbreviations

ALP	Australian Labor Party
ASBO	Anti-Social Behavioural Order
BNA	*British North America Act*
BORI	Bill of Rights Institutionalization
CBORA	*Canadian Bill of Rights Act*
CCF	Co-operative Commonwealth Federation
CEDAW	*Convention on the Elimination of All Forms of Discrimination Against Women*
CORAF	*Canadian Charter of Rights and Freedoms*
DOCR	*Defence of Canada Regulations*
ECHR	*European Convention on Human Rights*
HPT	Hegemonic Preservation Thesis
HRA	*Human Rights Act*
ICCPR	*International Covenant on Civil and Political Rights*
ICERD	*International Convention on the Elimination of All Forms of Racial Discrimination*
ICESCR	*International Covenant on Economic, Social and Cultural Rights*
IPPR	Institute of Public Policy Research
JCHR	Joint Committee on Human Rights
NCCL	National Council for Civil Liberties
NDP	New Democratic Party
NZBORA	*New Zealand Bill of Rights Act*
NZCCL	New Zealand Council for Civil Liberties
OLS	Ordinary Least Squares
PCC	Press Complaints Commission
PTT	Postmaterialist Trigger Thesis
SIF	Society for Individual Freedom
SNP	Scottish National Party
UDHR	*Universal Declaration of Human Rights*

Part I

Foundations

1

Introduction

Bills of rights are instruments of critical importance, exerting, at least within advanced democracies, a systematic influence over the entire constitutional order. Legally, they define the basic rights of the individual or citizen. Politically, they demarcate the power and discretion of the State. Ideologically, they symbolize a society's commitment to, and understanding of, some of its most important values.

Most fundamentally, within political systems with the potential for strong 'support structures' for rights litigation (Epp, 1998), the presence and strength of a bill of rights significantly affects where a country's constitution should be placed along a continuum from political to legal conceptions. According to the political conception, which has traditionally dominated Westminster thinking on this subject, power is constituted and controlled via ordinary political institutions. There is no (non-controversial) demarcation between constitutional as opposed to ordinary legislation. Moreover, the guarantee of individual rights depends on the goodwill of the executive coupled with the ability of the parliament or legislature to hold ministers to account. In contrast, legal constitutionalism, which in the last hundred or so years has become increasingly dominant, is grounded in the idea that legally codified and entrenched provisions should exert a wide-ranging and prior authority over the determination of the legitimate as opposed to illegitimate and arbitrary exercise of power. Within this model, it is the judges who ultimately determine the normativity or otherwise of a particular state action. In other words

> The courts have been promoted from mere faithful executors of the legislative will to the high status of more or less equal protagonists. Representative institutions have been demoted from the sovereign entities of the nineteenth century and much of the twentieth to institutions hemmed in by legally enforceable constitutional limitations. (Mandel, 1998, p. 251)

Legally protected rights, as included in a bill of rights instrument, occupy a critical position within this later model. As Richard Bellamy states:

> Central to legal constitutionalism is the idea of constitutional rights. . . .
> [P]robably nothing has been so influential in driving constitutionalism
> along the paths of legal rather than political thought than the emphasis
> on rights, their entrenchment in a constitutional document and their
> interpretation and elaboration by a supreme or constitutional court. It is
> this rights focus that gives contemporary constitutionalism its whole
> juridical cast, whereby a constitution's task is viewed as being to embody
> the substance of fundamental law rather than to provide a fundamental
> structure for law-making. (Bellamy, 2007, p. 15)

Moreover, these rights encourage a reconstitution of the relationship between
the State and the individual. Political constitutionalism conceives this relationship as resting on the right of the individual citizen to participate in ordinary
political processes coupled with the concomitant duty of all to respect the
decisions of the democratic majority. In contrast, within a model of constitutionalized rights, the individual is conceived as being entitled to certain legal
protections even against the contrary wishes of this majority. This reconcep-
tualization may be linked to the increasing normative concern with the
individual and his or her rights that characterizes the modern era (Gearty,
2006).

   Such have been the effects of bills of rights that some argue that they can
transform the political system into nothing less than a juristocracy (Ewing,
1994; Hirschl, 2004*a*). In the rather less hyperbolic terms of this book, the
decision to enact a bill of rights undoubtedly involves an important delegation of power over the interpretation of rights from the ordinary political
branches to the judiciary. Whichever form of words is adopted, bills of rights
raise critical issues which touch the very nature and principles upon which the
political community is based. It is, therefore, surprising that their origins
have, with a few notable exceptions, received scant social scientific attention.
Instead, work in this area has been dominated by a legal profession concerned
largely with both an exegesis and normative critique of the bill of rights
case law.

   This book addresses this lacuna by constructing a socio-political explanation for the origins of bills of rights in stable, advanced, industrialized
democracies. This task is approached via the critical comparison of the
national experiences of four 'Westminster'-style democracies: Canada, New
Zealand, the United Kingdom, and Australia. These countries share a common political and legal culture which distrusts legalized protections of
rights. Despite this, national bill of rights outcomes exhibit a surprising
diversity, ranging from a constitutional bill of rights in Canada through to
no bill of rights at all in Australia. This combination of similarity and
divergence poses particular social scientific puzzles, the solutions to which

shed important light on the more general dynamics of bill of rights genesis in stable democratic settings.

1.1 CORE ARGUMENT: THE POSTMATERIALIST TRIGGER THESIS (PTT)

Through close consideration of these cases, I propose a new explanation for the deliberate adoption of a bill of rights in stable, advanced democracies, focused on a 'postmaterialist trigger'. This PTT argues that in such cases, bill of rights genesis has been secured by the confluence of the gradual development of background forces conducive to change (most notably the growth of a powerful postmaterialist rights constituency) and a political trigger which provides an immediate rationale and impetus for it. Turning first to the background element, social and economic development in the post-Second World War period weakened erstwhile ascriptive social ties and identities and encouraged the postmaterialist growth of a 'left–liberal' human rights constituency concerned to advance 'equal rights' (Inglehart & Welzel, 2005, p. 54) and 'self-expression' (*Ibid.*, p. 24). Influenced in part by transnational human rights developments, this new civil liberty and social equality constituency became attracted to bills of rights, forging a powerful and influential social movement in favour of reform. Nevertheless, incremental factors such as these, whilst important, are themselves insufficient to generate change. Instead, and secondly, a concrete trigger providing a clear and specific political rationale and impetus is also required. It is this trigger which determines the precise timing of any particular bill of rights. Such a trigger operates especially on incumbent political elites. Elite political actors must support reform if it is to succeed. However, given that bills of rights generally transfer decision-making rights away from these actors and to the judiciary, they will usually recoil from such proposals. This project has located two political triggers which can, temporarily at least, reorientate attitudes, thereby catalysing adoption of a bill of rights given the appropriate background conditions. Both triggers may be further galvanized by a strategically placed constitutional entrepreneur with clear normative preference for reform.

In the first place, this project may be championed by a newly ascendant political grouping as part of an 'aversive' reaction to prior negative political experiences during opposition. Here, a long period in opposition loosens prior attachment to a power-hoarding, executive-minded approach to political power. Additionally, specific perceptions of the previous government being heavy-handed and authoritarian leads to a new understanding of the value of restraints on political power which a bill of rights instantiates. As will be outlined in the subsequent chapters, this 'aversive' pattern explains the origins of the _Canadian Bill of Rights Act_ (CBORA 1960), the _New Zealand Bill of Rights Act_ (NZBORA 1990), and the _Human Rights Act_ (HRA 1998). Alternatively, a bill of rights project may develop in response to a 'threat to political stability' trigger. Here, in the face of destabilizing centrifugal regional or ethnic political forces, a bill of rights emphasizing common rights held throughout the country may be perceived by political elites as providing a critical mechanism for reasserting the primacy of the national polity and national political identity. The origins of the _Canadian Charter of Rights and Freedoms_ (CORAF 1982) fits this 'threat to political stability' pattern. Both the background postmaterialist and the contingent political trigger factors structure the nature of bill of rights genesis which is forthcoming. Regarding the strength of the bill of rights enacted, the type of political trigger appears especially important. The 'aversive' trigger, rooted in reactions to past experience as opposed to clear, prospective self-interest, can generate only relatively weak bills of rights. It is, therefore, unsurprising that the CBORA (1960), the NZBORA (1990), and the HRA (1998) are all ordinary statutory enactments drafted so as to require executive-vetting of human rights compliance but not judicial overruling of governmental decision-making. In contrast, the 'threat to political stability' trigger, which is substantially grounded as an immediate and pressing self-interested concern to preserve the authority of national political institutions, engendered the stronger and constitutionalized CORAF (1982). Contrary to the dominance of trigger factors in determining the strength of bills of rights, their scope is shaped more by the background postmaterialist civil libertarian and social equality constituency. As Appendix A details, the various government-sponsored bills of rights enacted or proposed in Westminster democracies since 1960 have all included nine core legal and due process rights, five core civil rights, and a right to equality or non-discrimination. In contrast, socio-economic rights including, in particular, protections related to private property have generally been omitted. Even here, however, political triggers usually play a role. For example, the Canadian _Charter_'s particularly strong protection of equality rights, multicultural rights, aboriginal rights and, most especially, pan-national language rights reflects the goal of strengthening the common national identity against centrifugal threats. On the other hand, reflecting their 'aversive' origins, both the CBORA (1960) and the NZBORA (1990) emphasize core due process rights which were seen as having been threatened during the previous administration.

The PTT presented here contributes to broader debates on the origins of legal and political change. It links a growing literature on the concrete political effects of value change (Van Deth & Scarborough, 1995), the veto capacities of political elites (Tsebelis, 2002), and the role of both 'focusing events' (Baumgartner & Jones, 1993) and 'policy windows' (Kingdon, 2003) in triggering change. More specifically, the PTT's emphasis on the role of political triggers, even in stable democratic settings, importantly mirrors the finding (which will be outlined in Chapter 2) that the origins of formally strong bills of rights are generally associated with the particularly powerful political trigger of regime transition. Finally, the thesis also connects to a growing literature exploring the changing understanding and role of human rights within advanced industrialized society.

1.2 STRUCTURE OF THE BOOK

This book is structured into three parts and nine chapters. Most chapters are case-specific, exploring bill of rights outcomes in particular Westminster democracies. It is, therefore, important to reflect at the outset on how each chapter contributes to the broader demonstration of the value of the post-materialist trigger perspective.

The first three chapters (Part I) provide an overview of the basic material underpinning and structuring the entire project. This chapter has explained the importance of considering the socio-political origins of bill of rights genesis in stable, advanced democracies and provided a brief summary of the book's PTT. Chapter 2 is more analytical and comparative, outlining the basic concepts of bill of rights genesis, the history and worldwide development of bills of rights, and, finally, the specific puzzles which national bill of rights outcomes within the Westminster democracies raise for social science. Chapter 3 explores the PTT by comparing it to other theories of bill of rights genesis in the literature.

Part II, which comprises five chapters, explores bill of rights outcomes in each of the Westminster democracies under study, concentrating on both the social constituencies supporting reform and particular events or developments that may have engendered it. More specifically:

- Chapter 4 explores the origins of the CBORA (1960). It demonstrates that, in the lead-up to this enactment, bill of rights genesis was strongly supported by an increasingly politically salient social equality and civil libertarian constituency. The early interest of this constituency in a bill of rights is partially explained by the close cultural and people-to-people links between Canada and the United States. Finally, the Diefenbaker

Government's support for the CBORA is related to an 'aversive' reaction to perceived civil liberty abuses committed during the previous Liberal Administration.

- Chapter 5 focuses on the Canadian CORAF (1982). The chapter elucidates the origins of the *Charter* in an attempt to counter the centrifugal forces unleashed by the Québecois nationalist project. The critical role of civil libertarian and social equality forces in supporting the project is also outlined. Finally, the chapter explores how these two factors together determined both the *Charter*'s strength and scope.

- Chapter 6 concerns New Zealand, beginning with the proposal to enact a bill of rights during early 1960s. This failed because civil liberty and social equality groups were poorly developed, formalized legal rights protections were distrusted, and only a very weak trigger was present. In contrast, by the 1980s, a clear 'aversive' trigger rooted in the perceived authoritarian excesses of Robert Muldoon's National Party Government (1975–84) coupled with a strengthened civil liberty and social equality community, ensured the enactment of the albeit statutory and relatively weak NZBORA (1990).

- Chapter 7 examines bill of rights developments in the United Kingdom. Public debate gradually emerged from the late 1960s onwards, prompted by the increasing salience of a postmaterialist civil liberty and social equality lobby and growing European pressures to adopt more formalized protections for human rights. Attitudes among the political elite meanwhile ebbed and flowed in response to the emergence and then dissipation of specific triggers or focusing events. In particular, the Labour Party's interest in a bill of rights in the 1990s which led to the HRA (1998) was prompted by an 'aversive' reaction to its experience of the perceived abuses of executive authority under the Conservatives (1979–97), especially during the premiership of Margaret Thatcher (1979–90).

- Finally, Chapter 8 considers Australia, focusing on why it still lacks a national bill of rights. A strong civil liberty and social equality constituency, clearly committed to securing a bill of rights, has emerged since the late 1960s. Given the particularly large size of the 'multicultural' community, this constituency is at least as powerful as in other Westminster democracies, such as New Zealand and the United Kingdom. Nevertheless, elite political 'blockages' have prevented enactment. In particular, since the late 1960s, Australia has lacked the presence of a clear political trigger providing elites with an impetus for change.

The final concluding chapter (in Part III) draws together the main themes of the book and considers their broader implications. It considers the applicability of these findings beyond the Westminster world by examining the case of Israel. Finally, it reflects on the relevance of the PTT to broader debates on the origins of constitutional reform and the conceptualization of rights in postmaterialist societies.

2

The origins of bills of rights: concepts and comparative development

Before proceeding further, it is necessary to step back to consider some basic concepts. What exactly is a bill of rights? How can variation in the designed strength of bills of rights be captured and formalized? These definitional questions are addressed in Section 2.1. Section 2.2 then surveys the origins and global spread of bills of rights within the democratic world. Finally, Section 2.3 compares bills of rights in Westminster democracies with these overall patterns and reflects on the particular value for social science on exploring the four Westminster cases further.

2.1 CONCEPTS AND DEFINITIONS

2.1.1 National bill of rights

The bill of rights concept has been subject to considerable ambiguity and historical dispute. As Charles Parkinson (2007, p. 3) has noted, 'the phrase Bill of Rights has been used at various times in different contexts by different people. Even today there is no standard definition'. The first legal usage of the term can be dated to 1689 when, in the wake of the Glorious Revolution, the English Parliament enacted the *Bill of Rights* (1689). As has been widely remarked in the literature, this instrument was largely concerned with defining the rights of Parliament vis-à-vis the prerogative powers of the Crown (Schwartz, 1977, p. 22). In other words, it was primarily concerned with regulating and policing intra-State institutional relationships. In contrast, bills of rights today regulate the relationship between the State and its citizens (or, more widely, those subject to its jurisdiction). They achieve this aim by outlining, and giving legal effect to, a range of fundamental human or civil rights. In other words, a bill of rights, at least of the modern stripe, is an instrument which sets out a broad set of fundamental human or civil rights and grants these rights an overarching status within the national legal order.

2.1.2 Constitutional bill of rights

Overarching legal status for fundamental rights is usually achieved by including a bill of rights in the national constitution. Indeed, reflecting this, Parkinson argues that the term bill of rights should be reserved for such constitutional instruments. He defines a bill of rights as 'a set of provisions in a domestic constitution protecting individual rights that can be enforced by a court and can restrict the actions of the legislature and executive' (Parkinson, 2007, p. 4) (emphasis added). Nevertheless, in a number of situations, especially in the Westminster world, rights instruments have also been enacted in ordinary statutory form.[1] Parkinson labels these enactments 'Declarations of Rights'. However, far from being merely declaratory, such instruments, no less than their constitutional cousins, do make rights justiciable and grant them an overarching status within the law. As Lord Rodger has commented in relation to the United Kingdom's *Human Rights Act* (HRA 1998):

> The 1998 Act is unusual – perhaps unique – in its range. Whilst most statutes apply to one particular topic or area of law, the 1998 Act works as a catalyst across the board, whenever a Convention right is engaged. It may affect matters of substance, in such areas as the law of property, the law of marriage and the laws of torts. Or else it may affect civil and criminal procedure, or the procedure of administrative tribunals. (*Wilson v. First County Trust* (2003))

Given that both constitutionalized and statutory rights instruments serve such a similar function in the legal order, it would be inappropriate to exclude the latter from the definition of what constitutes a bill of rights.

2.1.3 National bill of rights institutionalization (BORI)

The fact that the designed strength of both constitutional and statutory rights instruments differ significantly provides a further reason for adopting this more inclusive definition. The strength of a bill of rights or, in other words, the extent of its effect on the legal and political system, depends in part on factors that emerge after its enactment including the degree of 'activism' by the judiciary and the extent to which it is used by potential litigants. Also important, however, are designed endogenous variables including

- the *status* of the bill of rights,
- its *rigidity*, and
- its *scope*.

The legal *status* of a bill of rights is determined by its relationship to, and effect on, other law. As previously noted, all bills of rights grant the rights they contain some form of overarching status within the legal system. These rights are usually supreme against any contrary non-constitutional legal provision. In other situations, however, the overarching status is weaker. Specific injunctions may be included, designed to limit the judicial function. For example, in Sweden, judicial invalidation of legislation under the bill of rights is possible but can be carried out only 'if the error is manifest' (Congleton, 2003, p. 143). In yet other cases, specified laws may be expressly exempted from compatibility with the bill of rights. The Jamaican Constitution contains a 'savings clause',[2] which 'preserves from invalidity all laws which were in force immediately before the Constitution came into effect, as well as all actions taken under the authority of those laws' (Barnett, 1977, p. 434). Near-identical provisions were also included in the independence constitutions of the Bahamas, Barbados, Belize, Guyana, and Trinidad and Tobago (Newton, 1988, p. 37). In Canada, a limiting provision of somewhat similar significance is included in the statutory *Canadian Bill of Rights Act* (CBORA 1960) (which applies only to the federal sphere) and the constitutional *Canadian Charter of Rights and Freedoms* (CORAF 1982) (which applies to all levels of government). Both instruments include 'notwithstanding' provisions allowing the federal parliament or provincial legislatures to exclude specified legislation from conformity with all (in the case of the *Canadian Bill of Rights*) or most (in the case of the *Charter*) rights which these instruments otherwise protect.[3] Finally, instruments such as the *New Zealand Bill of Rights Act* (NZBORA 1990) and the United Kingdom's HRA (1998) have an even weaker legal status. The rights these instruments set out must inform the interpretation of all other law[4] and, therefore, have an overarching effect. In neither case, however, may courts use the instrument to void the legal effect of primary legislation that is clearly incompatible with these rights,[5] though, in the case of the HRA (1998), they can issue a formal Declaration of Incompatibility.[6]

The *rigidity*, or designed durability, of a bill of rights depends on how easily it can be amended or repealed. As Lijphart (1999) has usefully outlined, it is possible to array rigidity (or by contrast flexibility) according to whether amendment or repeal requires a simple majority or a supermajority and, if so, how large any required supermajority is. Some bills of rights, such as the *Basic Law on Human Dignity and Liberty* enacted in Israel, are not especially legally protected at all. However, as Tom Ginsburg (2003, p. 5) notes, even in these cases, the enactments are likely to 'maintain great

normative power as constitutional legislation and politically are more difficult to amend than legislation concerning routine matters of governance,
even if not institutionally protected'. At the other extreme, at least parts
of a bill of rights may be completely insulated from lawful change. For
example, Section 79.2 of the German *Basic Law* prohibits amendment of 'the
essence' of any constitutionally enshrined right. Between these two types,
legal amendment procedures differ widely. Difficult procedural hurdles are
found in the United States where, under Article V of the constitution,
amendment of the *US Bill of Rights* requires the assent not only of
two-thirds of both the House of Representatives and the Senate but also
three-quarters of the State legislatures.[7] In contrast, under Article 138 of the
Italian Constitution, amendment of the bill of rights requires only
an absolute majority in both chambers of the Italian Parliament followed
by a referendum.[8]

Finally, the *scope* of a bill of rights depends on the range of rights it
includes. Many bills of rights, especially in the advanced industrialized
world, focus on protecting only a limited range of civil and political rights.
But others extend further. For example, the *United States Constitution*
(Amendment V (1791)) includes wide-ranging negative protections for
private property vis-à-vis the government. Even more extensively, the new
South African bill of rights protects a wide range of positive linguistic,
social, and economic rights.[9] Finally, the scope of a bill of rights should
be discounted (or, in Lijphart's language, 'demoted' (1999, p. 213)) if it
only protects rights that the State is already bound to respect through an
international mechanism. This applies to the United Kingdom's HRA.

The concept of 'bill of rights institutionalization' captures these important
differences in designed strength. It measures the extent to which a bill of
rights is designed to affect the overall legal and political system. Other things
being equal, a bill of rights exhibits greater *institutionalization*: the stronger is
its legal *status*, the greater its *rigidity*, and the greater the *scope* of the rights it
protects. Given that, in advanced democracies with well-developed legal
structures, all bills of rights are likely to have important systematic effects,
even low institutionalization matters. Meanwhile, high institutionalization is
designed to have a genuinely radical effect that fundamentally alters the
pattern or model of democracy within a country (Flinders, 2009). Chart 2.1
summarizes the concept of BORI both as an integrated measure and as
divided along the three dimensions of *status*, *rigidity*, and *scope*. (The precise
construction and operationalization of this variable is further outlined in
Appendix B).

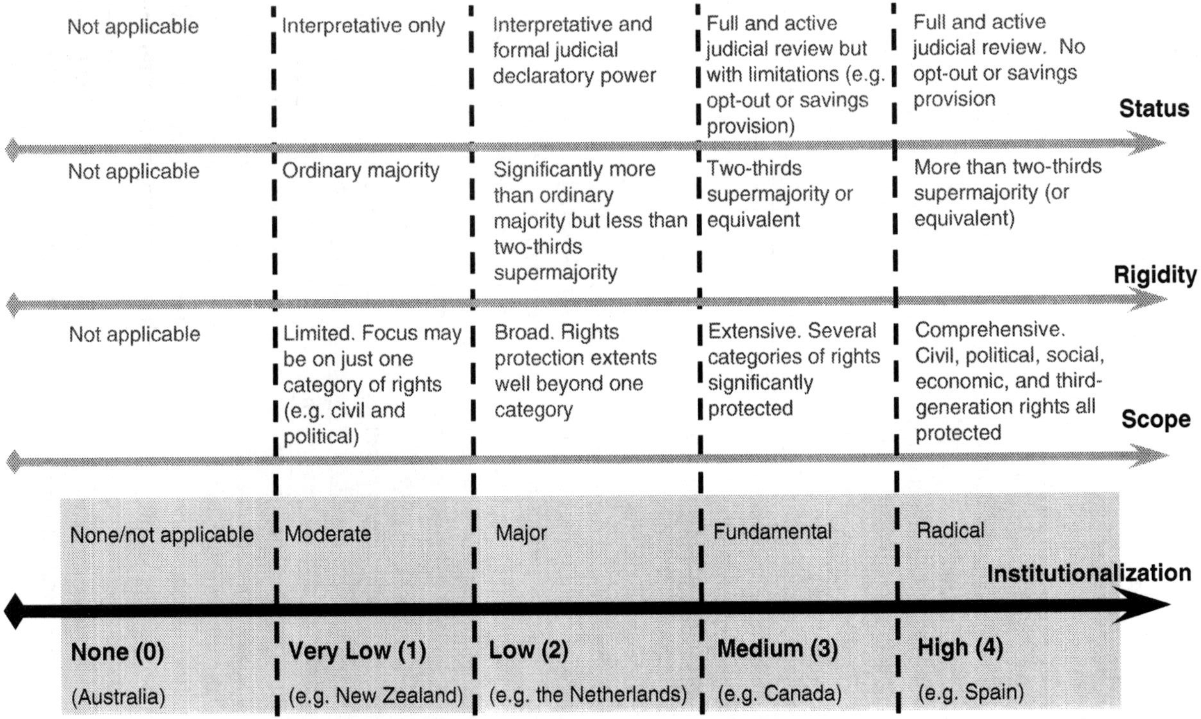

	None (0) (Australia)	Very Low (1) (e.g. New Zealand)	Low (2) (e.g. the Netherlands)	Medium (3) (e.g. Canada)	High (4) (e.g. Spain)
Status	Not applicable	Interpretative only	Interpretative and formal judicial declaratory power	Full and active judicial review but with limitations (e.g. opt-out or savings provision)	Full and active judicial review. No opt-out or savings provision
Rigidity	Not applicable	Ordinary majority	Significantly more than ordinary majority but less than two-thirds supermajority	Two-thirds supermajority or equivalent	More than two-thirds supermajority (or equivalent)
Scope	Not applicable	Limited. Focus may be on just one category of rights (e.g. civil and political)	Broad. Rights protection extents well beyond one category	Extensive. Several categories of rights significantly protected	Comprehensive. Civil, political, social, economic, and third-generation rights all protected
Institutionalization	None/not applicable	Moderate	Major	Fundamental	Radical

Chart 2.1 Bill of rights institutionalization (BORI)

2.2 THE DEVELOPMENT OF THE BILL
OF RIGHTS MODEL

Table 2.1 outlines bill of rights outcomes within thirty-six democracies. Whilst less than a full set of democratic countries, this group provides a broadly representative sample, including both less-developed and more-developed countries and examples of each of the three waves of democratization identified by Huntington (1991). Significantly, the countries comprise the same set as used in Lijphart's seminal study *Patterns of Democracy* (1999), thus allowing comparison between bills of rights (not directly explored by Lijphart) and other constitutional features. This set also includes all the Westminster democracies examined in this study.

The table first shows whether a country has a national bill of rights and, if so, whether this is formally part of the constitution or not. It then details the level of BORI, both at the time the bill of rights was first adopted (column three) and currently (column four).[10] These figures are presented to the nearest two decimal places. They can then be recalibrated to the nearest integer. Very roughly 0=no BORI, 1=very low BORI, 2=low BORI, 3=medium BORI, and 4=high BORI. Within these categories, the extensive variation between the countries should also be noted. Years of enactment of the national bill of rights currently in force are given in the fifth column.[11] Finally, columns six to eleven summarize factors that might explain variation in levels of institutionalization. Column six indicates the adoption context, namely, whether a bill of rights was adopted at a moment of clear general political transition (e.g. independence, regime change) or not. Column seven lists whether the judiciary is structured to provide review over national bill of rights matters via a centralized Kelsenian constitutional court system (labelled 'Yes') or, contrawise, whether this review is diffused or decentralized throughout the regular court system (labelled 'No'). This variable distinguishes between two core types of system for resolving constitutional law disputes (Kelsen, 1942; Shapiro & Stone Sweet, 2002). Column seven states whether the country in question has a British heritage. This measure also captures a major distinction within legal and political systems. Finally, columns nine to eleven list three variables, namely, federalism, bicameralism, and central bank independence, which divide power within the political system. In each case, a higher score indicates a stronger division of power. By shifting rights protection responsibilities from the ordinary political branch to the judiciary, bills of rights also divide power. Therefore, according to the logic of Lijphart's *Patterns of Democracy* thesis (1999), we may expect a positive correlation between these variables and BORI.[12]

Table 2.1 National bill of rights institutionalization (BORI) in select democracies

Country	National bill of rights	BORI (time of adoption)	BORI (current/2006)	Year of adoption	Transition bill of rights	Centralized review	British heritage	Federalism	Bicameralism	Central bank independence
Australia	No	0.00	0.00	N/A	No	No	Yes	5	4	0.42
Austria	Constitutional	3.08	3.17	1945	Yes	Yes	No	4.5	2	0.53
Bahamas	Constitutional	2.58	2.58	1973	Yes	No	Yes	1	2	0.4
Barbados	Constitutional	2.17	2.17	1966	Yes	No	Yes	1	2	0.4
Belgium	Constitutional	2.83	3.58	1831	Yes	No	No	3.2	3	0.28
Botswana	Constitutional	2.58	2.58	1966	Yes	No	Yes	1	2.5	0.32
Canada	Constitutional	3.00	3.00	1982	No	No	Yes	5	3	0.52
Colombia	Constitutional	3.33	3.33	1991	No	Yes	No	1	3.2	0.33
Costa Rica	Constitutional	3.33	3.50	1949	Yes	No	No	1	1	0.39
Denmark	Constitutional	2.75	2.75	1953	No	No	No	2	1	0.46
Finland	Constitutional	3.67	3.67	2000	No	No	No	2	1	0.28
France	Other	2.42	2.58	1971	No	Yes	No	1.3	3	0.29
Germany	Constitutional	3.42	3.42	1949	Yes	Yes	No	5	4	0.69
Greece	Constitutional	3.00	3.33	1975	Yes	Yes	No	1	1	0.38
Iceland	Other	2.75	2.75	1944	Yes	No	No	1	1.4	0.34
India	Constitutional	3.33	3.25	1950	Yes	No	Yes	4.5	3	0.35
Ireland	Constitutional	2.50	2.50	1937	No	No	Yes	1	2	0.41
Israel	Other	1.08	1.08	1992	No	No	Yes	3	1	0.39
Italy	Constitutional	3.33	3.33	1948	Yes	Yes	No	1.5	3	0.26
Jamaica	Constitutional	2.50	2.92	1959	Yes	No	Yes	1	2	0.35

Japan	Constitutional	3.75	3.75	1949	Yes	No	No	2	3	0.25
Luxembourg	Constitutional	3.00	3.08	1868	Yes	No	No	1	1	0.33
Malta	Constitutional	3.25	3.25	1964	Yes	No	Yes	1	1	0.41
Mauritius	Constitutional	3.17	3.17	1968	Yes	No	Yes	1	1	0.43
The Netherlands	Constitutional	2.17	2.17	1983	No	No	No	3	3	0.48
New Zealand	Other	1.17	1.17	1990	No	No	Yes	1	1	0.2
Norway	Constitutional	2.67	3.00	1814	Yes	No	No	2	1.5	0.17
Papua New Guinea	Constitutional	3.17	3.17	1975	Yes	No	Yes	3	1	0.42
Portugal	Constitutional	3.67	3.67	1976	Yes	Yes	No	1	1	0.28
Spain	Constitutional	3.58	3.58	1978	Yes	Yes	No	3	3	0.25
Sweden	Constitutional	1.83	2.50	1975	No	No	No	2	1	0.29
Switzerland	Constitutional	2.83	2.83	1999	No	No	No	5	4	0.63
Trinidad and Tobago	Constitutional	2.58	2.58	1976	No	No	Yes	1.3	2	0.39
United Kingdom	Other	1.50	1.50	1998	No	No	Yes	1	2.5	0.28
United States	Constitutional	3.25	3.25	1789	Yes	No	Yes	5	4	0.56
Venezuela	Constitutional	3.33	3.33	1999	No	No	No	4	3	0.37
Average		2.74	2.82							

What can be gleaned about the origins of bills of rights both from this table and other relevant comparative material? In the first place, column three demonstrates that in the majority of cases, the bill of rights currently in place was adopted since the Second World War. To an extent, this reflects the historical rarity of constitutional stability (Elkins, Ginsburg, & Melton, 2007). In addition, however, it suggests that the bill of rights model may have emerged as a regular part of the constitutional furniture only relatively recently. Analysis of wider historical material indicates that this is correct. Whilst a constitutional bill of rights was enacted in the United States as early as the eighteenth century (Schwartz, 1977), this country remained in a generally anomalous situation until at least the twentieth century. A few other political systems did accept the value of abstract rights declarations somewhat earlier. The French Constituent Assembly adopted *La Déclaration des droit de l'Homme et du citoyen* (the Declaration of the Rights of Man and the Citizen) in 1789, whilst Austria adopted the *Staatsgrundgesetz über die allgemeinen Rechte der Staatsbürger* (State Fundamental Law on the General Rights of Citizens) in 1867 (Hausmaninger, 2000). However, these instruments rejected strong judicial oversight over the enforcement of the enunciated values. In particular, as Baker has noted, the idea underpinning the *Déclaration* was enlightenment through the act of publication, rather than any notion of judicial control (Baker, 1994). Similarly, full judicial review of the *Staatgrundgesetz* was not possible since, as Kelsen (1942, p. 185) notes, '[b]efore the [Austrian] Constitution of 1920 came into force the Austrian courts had the power to test the constitutionality of statutes only in so far as the due publication of the latter was concerned'. In the aftermath of the First World War, a number of the defeated States, including Germany (1919) and Austria (1920) did include broad rights guarantees within their new constitutional documents (De Smith, 1961). Ensuring respect for these rights was theoretically overseen by a centralized court whose sole responsibility was to enforce constitutional norms (Kelsen, 1942). Nevertheless, the extent of such oversight was severely curtailed, in particular, by very restrictive rules of standing. As Kelsen (1942, p. 195) notes, under the 1920 Austrian Constitution '[p]rivate parties could only suggest judicial review, they had no legal right to demand it'.

Secondly, however, it is clear that bills of rights have now become nearly ubiquitous in democratic countries. All but one of the samples of thirty-six countries has a national bill of rights of some sort. Moreover, in the great majority (86%) of cases, this instrument is part of a written and entrenched constitution. Turning directly to the BORI measure, the average-level institutionalization is 2.74 at the time of adoption or 2.82 currently. This reflects a 'medium' level of formal bill of rights development in both cases.

Turning to the potential correlates or explanatory variables of BORI, it is helpful to run some simple statistical regressions. Given that the dependent variable is specified according to a considerable number of potential values, Table 2.2 estimates an ordinary least squares (OLS) regression with Hubert/ White robust standard errors. The first column of the table reports the OLS results for institutionalization levels at the time of bill of rights adoption. As can be seen, these results demonstrate that adopting a bill of rights at a moment of political transition is positively correlated with high levels of BORI (significant at the 5% level). In fact, adoption at transition is associated with a 0.66 increase in the BORI score. Meanwhile, a British heritage is correlated with lower levels of BORI (also significant at the 5% level). Specifically, having a British heritage correlates to having a BORI score 0.70 lower than non-British heritage countries. By contrast, there is no evidence of a significant relationship between BORI and any of the other variables included. The third column of Table 2.2 reports the OLS result for current institutionalization levels. Again, political transition and British heritage are significant at the 5% level. Since BORI is measured on an ordinal scale, columns two and four of Table 2.2 re-estimate the specification from columns one and three, respectively, in an ordered probit model.[13] The

Table 2.2 Determinants of bill of rights institutionalization (BORI)

	Time of adoption		Current	
	OLS	Ordered probit	OLS	Ordered probit
Transition	0.66**	1.02**	0.70**	1.20***
	(0.26)	(0.40)	(0.25)	(0.42)
Centralized review	0.10	0.27	−0.02	0.20
	(0.24)	(0.52)	(0.22)	(0.50)
British heritage	−0.70**	−1.07***	−0.83**	−1.37***
	(0.31)	(0.40)	(0.31)	(0.42)
Federalism	−0.06	0.06	−0.04	0.08
	(0.19)	(0.19)	(0.13)	(0.18)
Bicameralism	0.04	0.04	−0.01	0.06
	(0.25)	(0.25)	(0.14)	(0.25)
Central bank independence	0.71	0.71	1.28	−0.49
	(1.88)	(1.88)	(1.30)	(1.80)
Observations	36	36	36	36
R-squared (pseudo)	0.37	(0.08)	0.43	(0.10)

***, **, and * denote significance at the 1, 5, and 10% levels, respectively.

finding that both political transition and British heritage are important predictors of BORI is robust using this alternative model.[14] Chapter 9 of this book will return to a consideration of some of these comparative results and their relevance to this study.

2.3 WESTMINSTER PUZZLES AND THE WIDER VALUE OF THIS STUDY

More directly and immediately related to this project, it is clear that whether a country is a Westminster democracy significantly influences the timing and extent of BORI. The current average level of national BORI in Westminster democracies is 1.42, which is considerably lower than the average across all thirty-six democracies of 2.82. This result underpins the first rationale for

Table 2.3 National bill of rights outcomes in Westminster democracies

Country	National bill of rights	Key features
Canada	*Canadian Bill of Rights Act* (CBORA 1960)	• Statutory instrument • Covers federal action only • Protects mainly civil and political rights • 'Notwithstanding' opt-out (rarely invoked)
	Canadian Charter of Rights and Freedoms (CORAF 1982)	• Constitutional instrument • Protects civil, political, linguistic, and aboriginal rights • Covers federal and provincial action • 'Notwithstanding' opt-out for most civil and political rights (rarely invoked)
New Zealand	*New Zealand Bill of Rights Act* (NZBORA 1990)	• Statutory instrument • No judicial strike-down power • Protects civil and political rights
United Kingdom	*Human Rights Act* (HRA 1998)	• Statutory instrument • No judicial strike-down power (but explicit Declaration of Incompatibility power) • Protects mainly civil and political rights but also rights to education and property
Australia	None (but limited sub-national statutory bills of rights adopted in Australian Capital Territory (Human Rights Act (ACT) (2004)) and the State of Victoria (*Charter of Rights and Responsibilities Act* (2006)))	

examining bill of rights origins specifically in these cases: Westminster democracies appear particularly reluctant to adopt the bill of rights model.

Secondly, it is significant that, even in this subset, three out of four countries have proceeded, albeit within limits, along the path of national BORI. This raises critical questions about the particular social and political origins of these instruments and, given that none was correlated with any general political transition, their specific timing. Table 2.3 summarizes key aspects of these cases.

Thirdly, and most significantly, despite their shared legal and political heritage, there is substantial variation among the Westminster cases in their level of national BORI. Canada sits within the 'medium' category of BORI. Its institutionalization level of 3.0 is still marginally higher than the average for all the thirty-six democracies. By contrast, Australia has no national bill of rights. In between these two cases, both the United Kingdom and New Zealand exhibit BORI, albeit of a rather low level. Explaining this intra-Westminster variation should shed interesting light on variation elsewhere, especially in other non-transition cases.

2.4 CONCLUSIONS

The first part of this chapter outlined the basic concepts or variables which this book studies. It defined the term bill of rights and constructed a measure of its designed strength which it labelled 'bill of rights institutionalization'. The second part measured this institutionalization in the thirty-six democracies analysed by Lijphart (1999) and correlated it against a range of potential independent variables. Whether a bill of rights was adopted at a moment of general political transition or not was found to be important, with higher BORI being associated with adoption during such transition. By contrast, having a British legal and political heritage was systematically correlated with lower levels of BORI. More specifically, the very anomalous position of the Westminster democracies was vividly highlighted: Westminster democracies exhibited markedly lower average institutionalization than other democracies. Significant intra-Westminster variance was also apparent. These results confirm the broader relevance of studying national bill of rights outcomes in Westminster democracies as explored in Section 2.3.

This book is principally conceived as a qualitative study of specific cases. However, the operationalization of BORI and the quantitative results generated in this chapter will inform the analysis that follows. The concluding section of this book will return explicitly to the broader relevance of these results. Before turning to particular cases, it is also important to critically analyse social science theories of bill of rights genesis including, in particular, the Postmaterialist Trigger Thesis which this book forwards. This is the task of Chapter 3.

3

Theorizing the origins of bills of rights

Although substantively focused on the study of four Westminster democracies, this book contributes to a broader theorization of the origins of bills of rights. More specifically, it forwards a Postmaterialist Trigger Thesis (PTT) designed to explain the deliberate adoption of a bill of rights in stable, advanced democracies. This chapter provides a detailed overview of this theory exploring its understanding of both the long-term background and the contingent political triggers, which structure the bill of rights institutionalization (BORI). The PTT, however, did not develop within a theoretical vacuum. To the contrary, it was influenced, both negatively and positively, by other perspectives, including, in particular, theories within the existing literature. As will become evident, these theories not only influenced the PTT, they also constituted rival frameworks for the explanation of the origins of bills of rights in stable, advanced democratic settings.

3.1 POLITICAL TRIGGERS AND RISING TIDES: THE PTT

The PTT holds that the deliberate enactment of a bill of rights in stable, advanced democracies depends on two discrete forces: firstly, the development of long-range background pressures favouring a bill of rights (notably, the emergence of a postmaterialist rights constituency) and, secondly, the presence of a contingent and discrete political trigger. Both types of forces must be present for BORI to take place. Moreover, both pervasively structure key features of the bill of rights which is forthcoming, including, in particular, its timing, scope, and strength. This section elucidates these two types of factor including how they interact to bring about concrete reform.

3.1.1 Postmaterialism and background pressures
for bill of rights genesis

In order to explain the development of background forces favouring BORI, it is first necessary to consider the broader theory of postmaterialism. This theory argues that changes in socio-political values and attitudes emerge from more basic socio-economic developments. More specifically, postmaterialist theory holds that 'individuals pursue various goals in hierarchical order – giving maximum attention to the things they sense to be their most important unsatisfied needs at a given time' (Inglehart, 1971, p. 991). In societies with low socio-economic development, an overwhelming emphasis is placed on the need to secure 'physical substance and safety' (Inglehart, 1971, p. 66). Moreover, the fact that people tend to interact economically and socially within closely knit, and often small, groups leads to the construction and maintenance of tight ascriptive identities and relatively sharp boundaries between insiders and outsiders. These societal features, however, are gradually undermined by socio-economic development. In particular, an advanced industrial society is associated with greatly increased material prosperity, which, it is argued, leads citizens to place 'less intense emphasis on economic growth' (*Ibid.*, p. 57) and concomitantly more emphasis on non-economic issues such as 'belonging, self-expression and the quality of life' (*Ibid.*, p. 66). The development of this broader, postmaterialist outlook is also encouraged by the growth of the number of jobs requiring higher cognitive education and skills and more intellectually demanding and autonomous work patterns. At the extreme, '[h]uman efforts are no longer so much focused on producing material objects as on communicating with others and processing information; the crucial products are innovation, knowledge and ideas' (Inglehart & Welzel, 2005, p. 28). An advanced industrial economy is also associated with a diversification of human exchanges. '[H]uman interaction is increasingly freed from the bonding ties of closely knit groups, enabling people to make and break social ties readily' (*Ibid.*, 2005, pp. 28–9). In the more 'individualized' (Beck & Beck-Gernstein, 2001) society which results, a new emphasis is placed on the fundamental value of each individual. This may also lead to a reduced support for traditional and hierarchical organizations and authorities such as the police, armed forces, and big business (Dalton, 2004, p. 105). At the same time, however, these developments can leave citizens feeling more exposed, at risk, and vulnerable, thus encouraging 'growing demands for greater regulation and social control' (Durodié, 2007, p. 441).

Finally, given both that value preferences are largely fixed during early socialization and that postmaterialist values are engendered by higher levels of education and material prosperity, the postmaterialist thesis holds that postmaterialist values will be particularly prominent within a young, middle-class, and university-educated constituency (Inglehart, 1990). Despite their generally above-average earning capacity, these individuals will often associate with the left of the political spectrum. This linkage flows from postmaterialists' strong commitment to projects of 'radical social change' (Inglehart, 1971, p. 992) which often engage the power of the State for their implementation. A left–postmaterialist alliance is also encouraged by the declining size and political salience of the working class and the concomitant decline of traditional Marxist-inspired ideology (Inglehart & Rabier, 1986, p. 464). These other results of socio-economic development reduce the power of the traditionalist left's political constituency, encouraging it to reach out to new groups of citizens including postmaterialists.

The emergence of a general postmaterialist value orientation, which has been documented throughout the advanced industrialized world (Scarborough, 1995), leads to a more particular reorientation as regards attitudes towards human rights. In the first place, a growing public emphasis on a wider array of (non-economic) values and concerns encourages an increased focus on questions connected with civil liberties and human rights more generally. Secondly, and more particularly, the declining salience of traditional ascriptive identities and communities engenders increased support for the value of social or human equality. As Inglehart and Welzel (2005, p. 54) state: 'Equal rights for women, gays and lesbians, foreigners and other out-groups tend to be rejected in societies where survival seems uncertain but are increasingly accepted in societies which emphasize self-expression values'.

Thirdly, this greater emphasis on civil liberties, social equality, and self-expression leads to increased demands that fundamental civil and political liberties be subject to more formal protection (*Ibid.*, p. 2). A new focus on the need for formalization may be further encouraged by the growing sense of vulnerability to arbitrary action which a more individualized society tends to produce. Fourthly, however, increased emphasis on civil liberties, social equality, and self-expression should not be confused with the development of an outlook based on a presumption of State non-interference. To the contrary, given that postmaterialism engenders a broadening out of areas seen as appropriately regulated publicly, this development is associated with 'increasing pressures on governments to deal with all manner of problems' (Van Deth, 1995, p. 3). Additionally, the growing perception of risk that individualization engenders, as well as a weakening of informal mechanisms for responding to such risks, stimulates demands that the State take a more active role in supervising, auditing, and certifying both itself and others so as to ensure an increasingly 'risk-free' society.

The PTT holds that the growing salience of the postmaterialist rights constituency constitutes the most pervasive and important background factor favouring (and structuring) BORI in stable, advanced democracies. In each of the countries analysed in this study, a coalition of civil liberty and social equality groups came to support a bill of rights, seeing it as a potentially powerful mechanism for furthering its interests and values.[1] Moreover, these groups also exerted an important influence over the content of the bills of rights enacted or proposed. As Appendix A details, all the government-sponsored national bills of rights enacted or proposed within Westminster democracies since 1960 have included nine core legal and due process rights, five core civil rights, and a right to equality or non-discrimination. Furthermore, the imprint of postmaterialism's rejection of a presumption of State non-interference is also apparent, most obviously, in the absence of a general right to private property in a majority of the bills of rights enacted or proposed by Westminster governments since the Second World War.

The PTT does not claim that the development of a postmaterialist rights constituency constitutes the only background factor impacting on BORI. To the contrary, whilst asserting its centrality, it recognizes that other factors will exert important effects, both negative and positive. Firstly, as recognized within postmaterialist theory more generally (Inglehart & Welzel, 2005, pp. 48–76), existing cultural traditions will continue to exert a systematic influence. In particular, British-descended Westminster political culture, with its strong defence of parliamentary sovereignty and distrust of formalized rights provisions, pervasively limits the nature of BORI. This is reflected in the much lower average BORI score for Westminster democracies compared even to other non-transition cases. Nevertheless, these traditions do evolve over time. There is, for example, substantial evidence that Westminster political culture is becoming more supportive of the special legal protection of human rights (Scarman, 1974; Woolf, 1995). Secondly, transnational forces encouraging a formalized approach to human rights governance also exert an independent effect on bill of rights outcomes. These forces have operated in a highly asymmetric fashion in the Westminster cases. Australia and New Zealand have been subject only to distant and diffuse normative and mimetic transnational influence through international initiatives such as the *Universal Declaration of Human Rights* (UDHR 1948) and the *International Covenant on Civil and Political Rights* (ICCPR 1966/1977) and the widespread adoption of constitutional bills of rights throughout the democratic world in the post-Second World War period. Meanwhile, Canada, with its much stronger cultural and people-to-people ties with the United States, has been affected by rather more powerful transnational forces. These have, nevertheless, remained indirect, normative, and mimetic in nature. In contrast, the United Kingdom has been subject to much more direct pressures as a result of its membership of the *European Convention on Human Rights* (ECHR) system. This combines normative, mimetic, and ultimately coercive elements. Its strong influence is reflected in the fact that the UK *Human Rights Act* (HRA) is closely modelled on the transnational ECHR.

Chart 3.1 summarizes the PTT's understanding of the development of postmaterialist background forces favouring BORI in stable, advanced democratic settings. The chart first details important system-level transformations which are prompted by socio-economic development within advanced industrialized society. Then, changes in individual social value orientations which flow out of these broader transformations are outlined. Finally, the chart details those directly political value reorientations relating especially to constitutions and rights which arise from the more abstract social value reorientations. Included here in shaded boxes are other specific influences not directly associated with postmaterialist developments. As the last column indicates, all these changes encourage, and shape, an important system-level development, namely, BORI.

3.1.2 Political triggers and bill of rights institutionalism

Notwithstanding the clear importance of these background factors, they are not sufficient to bring about BORI. In particular, in the light of the fact that bills of rights transfer scarce decision-making rights from the political elite to the judiciary, the development of background postmaterialist pressures on its own will not convince incumbent political elites to champion change. And the active support of the incumbent political elite is invariably required for successful BORI. Nevertheless, the emergence of a political trigger providing actors with an immediate impetus for change can transform the elite political environment, making BORI possible. As well as determining the precise timing of change, the nature of the political trigger influences the type of bill of rights adopted, including its strength and, generally, its scope. Such a trigger will be particularly powerful if it is exploited by a strategically placed constitutional entrepreneur with a strong ideological commitment to reform. By contrast, if, as in Australia, no such trigger is present, efforts to secure such a reform will prove unsuccessful. This study has located two political triggers which can catalyse change.

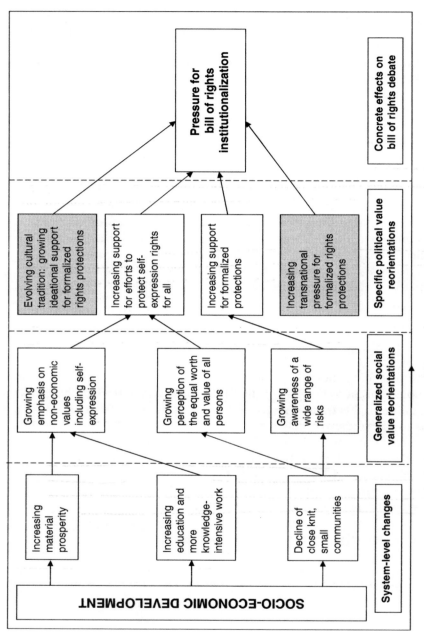

Chart 3.1 Background forces favouring bill of rights institutionalization (BORI): the Postmaterialist Trigger Thesis (PTT) model (after Inglehart, 1977)

'Aversive' political trigger

An 'aversive' political trigger arises when a newly resurgent political elite is motivated to champion a bill of rights in reaction to prior negative political experiences in opposition. Here, a long period in the political wilderness loosens commitments to the power-hoarding, executive-minded approach associated with parties of government. Additionally, an experience of such opposition under a government perceived as heavy-handed and authoritarian leads to growing support for specific institutional restraints on political power.[2] As such an elite senses a change in its electoral fortunes and, there-fore, a new chance to return to power, self-interest may result in a faltering of interest in these reforms. Nevertheless, normative self-entrapment and policy drag still ensure that real reform can occur. Given that 'aversive' constitution-alism is not based on a strictly rational, prospective calculation of self-interest, however, only a relatively weak bill of rights is likely to be adopted. Moreover, given the nature of these experiences, the resulting bill of rights will likely emphasize protection against the 'procedural' abuses of the past, as opposed to active promotion of more 'substantive' values such as a strong right to equality.

The genesis of the *Canadian Bill of Rights Act* (CBORA 1960), the *New Zealand Bill of Rights Act* (NZBORA 1990), and the HRA (1998) all fit within this 'aversive' template. In each case, only a relatively weak, statutory instru-ment was enacted. Both the CBORA (1960) and the NZBORA (1990) were clearly worded to provide a bulwark against the perceived procedural abuses committed by the previous government. In relation to CBORA, Christopher MacLennan (2003, p. 127) notes that it 'was designed with the 1940s civil liberties infringements clearly in mind'. Similarly, Kenneth Keith, a key adviser on the NZBORA, stated in 1985 that

> [t]he draft New Zealand Bill places major emphasis on the processes of government – writ large and small. There is consequently less emphasis on . . . substantive rights than is to be seen in some instruments. That is to say, substantive rights are left rather more to the political processes, processes which are protected and enhanced by some of the provisions. (Keith, 1985, p. 312)

Meanwhile, in the United Kingdom, the centrality of European factors ensured that the HRA (1998) was not framed as a free-standing instrument, but rather was almost entirely derived from the wording of the ECHR. Nevertheless, it bears notice that the ECHR itself is a highly proceduralist instrument designed to offer strong protection only of a very narrow range of largely procedural civil liberty and democratic rights. Moravcsik finds that, in contrast to the abstract and broad-ranging UDHR (1948), 'the precise enumeration of rights [in the ECHR] ... was considerably narrower than that granted by any member state [of the Council of Europe] with such a constitutional enumeration. ... The final document ... was constrained to include only the least controversial among basic political and civil rights' (Moravcsik, 2000, pp. 234–5).

'Threat to political stability' trigger

Under the 'threat to political stability' trigger, commitment to enacting a bill of rights emerges within political groupings challenged by centrifugal threats to the continuing stability of a country's political regime. Through such a project, they aim to construct institutions which can bolster national political allegiance in preference to the development of fissiparous regional identities. Given this, any bill of rights proposal emerging from such a dynamic will likely emphasize a set of substantive understandings and rights broadly shared by citizens across a wide geographical area. This trigger is also substantially grounded on a clear, prospective, and self-interested rationale, namely, a desire among elites to preserve and enhance their existing institutional position. Therefore, the threat to political stability trigger will generally be associated with elite support for relatively strong BORL.

The genesis of the *Canadian Charter of Rights and Freedoms* (CORAF 1982) fits the 'threat to political stability' trigger. The *Charter* was clearly designed to re-establish the dominance of pan-Canadian identity and institutions in the wake of the development of a potent Québécois nationalism, which threatened to destabilize the entire political system. The resulting instrument gave particular emphasis to substantive rights which transcended provincial identities, including a powerful open-textured equality provision (*Constitution Act* (1982), Section 15), the protection throughout the country of the linguistic rights of both the anglophone and francophone communities (Sections 16–23), the promotion of Canada's multicultural heritage (Section 25), and the special safeguarding of its aboriginal communities (Section 35). Meanwhile, throughout the process, the federal political elite remained strongly committed to a strong, fully constitutional, as opposed to merely statutory, model for the bill of rights. This was eventually achieved, albeit with the inclusion (added as a result of the vigorous efforts of eight out of ten provincial leaders) of a 'notwithstanding' clause allowing for an opt-out from conformity with some of the civil and political rights that the *Charter* enunciated (*Constitution Act* (1982), Section 33).

3.2 THE PTT AND EXISTING THEORY

Whilst there is a rich literature on bills of rights, this body of work has generally not developed a tight theoretical perspective on the origins of these instruments. Ran Hirschl (2004*a*, p. 4) notes that 'despite the fact that courts now play a key role in dealing with the most contentious social and political issues, the field of comparative judicial studies in general, and the study of the political origins and consequences of judicial empowerment in particular, remain relatively underresearched and undertheorized'. Instead of examining socio-political origins, scholarship on bills of rights has focused on doctrinal issues, from either an empirical or, more usually, normative standpoint. This focus reflects the dominance of lawyers within this area of study. As Kahn-Freund (1974, p. 27) famously argued, most lawyers have proved averse to exploring law's 'social, and above all its political context'. Meanwhile, work that is directly relevant to the analysis of the origins of bills of rights in internally stable, advanced democratic settings is spread across a wide range of academic disciplines, including political science and history, as well as law. As a result, many of these perspectives have engaged little with each other. The PTT builds on these diverse perspectives. This section elaborates them in turn. To begin with, existing approaches that relate to the longer-range or background aspects of the PTT will be considered, including constructivist theory, institutionalist theory, transnational diffusion theory, the Knowledge Class Thesis, and neo-Marxist theory. Thereafter, two theories which relate more to the political trigger aspect of the PTT – the Political Insurance Thesis and the Hegemonic Preservation Thesis (HPT) – are considered. This division broadly maps on to the 'demand/supply' (or 'push/pull') continuum proposed by Tom Ginsburg (2003, p. 11). At one pole on this continuum are 'push' or 'demand' theories, which hold that bill of rights outcomes depend on the strength of long-term, background demands to enact a bill of rights. At the other pole are 'pull' or 'supply' theories which, contrariwise, argue that outcomes are determined within the elite political realm by factors structuring the incentives to supply such an instrument.[3] Table 3.1 briefly summarizes the core tenets of each of these theories alongside that of the PTT.

Delegating Rights Protection

Table 3.1 Rival theories of bill of rights origins in stable, advanced democracies: key claims

---

Postmaterialist Trigger Thesis (PTT)

- Rising demand for bill of rights institutionalization (BORI) linked to growing postmaterialist emphasis on self-expression, social equality, and need for formalization.
- Concrete reform also requires, and is shaped by, a political trigger providing elites with an immediate impetus for change.
- Political trigger need not be rooted in prospective self-interest of elite but may instead reflect an 'aversive' reaction to perceived authoritarian excesses experienced during opposition.

Constructivist theory

- Bill of rights outcomes structured by normative processes such as socialization and persuasion.
- Spread of bill of rights model reflects moral reaction against the Second World War atrocities.
- Reticence of Westminster world to adopt bill of rights model linked to cultural allegiance to parliamentary sovereignty and organic common law.

Institutionalist theory

- High BORI correlated with presence of other institutions that divide power (e.g. federalism, bicameralism, and central bank independence).
- Divided power institutional matrix correlated with larger and more heterogeneous populations.
- Claim that in situations of high social pluralism political stability requires such explicit constraints.

Transnational diffusion theory

- Bill of rights outcomes pervasively influenced by policies adopted or pursued in other countries.
- Precise bill of rights outcome reflects nature of country's transnational relationships.
- Transnational influence most likely persuasive or mimetic in nature, but may also be coercive.

Knowledge Class Thesis

- BORI results from agency of cultural left special interests.
- Lack of electoral clout coupled with easy access to legal resources make such reform efforts attractive.
- Cultural left's disproportionate influence on political elite ensures reform success.

Neo-Marxist theory

- BORI results from agency of capitalist economic elite.
- Alleged conservatism of judiciary and egoistic nature of rights make such reform efforts attractive.
- Growing democratic threat to capital's interests provide further impetus for reform.

Background/demand-focused theories

Political Insurance Thesis

- Bill of rights outcomes reflect power and positional self-interest of political elite who must supply such an instrument.
- Political elites facing uncertain political future will support BORI as 'insurance' against potential damage inflicted by their political opponents.
- If such elites currently hold power, then bill of rights reform likely.

Hegemonic Preservation Thesis (HPT)

- Bill of rights outcomes reflect power and self-interest of political elites representing cultural and economic elite.
- Such elites will support BORI if threatened by peripheral minority groups.
- Bill of rights project will also be supported by neo-liberal economic elite and conservative judicial elite.

Trigger/supply-focused theories

3.2.1 Background/demand-focused explanations of BORI

Constructivist theory

Within much of political science, actors' preferences are assumed to be fixed and to reflect self-interested goals such as the maximization of resources. Interaction between agents is strictly strategic, each seeking to maximize their utility in the light of both their own and other actors' preferences and resource constraints. In other words, a logic of power predominates. In contrast, constructivist theory proceeds from the assumption that actors' preferences, and even their very identities, are products of socialization, including the internalization of the norms of a particular political culture. Constructivist theory also holds that actors' preferences and identities remain subject to change through norm-altering processes such as intersubjective persuasion. Intersubjective persuasion refers to a process where agents 'actively assess the *content* of a particular message – a norm, practice or belief – and change their minds' (Goodman & Jinks, 2004, p. 635).

As previously noted, the legal discipline, long dominant within scholarship on bills of rights, has generally concerned itself with doctrinal matters. Nevertheless, when attention has shifted to the origins of these instruments, a constructivist account, albeit rather under-theorized, has often been preferred. Within this perspective, the ideational origins of bills of rights is sometimes traced back many centuries including to Enlightenment thinking (Weinrib, 1999, p. 26) or even the Magna Carta of 1215 (Schwartz, 1977). More immediately, the global spread of bills of rights throughout the second half of the twentieth century is interpreted as a normative reaction to the atrocities of war and Nazism. Canadian legal scholar Lorraine Weinrib (1999, p. 25), one of the leading proponents of this constructivist approach, argues:

In the post-war period, in the aftermath of the most egregious transgres-
sion of the basic norms of civilized society, it became a priority for
liberal democracies to distinguish those norms from other fungible
preferences.... Just as the Universal Declaration reflected this new respect for human rights at the international level, so it was mirrored by the
institutional development of 'constitutional [bill of rights] guarantees' at
the level of the nation state.

These ideational imperatives, it is further argued, received a new boost following
the collapse of the ideological appeal of Marxism after the end of the Cold War.
According to Conor Gearty (2006, p. 27), this development allowed human
rights 'to step fully onto the centre-stage that the Universal Declaration had
erected for it. Socialists, trade unionists and radicals have found themselves
joining liberals and Christian democrats in the human rights camp'.

Within this legal constructivist literature, it is usually recognized that, notwithstanding their democratic and human rights credentials, Westminster democracies have generally rejected strong bills of rights. This rejection is explained by
widespread societal allegiance to specific normative understandings of the law and
the role of Parliament 'woven into the fabric of the English [and Westminster]
cultural tradition' (De Smith, 1961, p. 87). The Westminster understanding of law
is understood as being rooted in a common law which is organic and specific,
developed by precedents and linked to concrete remedies built up over many
centuries (Patapan, 1997a, 1997b). Bills of rights, being abstract *a priori* 'declarations or definitions of rights' (Dicey [1908] 1959, p. 197), are in clear tension with
such an understanding. The eminent British and Commonwealth constitutional
scholar, Stanley De Smith (1961, p. 86) commented that '[t]he English lawyer
finds political manifestoes out of place in a legal document, particularly when
their philosophical foundations are insecure. He instinctively prefers brass tacks to
noble phrases, pragmatism to metaphysics, and obstinately insists that the proof
of the pudding is in the eating'.

Westminster culture is also underpinned by the principle of parliamentary
sovereignty. Contemporary theorists such as Jeffrey Goldsworthy (1999)
argue that the Westminster political tradition has considered Parliament to
be the most authoritative voice of the people, with the right of the nation to
legislate through Parliament recognized as the highest form of liberty which
the law must uphold.[4] Meanwhile, Albert Venn Dicey ([1908] 1959, p. 40),
writing on the British Constitution in the nineteenth century, famously stated
that Parliament had 'the right to make or unmake any law whatever' and,
further that 'no person or body is recognized by the law of England as having
a right to override or set aside the legislation of Parliament'. In stark contrast,
the bill of rights model conceives constitutional protections as 'a thing
apart' which the judiciary must use to constrain legislators, just as much as

individuals, should their acts conflict with it (Tocqueville, [1835/40] 1969, p. 101). Within this understanding, it is the bill of rights document itself, rather than Parliament, which 'represents the will of the whole people' (*Ibid.*, p. 101).

Institutionalist theory

A rather less abstract background theory argues that bills of rights will be associated with related constitutional constraints. For example, Arend Lijphart (1984, 1999) links judicially enforced rights protections to a written constitution and a supreme court. In turn, he finds these constraints correlated with other institutions which divide political power, namely, bicameralism, judicial review, federalism, and central bank independence. This suggests that bills of rights should be seen not as discrete entities, but rather as integral parts of what Lijphart labels 'federal' institutions.

Lijphart argues that the presence of strong 'federal' institutions is best explained, not only by the size of a country's population, but also by the degree of social pluralism. Exactly how these variables influence institutional design is left rather opaque. In relation to population size, it is often suggested that the increasing size of the State leads to a complexity in governance that is best eased through a division of labour across multiple governmental institutions. Meanwhile, the linkage between social pluralism and 'federal' institutions can be explained in both ideational and more instrumental terms. Ideationally, deciding fundamental matters through the ordinary democratic process poses a particular legitimacy problem where citizens are divided into discrete ethnic or religious groups. A need is, therefore, created for special institutions to police fundamental matters. More instrumentally, these societies may be plagued by political instabilities which can be overcome only via the construction of explicit, durable, and binding rules establishing a relatively rigid framework of government. In this vein, Barry Weingast (1997, pp. 256–7) argues that 'instability plagues democracy in most divided societies because ethnic divisions impede resolution of the coordination dilemma about the appropriate role of the state. . . . Where divided societies have risen above their divisions, they do so by constructing explicit and self-enforcing constraints on the government that protect the various groups'.

Transnational diffusion theory

Transnational diffusion theory holds that policy change is strongly influenced by the courses of action pursued in other jurisdictions. Policy diffusion occurs when 'government policy decisions in a given country are systematically conditioned by prior policy choices made in other countries (sometimes mediated by the behavior of international organizations or even private actors or organizations)' (Simmons, Dobbin, & Garrett, 2006, p. 787). In relation to the decision to adopt bills of rights, this approach argues that '[h]uman rights laws and institutions have not only proliferated across the globe but, as some evidence suggests, also look increasingly similar in very different states. And more strikingly, different states have adopted rather similar national rights laws and institutions' (Versteeg, 2008, p. 8). Therefore '[t]here seems reason to believe that the global proliferation and alleged convergence of rights institutions – both national and international – reflect processes of diffusion' (*Ibid.*, p. 36).

Despite this common focus on transnational diffusion, works within this literature have identified divergent mechanisms by which it may occur. Some mechanisms, namely persuasion and acculturation, are transnational cognates of the constructivist processes identified above. However, both transnational coercion and transitional competition are also possible. These refer to situations '[w]hereby states and [transnational] institutions influence the behavior of other states by escalating the benefits of conformity or the costs of nonconformity through material rewards and punishments' (Goodman & Jinks, 2004, p. 633). These 'material rewards and punishments' may encompass anything from use of brute force through to softer forms of economic and diplomatic pressure.[5]

Generally, the transnational diffusion literature on human rights has emphasized the dominance of persuasion and acculturation (Goodman & Jinks, 2004; Versteeg, 2008). For example, American constitutional scholar Frederick Schauer (2005, p. 907) writes on the 'migration of constitutional ideas', giving emphasis to informal ideational influence in his account. According to Schauer, it is this influence which

> makes nationhood without a single written document now unthinkable, the positive experiences of the United Kingdom, New Zealand, and perhaps Israel notwithstanding. It is a process that leads television-watching Chinese to demand their *Miranda* rights when they are arrested. And it's a process that has engendered an increasingly well-known and acrimonious Supreme Court debate in the United States as the Court debates the propriety of references to foreign law. (*Ibid.*, pp. 915–16)

In this sense, the transnational diffusion theory and the constructivist account elucidated above overlap. At the same time, however, even Schauer admits to the presence of other non-ideational transnational processes, arguing that 'political influence [and] economic interests' (*Ibid.*, p. 916) also play a role in the birth of the 'transnational constitution' (*Ibid.*, p. 913).

Whatever the particular mechanisms or processes posited, an important common claim of transnational diffusion theorists is that policy outcomes within particular states reflect the nature of their transnational relationships. Within this perspective, the continued reluctance of Westminster democracies to fully embrace the bill of rights model is related not only to the cultural understandings of these countries themselves, but also to the continued strong cultural links between them, especially in the legal arena (Zines, 1991). At the same time, however, new forms of transnational interaction, such as the United Kingdom's engagements with the European Union and European Convention system, may underpin a reorientation of attitudes (Nicol, 2001; Madsen, 2004).

Knowledge Class Thesis

A more self-evidently power-based background theory is the Knowledge Class Thesis, developed in relation to Canada by F. L. Morton and Rainer Knopff (Morton, 1992; Morton & Knopff, 2000) and given a comparative treatment by Robert Bork (2002). This thesis has the following structure. Firstly, it suggests that the postmaterialization of advanced industrialized democracies has resulted in the development of a coterie of strategically placed, power-hungry cultural left special interests with 'an ambitious agenda for social reform' (Morton & Knopff, 2000, p. 86). Secondly, however, it holds that these groups lack 'electoral clout' (Morton & Knopff, 2000), particularly on specific controversial issues: 'The New [or Knowledge] Class's problem in most nations is that its attitudes command only a political minority. It is able to exercise influence in many ways, but, when cultural and social issues become sufficiently clear, the intellectual class loses elections' (Bork, 2002, p. 8). Nevertheless, and thirdly, these actors possess disproportionate access to the political elite, especially on the left on the political spectrum (*Ibid.*, p. 9). Finally, such groups also possess disproportionate legal resources including skilled lawyers and sympathetic judges who, it is alleged, support reform with the aim of exerting 'judicial activism' and even 'judicial imperialism' (*Ibid.*). As a result, it is claimed that these groups find it both possible and in their interests to push for BORI, thereby moving power to the courts and subverting the legitimate democratic interests of the majority of citizens (Morton & Knopff, 2000, p. 149).

Focusing on the origins of the Canadian *Charter*, Morton and Knopff (2000) argue that three specific interests make up this 'knowledge' or 'new' class: 'unifiers', civil libertarians, and social equality seekers. 'Unifiers' aim to counter 'the forces of decentralizing regionalism and provincialism' (*Ibid.*, p. 60). Civil libertarians aim to 'set limits to the power which the ruler should be suffered to exercise over the community' (*Ibid.*, p. 54). Social equality seekers work to ensure equality for groups facing not economic, but rather social discrimination rooted in 'life-style issues and the politics of identity' (*Ibid.*, p. 67). More generally, Morton and Knopff argue that 'social engineers' will support bill of rights genesis. This more amorphous grouping is composed of those who

> take the view that the social evils of this world are caused not by human nature but rather by defective social institutions. Cure the institutional ills, they believe, and natural human goodness will prevail. Such a cure, of course, implies comprehensive reconstruction of the defective social structures; i.e. social engineering. For example, social engineers believe that crime has no natural causes, that it can be explained almost completely by such structural factors as class inequality, and that it can be cured through appropriate structural change. (*Ibid.*, p. 74)

Neo-Marxist theory

Similarly to the Knowledge Class Thesis, neo-Marxism has also developed a strongly power-based understanding of BORI. However, in stark contrast to the Knowledge Class theorists' focus on the role of the 'cultural left', neo-Marxist scholars including J. A. G. Griffth in the United Kingdom and Michael Mandel in Canada have argued that bill of rights projects have been engineered by the capitalist economic elite in order to protect their hegemonic power and interests.

Three principal claims underpin this understanding. In the first place, neo-Marxists argue that the rights usually included in bills of rights do not protect fundamental aspects of human personhood. Rather, they entrench atomistic, egoistic, and antagonistic relations among individuals and between individuals and the State. These relations, whilst socially harmful, are argued to be intrinsic to the capitalist system. Michael Mandel (1998, p. 254) claims that bills of rights are designed

> to draw a sharp line between the political and economic, to declare the economic a 'private sphere', despite the enormous social power wielded there, a realm of 'freedom', even though the only thing that was free was the exercise of powerful and massively unequal market forces, and where, far from being 'free', each vote had to be bought in hard currency according to the principle of 'one dollar, one vote'.

It is possible to trace this perspective back at least to Marx's own writings. In particular, in *On the Jewish Question* (1843), Marx writes on what he mockingly labels 'human rights in their authentic form, the form they have in the writings of their discoverers, the North Americans and the French!' (Marx

[1843] 1978, p. 59). The context indicates that he principally has in mind those rights instantiated in the *US Bill of Rights* (1791) and also the *French Déclarations des droit de l'Homme et du citoyen* (1789). According to Marx, these rights are 'nothing but the rights of ... egoistic man, man separated from other men and the community' (*Ibid.*, p. 60). Moreover, the alleged freedom or emancipation they offer is only 'that of man treated as an isolated monad and withdrawn unto himself' (*Ibid.*, p. 60).

A second claim relates to the nature of the judiciary which, as a result of bill of rights genesis, is given an enhanced role in the formation of public policy. Far from being the figures of probity and neutrality often assumed by the cultural theories discussed above, neo-Marxists argue that the judiciary re-presents the interests of the capitalist ruling class. In particular, it is noted that the higher judiciary are recruited from a narrow socio-economic stratum of society and occupy high positions of authority alongside others 'in Govern-ment, in the City or in the Church' (Griffith, 1977, p. 214). For neo-Marxists, rather than following any abstract principles, judges' attitudes are reflective of the 'viewpoint of their own class' (*Ibid.*, p. 195), especially when political concerns come to the fore: 'The politics of the judiciary are not based on a developed philosophy, still less on a mature theology. [Instead] [t]hey are based on emotions and gut reactions' (Griffith, 1981, p. 12). From this, according to Griffith, it follows that '[t]he judicial conception of the public interest ... is threefold. It concerns, first, the interests of the State (including its moral welfare) and the preservation of law and order, broadly interpreted; secondly, the protection of property rights; and thirdly the promotion of certain political views normally associated with the Conservative party' (Griffith, 1977, p. 195). Given the enhanced role which such an instrument allocates the judiciary, it follows that the enactment of a bill of rights (at least in its constitutional form) will 'as night follows day' result in 'the strengthen-ing of the conservative right' (Griffith, 1993, p. 118).

Third, and finally, neo-Marxists link the growing interest in enacting bills of rights during the latter half of the twentieth century less to a moral reaction against the atrocities of the Second World War and more to an increased threat to hegemonic economic power resulting from the growth of a mass electorate. In particular, according to Mandel (1998, p. 253), it was as a result of these threats that '[t]hey [the ruling elite] changed everything (namely constitutional theory) so that everything (namely the oligarchy of the wealthy) would remain the same. They placed boundaries around govern-ment action and called on the legal profession to police the boundaries'. In other words, BORI 'was intended to operate and does operate as an antidote to democracy, that it was meant to preserve the oligarchy of private property from the mortal danger posed by representative institutions elected by the people without property, a. k. a., *the demos'* (*Ibid.*, p. 252).

The relationship of the PTT to demand/push-focused explanations

The PTT had been developed in engagement with all five theories outlined above and borrows positively from at least three of them. In particular, according to the PTT, constructivist theory correctly identifies a role for entrenched cultural traditions and dynamic intersubjective normative debate in structuring political outcomes. In fact, postmaterialist theory generally has increasingly recognized that cultural traditions not only persist but also continue to systematically structure political attitudes (Inglehart & Welzel, 2005). Additionally, a nuanced understanding of postmaterialism understands that the relationship between socio-economic development and preference development relates only to the development of broad tendencies or value orientations. This leaves an important role for not only strategic, but also normative, interaction amongst agents over the formulation of specific policy outcomes. Secondly, transnational diffusion theory valuably elucidates the various mechanisms through which transnational developments influence domestic policy change. Nevertheless, the PTT rejects both constructivist and transnational diffusion theory as dominant explanations even of the background forces structuring BORI. It argues that these theories fail to properly appreciate the critical role of value change rooted in domestically situated socio-economic development. Moreover, these theories generally offer little explanation of the particular modalities through which change occurs, thereby downplaying the role of both agency and of individual and group preference formation.

The PTT shares most in common with the Knowledge Class Thesis. In particular, both theories hold that the development of postmaterialist rights constituencies constitutes the most powerful factor favouring BORI in stable, advanced democracies. Nevertheless, even at the level of this background factor, there are important differences. In particular, in contrast to the Knowledge Class Thesis's focus on a coterie of 'special interest' groups, the PTT emphasizes broader societal value shifts in underpinning support both for these groups and for constitutional change more generally. Secondly, the PTT disputes the assumption of an inherent linkage between supporters of national authority ('unifiers') and postmaterialism. In fact, as Inglehart has cogently argued, other things being equal, postmaterialists will actually tend to favour decentralization and regional autonomy, seeing this as a valuable mechanism for building a more pluralist democracy (Inglehart, 1990, p. 302).[6]

The PTT shares least, meanwhile, with neo-Marxist theory. Neo-Marxist theory is correct to argue that bills of rights have been rooted in classic liberal understandings of the human person and his or her relationship with the State. Nevertheless, whilst historically this has entailed a defence of economic freedom, this connection has been significantly undermined during more recent times. As previously mentioned, it is notable that only a minority of the bills of rights enacted or proposed in Westminster democracies have included rights to private property. Moreover, even in such cases, the protections offered have been significantly less substantial than in classic instruments such as the *US Bill of Rights*. This reflects the fact that recent bills of rights genesis has been championed and structured not by neo-liberal economic actors (as neo-Marxists contend), but rather by postmaterialist rights interests including civil libertarians and social equality seekers.

A final problem with all five of these theories is that none grapple effectively either with the critical and independent role of incumbent political elites or with the need for a clear political trigger. Section 3.2.2 examines two theories which do address these important, and related, issues.

3.2.2 Trigger/supply-focused explanations of BORI

The Political Insurance Thesis

The Political Insurance Thesis, developed by Tom Ginsburg (2002, 2003) and later refined and expanded by others including Jodi Finkel (2004, 2005), rejects the notion that social demands or pressures are what fundamentally drive either BORI or other forms of constitution-making. Instead, this theory argues that these outcomes are primarily influenced by variables which determine whether and, if so, how and to what extent it is in the interest of elite politicians to supply a bill of rights. Ginsburg (2002, p. 51) argues that 'constitution-making is dominated by the short-term interests of the designers rather than the long-term interests of the citizenry. Under such circumstances, it is likely that the politicians who draft the constitution seek to design institutions that benefit them narrowly rather than citizens broadly'. In these circumstances, the critical questions to ask are not which social interests support the genesis of a bill of rights and why but rather 'why is it that politicians would be interested in providing it?' (Ginsburg, 2003, p. 11).

Three factors underpin the political insurance theorists' focus on the interests of incumbent elites. Firstly, they argue that those who hold elite political office must actively support bill of rights genesis if it is to proceed. In other words, these actors occupy a key 'veto gate' position (Ginsburg, 2002,

p. 51). Secondly, they reject a pluralist understanding of political power which fuses the interests and priorities of political elites to the social interests they represent. Instead, they note that political elites possess distinct positional interests and priorities including, most particularly, maximizing their own power and discretion.[7] Thirdly, they argue that bills of rights systematically reduce incumbent power by transferring scarce policy-making rights from ordinary political institutions to the courts. Therefore, BORI has the potential to impose 'severe costs' (Finkel, 2004, p. 61) on incumbents and, in most cases, will be rejected by them. In contrast, opposition politicians may see an increase in 'judicial neutrality and authority' (Finkel, 2005, p. 101) as providing a welcome restraint on the power of their political opponents.[8] However, these actors are generally politically ineffective in Westminster systems.

Notwithstanding their general wariness or hostility, the Political Insurance Thesis holds that, in specific and relatively rare circumstances, BORI may dovetail with the power interests of incumbent elites. Specifically, when these actors expect to lose power in the future, it may be to their advantage to trade the 'upfront costs' of an immediate reduction in their power for 'future protection' in terms of additional constraints on the power of forthcoming governments (Finkel, 2005, p. 102). As Finkel (*Ibid.*) remarks:

> A ruling party with an uncertain future may decide to grant the supreme court independence and the power of judicial review in order to serve as a hedge against possible downturns in the party's political position. Granting the supreme court the right to declare political acts or national laws null and void reduces the costs a ruling party would face if it were to end up as an opposition party. In particular, a ruling party that has wielded arbitrary power in the past may seek to enable the court to limit the ability of future ruling parties to do likewise. In effect, a ruling party, unsure if it will control political power in the future, may seek to protect the political power of those parties that will not.

Hegemonic Preservation Thesis

In many respects, the HPT mirrors the Political Insurance Thesis sketched above. In common with this thesis, the HPT stresses that BORI 'transfer[s] policy-making from majoritarian decision-making arenas to courts', which 'run[s] counter to the [*prima facie*] interests of power-holders in legislatures and executives' (Hirschl, 2004b, p. 84). It contends that these projects will therefore only prove appealing to politicians who 'find their interests under threat from within majoritarian political institutions' (*Ibid.*, p. 138).

The key addition of the HPT is to draw on other perspectives including, most notably, neo-Marxist theory, so as to develop a 'thicker', more socially and ideologically situated account of bill of rights genesis. Firstly, the HPT argues that courts are conservative by nature and tend to rule in accordance with 'hegemonic ideological and cultural propensities' (Hirschl, 2000*a*, p. 138). Only those politicians 'representing cultural and economic elites' (*Ibid.*) and facing opposition from 'peripheral minority groups' (Hirschl, 2004*a*, p. 49) are, therefore, likely to find BORI in their interests. Secondly, the HPT argues that BORI derives vital non-governmental support from both neo-liberal economic actors and the judicial elite. Neo-liberal actors will see the constitutionalization of rights as a valuable 'means to promote economic deregulation and to fight what its members often understand to be the harmful large government policies of the encroaching state' (Hirschl, 2000*a*, pp. 104–5). Meanwhile, the judicial elite will see a bill of rights as enhancing their 'symbolic power' (*Ibid.*, p. 105) as well as their 'political influence and international reputation' (Hirschl, 2004*a*, p. 12). Finally, the logic of the HPT implies that 'peripheral minority groups', whose growing power threatens the hegemonic actors, should constitute the principal opponents of BORI. Groups specifically singled out by the HPT include advocates of 'environmentalism, disarmament, multiculturalism, non-mainstream sexual preferences, [and] regional and religious separatism' (Hirschl, 2000*b*, p. 433).

The relationship of the PTT to trigger/supply-focused explanations

The PTT is heavily influenced by the Political Insurance Thesis' understanding of BORI. In particular, it accepts this thesis' claims that incumbent political elites occupy a strategic position, that they have particular power interests which encourage a general wariness towards bills of rights, and that a specific political trigger is required if BORI is to take place.

Despite this, the PTT disputes the idea that such a trigger may only be related to a strictly rational, prospective, power-focused calculation on the part of incumbents. To the contrary, as will be further outlined in three of the four case studies to come, the PTT holds that BORI can also be triggered by a reactive or 'aversive' response rooted in past negative political experiences. This broader notion of 'political trigger' is closely related to the concepts of 'critical junctures' (Collier & Collier, 1991) and 'punctuated equilibria' (Baumgartner & Jones, 1993) found within the historical institutionalist literature of political science. Whilst never so far applied to the phenomenon of BORI, this literature also emphasizes the importance of discontinuities in the formation of policy: innovation occurs in time-bound 'policy windows' (Kingdon, 2003, p. 169), when multiple factors converge to make change more likely.

The HPT shares the Political Insurance Thesis' strictly forward-looking, prospective, power-based understanding of the trigger behind the change; the

PTT rejects this. In addition, the PTT also disputes the HPT's understanding of the social and ideological origins of bills of rights which, mirroring that of neo-Marxist theory, have already been addressed above. The PTT also identifies many of the HPT's 'peripheral minority groups' as core members of the postmaterialist rights constituency who champion, rather than oppose, change. Finally, unlike the HPT, the PTT does not identify the judicial elite as a necessary member of the coalition supporting BORI. Whilst such support can be helpful and is sometimes present (e.g. in the United Kingdom prior to the enactment of the HRA (1998)), it is by no means guaranteed. In fact, judicial figures may exhibit hostility towards such a project seeing it as conflicting with their apolitical and passive understanding of the role of the law (Conklin, 1989). The examples of the CBORA (1960), the Canadian *Charter* (1982), and the NZBORA (1990) all indicate that strong *ex ante* judicial support for bills of rights is not essential.[9]

Whilst rejecting its particular substantive understanding of the origins of bills of rights, the PTT finds the basic shape of the explanation put forward by the HPT compelling. Specifically, in contrast to other theories' overemphasis either on social/background forces (as with the theories examined in Sections 3.2.1.1–3.2.1.5) or political elites (as with the Political Insurance Thesis), the HPT correctly identifies the important roles of both types of factors in BORI. Additionally, in common with the HPT, the PTT argues that, whilst the factors determining political elite and social actor preferences do differ markedly in terms of their dominancy, these factors also overlap. In particular, alongside more short-term considerations, ideological factors remain important in determining elite political support for bill of rights genesis.

3.3 CONCLUSIONS

This chapter has elucidated not only the new PTT, but also relevant theories of BORI extant in the literature. Whilst these theories have certainly influenced the development of the PTT, they also constitute rival explanations for the origins of bills of rights in stable, advanced democracies.

The case studies examined in Part II of this book explore the potential of the PTT to explain BORI in Westminster settings. Where relevant, evidence both for and against the other theoretical paradigms discussed in this chapter are also noted and elaborated. This chapter therefore provides both an analytical overview, and a theoretical reference, for the more empirically focused chapters which now follow.

Part II

Westminster Case Studies

4

Canada and the *Canadian Bill of Rights Act* (1960)

Compared with the other Westminster democracies, bill of rights develop-ments in Canada both started early and have progressed extensively. In 1960, the statutory *Canadian Bill of Rights Act* (CBORA) was enacted. Although binding only at the federal level and arguably weakly worded, CBORA was a pioneering reform within the Westminster world. Not until some three decades later was a similar piece of legislation – the *New Zealand Bill of Rights Act* (NZBORA) – enacted elsewhere. Moreover, by then Canada had acquired a fully constitutionalized rights instrument in the form of the *Canadian Charter of Rights and Freedoms* (1982).

In the light of both its complexity and richness, this book devotes two chapters to Canada. Whilst the next chapter examines the genesis of the Canadian *Charter*, this chapter provides a socio-political account of the rather overlooked CBORA. Having briefly set out the relevant background and chronology (Section 4.1), the chapter analyses, firstly, the development of background factors favouring the genesis of a bill of rights (Section 4.2) and, secondly, the presence of any political trigger which may have catalysed the project (Section 4.3). This analytical separation reflects the theoretical logic developed in Chapter 3.

The chapter argues that the genesis of CBORA broadly comports to the Postmaterialist Trigger Thesis (PTT). As Section 4.2.1 elucidates, pre-CBORA pressure for a bill of rights was primarily spearheaded, and shaped, by a group of civil libertarians and social equality seekers who shared a post-material orientation towards human rights. What is particularly notable is that these groups (and the Canadian public more broadly) came to embrace the idea of a bill of rights significantly in advance of their counterparts elsewhere in the Westminster world. This acceptance helps explain the early enactment of CBORA. Section 4.2.2 will examine this puzzle, arguing that alongside the precocious development of a postmaterialist economy and society in Canada, strong cultural and people-to-people ties between Canada and the bill of rights-infused United States also proved important. Thus, as the PTT itself

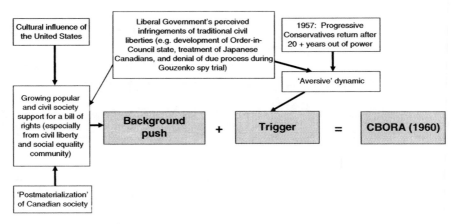

Chart 4.1 Stylized path to the *Canadian Bill of Rights Act* (CBORA 1960)

acknowledges, postmaterialist forces were not the only background pressures of importance. Finally, as Section 4.3 will demonstrate, the actual enactment of CBORA was prompted by an 'aversive' political trigger which developed within, and around, the Progressive Conservative Party. This party had returned to power in 1957 after over twenty years in opposition, much of it experienced during a time when concerns over civil liberty infringements were particularly acute. The idea of enacting a bill of rights emerged as a reaction against these negative political experiences which left a deep impression on key actors including in particular the new Prime Minister John G. Diefenbaker. Given that the momentum behind CBORA was, therefore, largely retrospective and backward-looking, it is unsurprising that it was (and is) a relatively weak, statutory enactment, which gives particular prominence to the specific civil liberty interests which had allegedly been undermined by the previous administration.

Chart 4.1 presents a stylized account of the genesis of CBORA which underpins the analysis of Sections 4.2 and 4.3 in particular. However, before turning to this analysis, the chronology of the debate will be outlined.

4.1 BACKGROUND AND CHRONOLOGY

Table 4.1 sets out the most important developments related to the genesis of the CBORA in 1960. As can be seen from this, the founding of modern Canada dates from the enactment of the *British North America* (BNA) *Act*

Table 4.1 Canadian bill of rights developments up to 1960

Date	Development
1867	*British North America Act* (BNA Act 1867) creates the Canadian federation of British North American colonies. The Act includes very limited language and denominational schooling rights but no general human rights provisions.
1935	League for Social Reconstruction/F. R. Scott pens first public call for a bill of rights. Followed by Native Sons of Canada in 1937.
1938	Canadian Supreme Court strikes down Alberta's *Accurate News and Information Act* on federalism grounds. Important 'implied bill of rights' *obiter.*
1945	Tommy Douglas, Co-operative Commonwealth Federation (CCF) Premier of Saskatchewan calls for a constitutional bill of rights. Alistair Stewart (CCF MP for Winnipeg North) introduces a parliamentary motion supporting the idea, which CCF party itself commits to.
1946	John. G. Diefenbaker (Progressive Conservative MP for Lake Centre) proposes a statutory bill of rights.
1950	Senate Special Committee on Human Rights and Fundamental Freedoms backs the idea of a constitutional bill of rights. Proposal is endorsed by Canadian Senate.
1952	Diefenbaker re-proposes a statutory bill of rights in Parliament. This is now Progressive Conservative official policy.
1953	Canadian Supreme Court in *Samur* case strikes down Québec city by-law restricting proselytization (by Jehovah's Witnesses). The decision is based on incompatibility with Québec provincial law but includes important 'implied bill of rights' *obiter.*
1955	Diefenbaker reintroduces resolution supporting a statutory bill of rights. Major Coldwell (federal leader of CCF Party) proposes constitutional bill of rights.
1956	Diefenbaker elected leader of the Progressive Conservatives.
1957	Canadian Supreme Court in *Switzman* case declares invalid Québec *Padlock Act* (1941), aimed at the suppression of 'communistic propaganda'. Decision is grounded in federalism rationale but includes important 'implied rights' *obiter.*
1957	General election sees Progressive Conservatives returned to power as a minority government.
1958	New general election results in a landslide victory for Progressive Conservatives. Policy of a bill of rights strongly emphasized during campaign.
1958	First draft of Canadian Bill of Rights Bill unveiled. Withdrawn for further scrutiny and consultation.
1960	New draft Canadian Bill of Rights Bill presented (July). Limited amendments accepted before unanimous enactment (August).

in 1867. This instrument established a new federal (or confederal) union composed of a predominantly francophone Québec, a predominantly anglophone Ontario (both of which had previously been fused within the Union of Canada), alongside the predominantly anglophone colonies Nova Scotia and New Brunswick.[1] This innovation marked the first time in which federal principles were 'appropriated and juxtaposed onto a British constitutional system' (Patapan, 1997*a*, p. 121). Additionally, the Act did explicitly protect a few discrete language and religious rights of both francophone Catholics and anglophone Protestants. In particular, Section 133 protected the right to use either the English or French language in the courts and Parliament of both federal Canada and Québec, whilst Section 93 protected any rights or privileges to denominational schools which existed pre-confederation in any of the provinces. Nevertheless, these rights were narrow both in terms of subject matter and philosophically.[2] Generally speaking, the Canadian founders exhibited a preference, so far as circumstances would allow, for 'a Constitutional Similar in Principle to that of the United Kingdom' (Preamble, BNA Act (1867)). This linkage to 'British laws, British connection, and British Freedom' (John A. MacDonald in Canada, Parliament, 1865, p. 31) was underscored not only by the Act's formal enactment in London, but also by the fact that revision and maintenance continued to depend on the British Parliament. Unsurprisingly, there was no attempt to adopt any generalized bill of rights at this time.

Interest in enacting a bill of rights did emerge in the 1930s. In 1935, constitutional lawyer Frank R. Scott suggested that, alongside further constitutional protection of anglophone and francophone rights, a national bill of rights protecting fundamental civil liberties could also be enacted (League for Social Reconstruction (Research Committee), 1935, p. 508). Two years later, under the name Native Sons of Canada, A. R. M. Lower, J. B. Coyne, and R. O. MacFarlane penned a brief for the Rowell–Sirois Commission on dominion–provincial relations which also favoured a bill of rights (MacLennan, 2003, pp. 26–7).[3]

Despite this important development, serious political support for a national bill of rights only developed in the aftermath of the Second World War. In August 1945, Tommy Douglas, who had led the Co-operative Commonwealth Federation (CCF) to power in Saskatchewan the previous year (the first such win by a democratic socialist party in North America), argued for a constitutional bill of rights at the Dominion–Provincial Conference on Reconstruction (Lambertson, 2005, p. 325).[4] This call was echoed in the Canadian Parliament by Alistair Stewart, CCF Member for Winnipeg North (Canada, Parliament, House of Commons, *Debates*, 11 October 1945, p. 900). The following year, John G. Diefenbaker, Progressive MP for Lake Centre, proposed appending a statutory bill of rights to the *Canadian Citizenship Bill*, then making its way through Parliament (Canada, Parliament, House of Commons, *Debates*, 7 May 1946, p. 1300). Finally, towards the end of 1949, the maverick, Liberal Senator Arthur Roebuck tabled a draft constitutional bill of rights in the Canadian Senate (Canada, Parliament, Senate, *Debates*, 3 November 1949, pp. 215–17). This led to the setting up of a Senate Special

Committee which, in June 1950, strongly backed this concept (Canada, Parliament, Senate, 1950, p. 104) but argued that such a bill could not responsibly be enacted without provincial concurrence (*Ibid.*, pp. 305–6). In the interim, the committee recommended that the federal Parliament adopt a non-binding 'Declaration of Human Rights to be strictly limited to its own legislative jurisdiction' (*Ibid.*, p. 306). These recommendations were then accepted by the Senate as a whole.

Although the emphasis on this issue somewhat reduced during the 1950s, it was not entirely abandoned. In the first place, by the early 1950s, both the CCF and Progressive Conservative parties had become committed to enacting such an instrument. Additionally, in both 1952 and 1955, Diefenbaker re-proposed a bill of rights (Canada, Parliament, House of Commons, *Debates*, 24 March 1952, p. 720; Canada, Parliament, House of Commons, Debates, 7 February 1955, p. 896). Finally, in a related development, a number of justices on the Supreme Court of Canada began to elaborate an 'implied bill of rights' within the existing BNA Act. This was especially evidenced in the cases of *Samur* (1953) (which concerned the legality of a Québec city by-law restricting the freedom of Jehovah's Witnesses to proselytize) and *Switzman* (1957) (which concerned the validity of the province of Québec's *Padlock Act* (1941) aimed at the suppression of 'communistic propaganda').

In late 1956, Diefenbaker was elected leader of the federal Progressive Conservatives and, in the general election the following June, he reaffirmed the party's commitment to enacting a bill of rights (Belliveau, 1992, p. 78). The Conservatives won the ensuing election but were only able to form a minority administration. In March 1958, however, a new election resulted in a landslide victory for the Progressive Conservative Party. The following September, the first draft of the statutory *Canadian Bill of Rights Bill* was introduced into Parliament (Canada, Parliament, House of Commons, 5 September 1958). The bill was then withdrawn from the order paper in order to allow for a further process of scrutiny and consultation both within the executive and beyond. In July 1960, a new draft of the *Canadian Bill of Rights Bill* was finally reintroduced. Reflecting the work of a Special Committee of the House of Commons established to consider the bill, some relatively minor amendments were then made (Canada, Parliament, House of Commons, 1 August 1960, pp. 7372–3; 7492). On 4 August, the House passed the amended bill unanimously with 186 votes recorded in favour (*Ibid.*, p. 7553). The bill then received a perfunctory passage through the Canadian Senate where it was passed without a formal vote being taken (Canada, Parliament, Senate, *Debates*, 5 August 1960, p. 1243). The CBORA came into force on 10 August 1960 following the Royal Assent (Canada, Parliament, House of Commons, *Debates*, 10 August 1960, p. 1948).

4.2 BACKGROUND PRESSURES BEHIND
CANADIAN BILL OF RIGHTS ACT

This section considers the development of background forces favouring bill of rights genesis in the period preceding enactment of CBORA in 1960. As Section 4.2.1 outlines, notwithstanding certain complexities, the push for a bill of rights clearly developed and was shaped by a coalition of civil libertarians and social equality seekers with a postmaterial conceptualization of human rights. The puzzle, however, is explaining why a bill of rights movement emerged decades earlier in Canada than elsewhere in the Westminster world. Section 4.2.2 demonstrates that alongside the early development of a postmaterialist economy and society, cultural and people-to-people influence from the bill of rights-infused United States proved important. Whilst the steady postmaterialization of Canadian society certainly aided the development of social pressure for a bill of rights, it was, therefore, not the only background factor of significance.

4.2.1 Social interests and bill of rights genesis

Core support for a national bill of rights emerged from within two identifiable groups in the Canadian case: civil libertarians and social equality seekers. The earliest advocacy was concentrated within the civil libertarian community. Professor Frank Scott, who penned the first demand for a bill of rights in 1935, was not only a strong civil libertarian personally but was also involved in efforts to set up the Canadian Civil Liberties Union (MacLennan, 2003, p. 19). Similarly, A. R. M. Lower, who in 1937 presented the first argument for a national bill of rights before an official governmental enquiry, was the chairman of the newly established Civil Liberties Association of Winnipeg (MacLennan, 2003, p. 26).[5]

This community continued to play an important catalytic and coordinating role throughout the period leading up to CBORA. During the 1950 Senate Committee hearings, the Association of Civil Liberties arranged for its pro-bill of rights brief to gain support from some twenty-one organizations across Canada (Canada, Parliament, Senate, Special Committee, 1950, p. 34). Similarly, in the lead-up to the passage of CBORA in the spring of 1959, the same association coordinated a delegation representing some thirty-five organizations who met Prime Minister Diefenbaker urging him to enact a stronger bill of rights than the one then proposed (Canada, Parliament, House of Commons, Special Committee, 1960, p. 169; MacLennan, 2003, p. 137). From at least the late 1940s onwards, a range of social equality actors, representing religious minorities, ethnic groups, and women, joined forces with civil libertarians to campaign for a bill of rights. The following groups were particularly significant, providing support for a bill of rights throughout the late 1940s and 1950s:

- Jehovah's Witnesses
- Canadian Jewish Congress
- National Japanese Canadian Association
- National Council of Women

The Jehovah's Witnesses are a small and fervent religious community who felt compelled in this period to aggressively proselytize their anti-state and anti-organized religion message as well as actively reject all state patriotic initiatives such as oaths of allegiance and flag salutes. As a result, the group faced opposition from the federal government (they were banned as an illegal organization between 1939 and 1943) and an even more extreme response, which continued on into the 1950s, from the Catholic-dominated Québec Government. Aware of the protections against such treatment which the *United States Bill of Rights* had afforded them there (Glen How, 1948, p. 793), this organization quickly became converted to the value of a bill of rights and went on to provide critical organizational and logistical support behind the campaign. For example, in 1949, the Witnesses organized a parliamentary petition in favour of a bill of rights signed by over 600,000 people (Canada, Parliament, House of Commons, 9 February 1949, p. 371). Similarly, vocal support was provided by representatives of the Canadian Jewish community including, in particular, the Canadian Jewish Congress (Canada, Parliament, Senate, Special Committee, 1950, pp. 70–7; Canada, Parliament, House of Commons, Special Committee, 1960, pp. 87–102). As both a minority religious and ethnic group, this community was acutely aware of wide-ranging discriminatory practices and attitudes including the use of restrictive covenants barring the transfer of property to Jews. A bill of rights was seen as a vital symbolic and legal mechanism for fighting these provisions.[6] The National Japanese Canadian Association, which represented individuals who had suffered even more extreme and directly State-sponsored discrimination, took a similar view. In particular, its Executive Secretary George Tenaka argued that a bill of rights was needed 'to encourage growth of one of the instructive and basic qualities of the human person – to the giving of consideration and justice to others' (Canada, Parliament, Senate, Special Committee, 1950, p. 270).[7] Finally, although not as central as they would later become,[8] women's organizations including, in particular, the National Council of Women also provided valuable and consistent support

Table 4.2 Rights content of proposed Canadian bills of rights (1935–50)

Proposal	Content
F. R. Scott/League for Social Reconstruction (1935)	Freedom of speech, association, public meeting, and press freedom (League for Social Reconstruction, 1935, p. 508)
Native Sons of Canada (1937)	Civil liberties (MacLennan, 2003, pp. 26–7)
Alistair Stewart MP (1945)	Minority rights; civil and religious liberties; freedom of speech; freedom of assembly; equal treatment before the law of all citizens, irrespective of race, nationality, or religious or political beliefs (Canada, Parliament, House of Commons, Debates, 10 October 1945, p. 900)
Senator Roebuck (1949)	Seventeen civil and political rights including right to equal protection of the law (article 5). Also limited right to private property based on UDHR (Appendix 3, MacLennan, 2003 pp. 166–9)
Association of Civil Liberties (1950)	Broad range of civil and political rights derived from the UDHR. Also limited right to private property (Canada, Parliament, Senate, 1950, pp. 34–8)

(Canada, Parliament, Senate, Special Committee, 1950, pp. 53–63; Canada, Parliament, House of Commons, Special Committee, 1960, p. 169).

From the beginning, the conceptualization of what a bill of rights should be designed to achieve was powerfully structured by its linkage to the civil liberty and social equality community. As Table 4.2 demonstrates, the various bill of rights proposals put forward from 1935 onwards concentrated on protecting a relatively narrow range of civil and political rights. Over time this rubric was expanded so as to explicitly encompass a positive right to equality and non-discrimination. By contrast, with the exception of a limited right to private property, social and economic rights of either a left-wing or right-wing hue were deliberately excluded.[9] The general inclusion of limited rights to private property reflected a dominant understanding amongst civil liberty activists that such rights were fundamentally civil, as opposed to economic, in nature. Indeed, the recently promulgated *Universal Declaration of Human Rights* (UDHR) (1948) had included a right to private property within the section dealing with civil and political rights issues.[10]

This focus on the protection of civil and political liberties was also reflected in the original draft of CBORA.[11] During the parliamentary passage of CBORA, the civil liberty and social equality community obtained a number of additional advantageous drafting changes, namely, the strengthening of the anti-discrimination provisions (Clause 1, CBORA) and the addition of a range of new procedural rights including the right not to be deprived of reasonable bail without just cause (Clause 2 (f)), and the right to the assistance of an interpreter in legal proceedings (Clause 2 (g)).

These linkages should not disguise certain complexities in the process leading to CBORA. Firstly, although most civil libertarians and social equality seekers were associated with the left,[12] the idea of a bill of rights also appealed to a number of individuals on the right, including, most notably, John G. Diefenbaker. These individuals were particularly concerned that aspects of the modern administrative state were undermining the traditional due process rights of individuals and saw a bill of rights as a useful mechanism for countering this (Belliveau, 1992, p. 82). Secondly, certain organizations of the economic right, notably the Canadian Chamber of Commerce, did publicly identify themselves with support for a bill of rights in the immediate lead-up to CBORA (Canada, Parliament, House of Commons, Special Committee, 1960, pp. 231–2). Despite its conceptualization as a primarily civil as opposed to economic right, these actors undoubtedly saw CBORA's right to private property clause as providing a potential economic benefit. Nevertheless, it is also notable that, despite its right-of-centre inclinations, the Diefenbaker Government actually rejected the proposals of the Canadian Chamber of Commerce and other economically libertarian organizations that an explicit right to follow a vocation of one's choice irrespective of non-membership of a trade union be included in the bill (Canada, Parliament, House of Commons, Special Committee, 1960, p. 232).[13] Additionally, it bears emphasis that, in contrast to civil liberty and social equality groups, none of these organizations dedicated significant resources to the bill of rights issue during this time.

Overall, therefore, the locus of social support for a bill of rights in the period preceding CBORA was concentrated around civil libertarians and social equality seekers. In turn, these actors powerfully structured the conceptualization of what a bill of rights should seek to achieve, thereby playing a critical role in determining the content of CBORA. All these findings mirror the hypotheses of the PTT.

4.2.2 Why did a bill of rights movement emerge in Canada (so early)?

As previously noted, the first public advocacy for a bill of rights in Canada emerged during the mid-1930s; moreover, by the end of the 1940s, this campaign had garnered widespread civil society support and high public visibility. In contrast, a movement for a national bill of rights elsewhere in the Westminster world only emerged in the late 1950s and early 1960s. This puzzling divergence is important since it largely explains the earlier genesis of a bill of rights in this case.

Postmaterialism

Throughout this period, moves towards a 'post-industrial' economy and society in Canada preceded apace. Samuel Huntington notes that by 1958 over 50% of the Canadian labour force was employed in service industries (Huntington, 1974, p. 169); additionally, this change was associated not only with higher living standards, but also with a more highly educated workforce and a more flexible, and less ascriptive, pattern of human exchange (*Ibid.*, pp. 171–2). At the same time, and relatedly, Canada also experienced significantly diversified immigration. In other words, basic economic changes did generate broader social change. Moreover, these changes were associated with support for action on human rights. Canadian historian Ross Lambertson (2005, pp. 5–6) notes:

> [E]conomic and demographic changes made Canadians increasingly sympathetic to the international discourse of human rights. As the country became increasingly well off in the immediate post-war years, and as political stability seemed assured, there was greater acceptance of ethnic differences and alternative political views... economic growth stimulated ethnically diverse immigration as well as a feeling that newcomers were potential contributors rather than threats to the Canadian way of life. In short, Canadians began to take the first halting steps towards the modern multicultural experiment.

Allied to the bill of rights movement was a growing social, organizational, and political movement for state efforts to tackle racial and other forms of social discrimination. This agenda particularly impacted on the left of the political spectrum; Christopher MacLennan (2003, p. 93) argues that 'by the 1950s fighting racial discrimination had become one of organized labour's most publicized and successful campaigns'. Reflecting this value change, legislation targeting instances of private, social discrimination were enacted throughout the 1950s. For example, fair employment measures (largely restricted to race and closely related categories) were adopted in Ontario (1951), Manitoba (1953), federal Canada (1953), Nova Scotia (1955), New Brunswick (1956), Saskatchewan (1956), and British Columbia (1956) (Evans Case, 2004, p. 79). Cognate legislation targeting discrimination against women in employment was also enacted in Ontario in 1951 (*Female Employees Fair Remuneration Act*) (Hill & Pollock, 1969, p. 194). In addition, legislation tackling discrimination in the provision of goods and services was enacted in Ontario (1954), Saskatchewan (1956), Nova Scotia (1959), and New Brunswick (1959) (Evans Case, 2004, p. 80).[14]

These developments, and linkages, mirror the predictions of the post-materialization thesis as applied to questions of human rights and the bill of rights. Nevertheless, they cannot provide a comprehensive explanation of the early development of background, that is, social support for what became CBORA. In particular, although postmaterialism did develop particularly rapidly in the Canadian case, other Westminster democracies experienced broadly similar trends. For example, Huntington notes that in 1965, only seven years after Canada, the United Kingdom also passed the mark where more than 50% of the workforce was employed in the service industry (Huntington, 1974, p. 169); Despite this, a bill of rights movement only emerged much later in the other cases. Given this, the rest of this subsection explores potential complementary explanations for the precocity of the Canadian developments derived from other theories examined in Chapter 3. These are ideational and institutional international developments after the Second World War, the presence of strongly consociational features in the Canadian polity, and, finally, Canada's particularly strong people-to-people and cultural linkages with the bill of rights-infused United States.

International developments

Alongside postmaterialist socio-economic change, Lambertson (2005, p. 5) argues that growing Canadian interest in a bill of rights reflected 'a shift in thinking, language, and law at the international level, beginning in the Second World War and gaining strength in the immediate post-war period'. This complex hypothesis combines an ideational and institutional element, thereby linking to both the constructivist and transnational diffusion theories. Certainly, as Lorraine Weinrib (1999) stresses, the atrocities of the Second World War did galvanize worldwide interest in human rights. This heightened ideational concern was reflected more concretely in, firstly, the *Atlantic Charter* (1941) and then the UDHR (1948). These developments did impact on the bill of rights debate in Canada. As MacLennan carefully documents, they encouraged the Liberal Government to set up a Special Joint Committee on Human Rights in both 1947 and 1948, thereby providing bill of rights proponents with a valuable platform for their cause (MacLennan, 2003, p. 53). Additionally, after the passage of the UDHR, the civil and political rights included in that document provided a useful template for the various model bill of rights which were drawn up. Indeed, even John G. Diefenbaker happily linked CBORA itself to a furtherance of the purposes of the UDHR.[15] Despite this, at least three factors indicate that the role of these forces was both limited and weak. Firstly, as Section 4.1 documented, societal interest in enacting a Canadian bill of rights had already started to emerge in the late

1930s, before the international developments referred to had taken place. Secondly, at least at an institutional level, whilst not quite stillborn, these developments were severely stunted within a few years by the onset of the Cold War.[16] Finally, what developments were forthcoming impacted virtually symmetrically on the other Westminster democracies. However, as previously stressed, these countries only became interested in enacting a bill of rights much later.

Institutionalist perspectives

Uniquely amongst the Westminster democracies, Canada exhibited all of the following elements:

- A semi-consociational relationship between anglophones and franco-phones
- A semi-consociational relationship between settlers and aborigines
- A written constitution setting out a federal relationship between the centre and the provinces and subject to judicial review.

As mapped out in Chapter 3, Lijphartian institutionalist theory suggests that such non-majoritarian features of the polity may be correlated with bill of rights institutionalization. In reality, these factors either played little role or acted more as a blockage than as pressure for reform. Regarding anglophone–francophone relations, it is apparent not only that 'throughout the 1940s and 1950s, there was a notable absence of francophone Québecers amongst those who demanded the better protection of human rights' (MacLennan, 1998, p. 115) but, further 'no francophones testified at all before the 1960 parlia-mentary committee' and '[t]he struggle for a bill of rights had been, and continued to be, almost entirely an English–Canadian affair' (Lambertson, 2005, p. 366). If anything, francophone Québecers saw a bill of rights as a potential threat to their valued autonomy.[17] For example, despite its clear restriction to the federal realm, in early 1960 the Legislative Assembly of Québec unanimously passed a resolution expressing concern at CBORA's potential to infringe Québec's provincial rights (Belliveau, 1992, p. 105–6).[18] Turning to the relationship between aborigines and the settler communities, this issue was barely visible during the pre-CBORA debates. Moreover, whilst bill of rights supporters sometimes referenced inequalities in the aboriginal–settler relationship as an argument for such an instrument,[19] others questioned what they saw as the illegitimately assimilationist logic behind both a bill of rights and the emerging 'human rights' movement generally.[20] Finally, the enactment of a national bill of rights was made significantly more complex and difficult as a result of the federal structure of Canada and, in particular, the danger of it being seen to encroach on the constitutional authority of not only Québec but also of the provinces more generally.[21]

Transnational ideational and people-to-people influence from the United States

In contrast to the international and consociational factors examined above, Canada's uniquely strong cultural and people-to-people relationship with the bill of rights-infused United States exerted a significant influence and does help explain its early interest in, and greater comfort with, bill of rights genesis compared with the other Westminster democracies. The closeness of this relationship impacted on the debate in a number of different ways. In the first place, many of the early proponents of a bill of rights in Canada had strong personal connections with America. For example, both A. R. M. Lower and R. O. MacFarlene (joint authors, along with J. B. Coyne, of the 1937 Native Sons of Canada submission favouring a bill of rights) had pursued extensive postgraduate study at Harvard University; moreover, for Lower, this experience clearly exerted an important effect on his intellectual development (Lower, 1967, p. 158). Personal experiences in the United States also proved significant both for the principal developers of the 'implied bill of rights' jurisprudence on the Supreme Court of Canada[22] and a number of the civil society supporters of a bill of rights.[23] More generally, diffuse yet powerful cultural ties ensured that the bill of rights proposal was often conceived, through the prism of American understandings, as an innately positive development. This dynamic particularly impacted on the thinking of Canadian civil society. Whilst representatives of eight civil society organizations[24] presented evidence to the 1950 Senate Special Committee favouring the rights protections of the *US Bill of Rights*, none spoke against.[25] Similar attitudes were also voiced by the politicians advocating for a Canadian bill of rights. Notably, in introducing CBORA to the House in July 1960 Diefenbaker stated that

> the first 10 amendments to the constitution [i.e. the *US Bill of Rights*] were added to that constitution as of December 15, 1791....These 10 amendments cover the fundamental freedoms of religion, speech, and security of the individual. In general, they are those which are in the bill of rights which I now bring to parliament. (Canada, Parliament, House of Commons, *Debates*, 1 July 1950, p. 5644)

Concluding thoughts

Most basically, the development of interest in enacting a bill of rights in Canada from the late 1930s onwards reflected the value change which accompanies a shift to a postmaterialist society and economy. Given that this postmaterialization was particularly advanced in the Canadian case, this factor also helps explain why this interest emerged so much earlier here than in the other Westminster democracies. Nevertheless, the extent of Canada's constitutional precociousness is too great to be fully explicable by this factor alone. The new international focus on formalized rights protections impacted symmetrically on the Westminster democracies and, therefore, cannot help explain this divergence. Neither can the generally strong existing non-majoritarian features of the Canadian policy be of help since these features suppressed as much as aided bill of rights developments during this period. In contrast, Canada's particularly strong cultural and people-to-people relationship with the United States did help create a public and civil society which was particularly receptive to the value of a bill of rights. Therefore, it should be concluded that both postmaterialization and, secondarily, transnational cultural diffusion from the United States powerfully structured the development of background pressure for what became CBORA.

4.3 CBORA AS 'AVERSIVE' CONSTITUTIONALISM

Operating alongside these background factors, the elite politics of bill of rights genesis in Canada was catalysed by the development of an 'aversive' trigger for reform. During the late 1940s and 1950s, serious elite political interest in a bill of rights was concentrated within the opposition parties (Progressive Conservative and New Democratic) and emerged in reaction to perceived abuses of power under the Liberal Government. This 'aversive' trigger was further galvanized by the Progressive Conservatives' experience of over twenty years in the political wilderness before returning to power. As well as determining the precise timing of change, this 'aversive' trigger also critically affected CBORA's strength and scope.

4.3.1 'Aversive' constitutionalism and the timing of CBORA

As previously noted, elite political interest in enacting a national bill of rights first emerged in the late 1940s. Especially amongst Progressive Conservatives, it was linked to a felt need to respond institutionally to both 'a long list of [perceived] civil liberty abuses by the Liberal Government' (MacLennan, 2003, p. 43) and the increasing concentration of power in the executive as opposed to Parliament. The following were seen as particularly problematic:

- Wartime regulations including the *Defence of Canada Regulations* (DOCR) especially if, as critics argued, the government was likely to continue these controls into the peacetime era (MacLennan, 2003, p. 37).

- The Liberal Government's response to former Soviet cipher clerk Igor Gouzenko's defection and the disclosure of a Soviet spy ring operating in Canada. Secret Orders-in-Council were enacted enabling suspects to be held with no formal charges being laid and with 'the traditional rights of access to legal counsel and habeas corpus' suspended (Lambertson, 2005, p. 145). Following this, a Royal Commission on Espionage was established in early 1946 which, in cross-examining suspects, suspended traditional safeguards including the right to counsel and the right for incriminating evidence not to be used in subsequent criminal prosecutions (*Ibid.*, pp. 152–3).

- The Liberal Government's post-war attempts to use Orders-in-Council to deport those of Japanese descent, including a number who were both born in, and citizens of, Canada.[26]

In March 1946, John G. Diefenbaker linked these various issues together in claiming not only that 'from 1939 on, the government has arrogated itself powers which ordinarily reside with parliament and the people' (Canada, Parliament, House of Commons, *Debates*, 21 March 1946, p. 138), but also that 'out of the events of the last few years a responsibility falls upon parliament to assure that Canadians . . . have established by their legislature a bill of rights' (*Ibid.*, pp. 137–8). Throughout the 1950s, a number of factors kept alive this 'aversive' opening towards reform. In particular:

- The Liberal Government continued to be associated with the inappropriate concentration of power including reliance on Orders-in-Council and disregard for parliamentary checks and balances. For example, in 1957, the Liberals were strongly criticized for imposing parliamentary closure in order to secure an immediate division on their controversial pipeline bill (Belliveau, 1992, p. 73).

- A number of 'cause célèbre' Supreme Court judgments, notably *Samur* (1953) and *Switzman* (1957) drew attention to serious violations of rights at the provincial level. Although not directly relevant to what became CBORA, these cases highlighted the importance of human rights whilst also apparently highlighting judicial support for the proposition that existing legal protections were potentially inadequate (Russell, Knopff, & Morton, 1989, p. 318).

- The Progressive Conservative's experience of over twenty years in the political wilderness encouraged a party *zeitgeist* which was open to restraints on executive power. Although tending to dissipate after their return to power, this culture continued to exert an influence during the early years of the new Progressive Conservative Government.

- Finally, John G. Diefenbaker became the leader of the Progressive Conservatives in late 1956. First elected an MP in the 1940s, Diefenbaker had his formative political experiences during the height of civil liberty concern with Liberal Government policies. As a result, he had become strongly personally committed to seeing a bill of rights enacted.

This combination of factors ensured that an elite political push to enact what became CBORA followed the re-election of the Progressive Conservatives to government in the late 1950s. In other words, an 'aversive' trigger fundamentally determined the precise timing of reform.

4.3.2 'Aversive' constitutionalism and the strength and scope of CBORA

In addition, this trigger influenced both the strength and scope of CBORA. Regarding the strength, the elite trigger behind CBORA was grounded in the Progressive Conservatives' reaction to negative political experiences under the Liberals. In their opposition period, key Progressive Conservative actors (notably John G. Diefenbaker) voiced support for a strong bill of rights which would

- be constitutionally entrenched and binding at both the federal and provincial levels,[27]
- grant clear rights to the courts to invalidate contrary law,[28] and
- be complemented by other mechanisms including a parliamentary watchdog committee on civil rights.[29]

Nevertheless, these commitments, which were rooted in past experiences, were increasingly seen to be in conflict with the prospective self-interest of the Progressive Conservatives as a party of government. It was in this context that, in the wake of the Progressive Conservative victory of 1958, the proposals morphed into a weaker model of protection which came to be enacted as CBORA.[30] In particular:

- Despite calls to include CBORA within the BNA Act (1867),[31] the government opted to draft it as a statutory as opposed to constitutional instrument.
- Notwithstanding evidence of increasing provincial support for a comprehensive instrument,[32] the government refused to examine (either through unilateral action or through negotiation with the provinces) whether a bill

of rights could be enacted which would apply not only to federal but also to provincial action.

- Aspects of the CBORA text appeared designed to shield government discretion from the threat of potential legal challenge. In particular, Section 1 of CBORA was drafted so as only to 'recogniz[e]' and 'declar[e]' that certain rights 'have existed and shall continue to exist'. Arguably, such wording made this part of the Act little more than a political declaration (Scott, 1959, p. 45). Additionally, the substantive provisions of the *War Measures Act* were directly excluded from the reach of the instrument (Section 6 (5), CBORA).

- The government failed to establish a parliamentary scrutiny committee on human rights. Moreover, it is now clear that, in private government discussions, the Minister of Justice, E. Davie Fulton expressed fears that 'in an attempt to justify its existence' such a committee 'might . . . embarrass the Government'.[33]

Alongside its effect on the strength of the instrument, the 'aversive' origins of CBORA also effected the scope of rights protection, producing an instrument with a distinct emphasis on protecting procedural rights.[34] As Mac-Lennan (2003, p. 127) has noted 'the Diefenbaker draft was designed with the 1940s civil liberties infringements clearly in mind'. Section 2 of CBORA protected various due process or civil liberty values which had been undermined during the previous Liberal Government. Harking back to the treatment of Japanese Canadians, one clause outlawed 'the arbitrary detention, imprisonment or exile of any person' (Clause 2(a), CBORA). Similarly, responding to the alleged infringements of suspects' rights during the Gouzenko affair, another granted a right to habeas corpus, to be informed promptly of the reason for arrest or detention and to the retaining and instructing of counsel without delay (Clause 2(b), CBORA). Moreover, in contrast to Section 1, this whole section was drafted so as to have a direct and overriding legal effect, unless a 'notwithstanding' declaration to the contrary was included in primary legislation. Finally, whilst leaving Parliament's fundamental freedom to legislate unmolested, the bill was framed so as to exert a controlling and binding effect on subsidiary legislation including, in particular, Orders-in-Council. This was reflective of a general concern over the abuse of Orders-in-Council under the previous Liberal Administration. Indeed, in introducing CBORA to the House, Diefenbaker stated that it was his primary intent that 'the tendency and trend toward passing orders in council with almost prodigal disregard of human freedoms should end' (Canada, Parliament, House of Commons, *Debates*, 3 August 1960, p. 7493).

4.4 CONCLUSIONS

As Chapter 5 will detail, an inhospitable judicial and legal environment combined with weak drafting seriously impeded CBORA's legal effect. It therefore proved something of a disappointment to its supporters. Despite this, as the first bill of rights enacted within the Westminster world, CBORA was path-breaking. Moreover, in the lead-up to enactment of the Canadian *Charter* (analysed in Chapter 5), it exerted an important symbolic influence in the fight for a genuinely legally effective, constitutional, and comprehensive instrument.

This chapter elucidated the socio-political origins of this important instrument. As the PTT suggests, these were rooted in two types of factors. To begin with, social interest in enacting a national bill of rights was associated with the influence of the civil libertarian and social equality rights communities, both given impetus by postmaterialization. The precocious postmaterialization of Canadian society and economy helps explain the early interest in bills of rights in Canada compared to the other Westminster democracies. Additionally, this interest was aided by the country's peculiarly strong cultural and people-to-people linkages with the bill of rights-infused United States. Alongside these background, social factors, the rise of a bill of rights project onto the elite political agenda depended on the presence of a clear 'aversive' political trigger for reform. This was engendered by a reaction amongst key Progressive Conservatives (notably John G. Diefenbaker) to negative political experiences during a lengthy period in opposition. A recoiling against the perceived abuses of procedural rights under the previous Liberal Government proved particularly important. The development of this backward-looking (as opposed to prospective and self-interested) dynamic helps explain not only CBORA's procedural rights focus, but also its relatively weak nature. Thus, whilst critical to the success of Canada's first national bill of rights project, the nature of this political trigger partially clarifies why CBORA failed to fully satisfy its natural supporters.

5

Canada and the *Canadian Charter of Rights and Freedoms* (1982)

Despite (indeed, perhaps, partially because of) its path-breaking character-istics, the *Canadian Bill of Rights Act* (CBORA) failed to have more than a marginal concrete impact on Canadian law. Nevertheless, social and political interest in protecting human rights through a bill of rights soon developed a new head of steam. In 1982, just over two decades after the enactment of CBORA, Canada adopted the *Canadian Charter of Rights and Freedoms* (CORAF), a fully constitutional instrument which, subject (in some cases) to a 'notwithstanding' provision (Section 33), was overriding against both federal and provincial law. In contrast to CBORA, the Canadian *Charter* has led to important, even radical, legal, and political change. Lorraine Weinrib, a prominent 'Charterphile', argues that it has altered the nature of the Canadian legal regime from one in which legislatures held 'free-ranging, law-making power' (Weinrib, 1999, p. 38) to one where '[t]he Canadian constitution now fetters legislative authority to pervasive constitutional norms that are judi-cially protected' (*Ibid.*), thus bringing about 'a revolutionary transformation of the Canadian polity involving every public institution' (Weinrib, 2002, p. 120). Similarly, and from across the political divide, F. L. Morton, a vociferous opponent of the change, argues that '[t]he adoption of the *Charter of Rights and Freedoms* in 1982 has transformed both the practice and the theory of Canadian politics. It has replaced a century-old tradition of parlia-mentary supremacy with a new regime of constitutional supremacy that verges on judicial supremacy' (Morton, 1992, p. 629).[1]

This chapter examines the origins of this important instrument, forward-ing an explanation in line with the Postmaterialist Trigger Thesis (PTT). Having outlined the basic chronology (Section 5.1), the chapter explores the political trigger behind the *Charter* (Section 5.2). It argues that the development of Québécois separatist sentiment from the late 1960s and, most particularly, following the provincial victory of the Parti Québécois in 1976, threatened the stability of the Canadian federal polity. Those with strong power, resource, and affectational ties to this system, notably federal

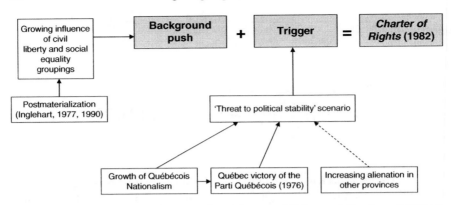

Chart 5.1 Stylized path to the *Canadian Charter of Rights and Freedoms* (CORAF 1982)

elite politicians, were confronted with the need to construct a powerful unifying mechanism to fight this new centripetal force. The political project of the *Charter* emerged out of this 'threat to political stability' dynamic. This trigger not only made the *Charter* possible, but also influenced both its strength and scope. Additionally, however, the growing political salience of postmaterialist rights groups also played a powerful role in aiding the success of this project and in determining its final shape. The important background role of postmaterialist forces is outlined in Section 5.3. Chart 5.1 presents a précis of the genesis of CORAF on which the material in both Sections 5.2 and 5.3 will rest.

5.1 CHRONOLOGY OF CANADA'S BILL OF RIGHTS DEBATE, 1960–82

Table 5.1 outlines the most important developments in the Canadian bill of rights debate between the enactment of CBORA in 1960 and the Canadian *Charter* in 1982. To begin with, the judicial reception of CBORA proved a significant disappointment to the civil libertarian and social equality communities. Notwithstanding the promise of the 'implied bill of rights' jurisprudence of the 1950s, the majority of Canadian judges continued to see themselves as 'passive' agents charged with enforcing a 'vertical hierarchy of all-encompassing, encyclopaedic rules' (Conklin, 1989, p. 98). Enactment of CBORA did not displace this understanding. Therefore, the bill was generally 'rejected as a foreign unassimilable object', rendering its formal protections largely 'ineffective' (Conklin, 1989, p. 85).[2] This development, however, did

Table 5.1 Canadian bill of rights developments (1960–82)

Date	Development
1963	Supreme Court in *Robertson and Rosetanni* declares *Lords Day Act* compatible with CBORA, adopting 'frozen' interpretation of its terms.
1968	Canadian Government forwards proposal for a new charter of rights, including linguistic rights, as part of a patriated Canadian Constitution.
1971	Victoria Accord – Provinces and federal government agree to entrenchment of political rights and some linguistic rights in patriated constitution. Collapses after Québec pulls out.
1978	Canadian Government issues proposals for a new charter of rights, including linguistic and aboriginal rights, as part of a patriated Canadian Constitution.
1980	Canadian Government launches a unilateral initiative for patriating Canadian Constitution with a new charter of rights, including linguistic rights. Six provinces initiate legal action in opposition.
January–February 1981	The proceedings and report of the Canadian Parliament's Joint Select Committee result in a strengthening of the charter of rights proposal in the area of equality and legal rights. Addition of aboriginal rights provisions.
September 1981	Supreme Court of Canada declares (7–2) that the unilateral government initiative is legal but (6–3) that it would violate constitutional convention absent a 'significant measure' of provincial support.
5 November 1982	Canadian Government and all provinces bar Québec agree to the patriation of the new constitution. It includes a constitutionalized Charter of Rights but subject to a 'notwithstanding' clause in relation to most rights. Aboriginal rights excluded.
23 November 1982	Federal government announces partial restoration of aboriginal rights protections and the exclusion of some gender rights from a 'notwithstanding' clause.
April 1982	Promulgation into law of the new *Constitution Act* (1982) including *Charter of Rights and Freedoms*.

not choke off interest in protecting human rights through the legal system; to the contrary, if anything, it tended to engender social and political support for a stronger, constitutional model of rights protection.[3]

In 1968, the Liberal Government proposed that such a charter of rights, including anglophone and francophone linguistic rights (see Chart 5.2),[4] should form part of a patriated and renewed *British North America* (BNA) *Act* (Pearson, 1968; Canada, Government, 1969). Negotiations with the provinces led to an agreement to constitutionalize only three core 'political' rights – to universal suffrage and free democratic elections; freedom of thought, conscience, and religion; and of peaceful assembly and association – together with certain very limited linguistic rights. Even this Victoria Accord agreement collapsed later in 1971.[5] The next federal push to enact a constitutional bill of rights, again conceived as part of a broader plan for constitutional reform, came in 1978 (Canada, Prime Minister, 1978).[6] Plans to unilaterally implement those aspects of the proposals relating to the federal sphere came unstuck, following a successful legal challenge.[7] The federal government remained committed to this constitutional vision,[8] although with the election of the Progressive Conservatives in May 1979, increasing emphasis was placed on both implementing reform on the basis of consent with the provinces and limiting the range of rights included in the charter.[9] In contrast, by mid-1980, when the Liberals had returned to power, the government returned to vigorous promotion of a strong charter of rights, secured if need be by a unilateral resolution to the British Parliament. This action led to a new legal challenge by six[10] out of the nine provinces which led in September 1981 to a Supreme Court ruling that unilateral federal action would be technically lawful but, in the absence of a 'substantial measure' of provincial support, a breach of constitutional convention.[11] This ambiguous decision led to new negotiation which culminated in the federal government and all the provinces bar Québec agreeing to entrench a charter of rights in the constitution, subject to a notwithstanding provision which would allow legislation to be excluded from compatibility with most of the included rights on a time-limited (five-yearly), yet renewable, basis.[12] Although this accord originally recommended excluding aboriginal rights, subsequent discussions led to this decision being partially reversed. Following endorsement by both the Canadian[13] and British Parliament,[14] on 17 April 1982, Queen Elizabeth (as Queen of Canada) promulgated these constitutional amendments into law on Parliament Hill in Ottawa, thus bringing the *Charter of Rights and Freedoms* into being.[15]

5.2 THE 'THREAT TO POLITICAL STABILITY' TRIGGER BEHIND THE *CHARTER*

To a greater extent than with any other bill of rights analysed in this book, the genesis of the *Charter* depended on and was shaped by the presence of a contingent political trigger. This 'threat to political stability' trigger resulted from a perceived need to find a unifying institutional mechanism to counteract the powerful centripetal forces unleashed by the development of a new form of Québécois nationalism. This section reflects on this political trigger and its importance. The basic nature of the trigger is first explicated. Then,

Table 5.2 Development of bill of rights English and French linguistic provisions (1969–82)

Categories of right	Canadian Government 1969 proposals	Victoria Accord (1971)	Constitutional Reform Bill (1978)	Canadian Charter (1982)
Parliament/ Legislature	Use of either language in all legislative proceedings.	Use of either language in all legislative proceedings bar British Columbia and Alberta.	Use of either language in all legislative proceedings (Section 14).	Use of either language in legislative proceedings of Canada and New Brunswick (Section 17).
	Records, journals, and enactments of, at a minimum, federal Canada, Ontario, New Brunswick, and Québec to be in both languages.	Statutes of all provinces to be printed in both French and English but both versions only authoritative in federal Canada, Québec, New Brunswick, and Newfoundland (Articles 11–13).	Statutes, records, and journals to be printed in both languages in federal Canada, New Brunswick, Ontario, and Québec. All equally authoritative (Section 15).	Statutes, records, and journals to be printed in both languages in federal Canada and New Brunswick. Both equally authoritative (Section 18).
Courts	Use of either language in any pleading or process originating from any judicial or quasi-judicial body established by constitution or Parliament of federal Canada or superior courts of, at a minimum, New Brunswick, Ontario, and Québec.	Right to use either language in pleading or process issuing from courts of federal Canada, Québec, New Brunswick, and Newfoundland. Right to all documents and judgments in both languages (Article 14).	Right to use either language in any pleading or process in or issuing from courts of federal Canada, New Brunswick, Ontario, or Québec and in any matter where any court exercising criminal jurisdiction conferred by Act of Parliament or matter relating to imprisonable offence (Section 16).	Right to use either language in any pleading or process in or issuing from courts of federal Canada or New Brunswick (Section 19).

(continued)

Table 5.2 Continued

Categories of right	Canadian Government 1969 proposals	Victoria Accord (1971)	Constitutional Reform Bill (1978)	Canadian Charter (1982)
Government communications and services	Right to communicate in either language with head office of every department and agency of, at a minimum, federal Canada, New Brunswick, Ontario, and Québec (56). Also principal office of every department or agency of Canada or provinces in any area where substantial proportion of population has that language as its mother tongue (58).	Right to communicate in either language with any central office of any department or agency of federal Canada, Ontario, Québec, New Brunswick, Prince Edward Island, and Newfoundland. Right to communicate in either French or English with any principal area office of federal Canadian department or agency in area where a substantial proportion have that language as a mother tongue (Articles 16 and 17).	Right to communicate in either language with any central office of any department or agency of federal Canada. Right to communicate in either language with the principal office of any department or agency of federal Canada or of any province in area where substantial number of persons use the official language (Section 19).	Right to communicate and to receive available services in either language from any office of New Brunswick government institution, any central or head office of a federal Canadian agency, and any other federal Canadian office where significant demand for such communications or services or where otherwise reasonable given the nature of the office (Section 20).
School education	Right to choose between English or French as main language of instruction in publicly supported schools where sufficient number of persons to justify provision of the necessary facilities (58).	None.	Citizens whose principal language of parent is either French or English have right to receive education in that language in publicly supported schools where such provision is reasonable. Right would only become active upon adoption of	Right to have either language as main language of instruction in publicly supported schools where numbers are sufficient to warrant this and either (a) they received their primary school instruction in Canada in that language or (b) have a sibling who is or

	has received primary or secondary school education in that language anywhere in Canada or (c) their parents' mother and still understood tongue is that language (Québec opt-out from latter provision) (Sections 23 and 59).	section by a province (Section 21).	Both languages have equal rights and privileges as to their use in all institutions of the Parliament and government of federal Canada and of New Brunswick (Section 16).
Other	None.	No federal or provincial law shall apply or have effect so as to affect adversely the preservation of English or French as the language spoken or otherwise enjoyed by an identifiable and substantial linguistic community in any area of Canada (Section 22).	Other provinces, may by parliamentary resolution, opt-in to rights relating to Parliament, courts, and communication with government central offices. Such a resolution would then only be repealable through vote of provincial legislature and Parliament of Canada (Article 50).

this trigger's specific impact on the shape and strength of reform is outlined. Finally, this book's understanding of the 'threat to political stability trigger' is briefly distinguished from the (quasi-Marxist) hegemonic preservation interpretation of the origins of *Charter* which has been forwarded elsewhere.

5.2.1 *Charter* genesis and the 'threat to political stability' trigger

The re-emergence of strong political support for a constitutional charter or bill of rights resulted from the crisis which engulfed the Canadian federal system, following the emergence of a new nationalism amongst francophone Québecers. Unlike previous forms of nationalism in Québec which were traditionalist in nature, this new nationalism was developmental, based on the goal of building an 'efficient technological society led by French Canadians and animated by a French spirit' (McRoberts, 1988, p. 129). From the mid-1960s onwards, the vigorous pursuit of this goal led to sharp disjunctures in the relationship between groups within Québec and also between that province and the rest of Canada. The following interrelated disjunctures are especially worthy of note:

- Laws were enacted to suppress the position of English, especially within the economic sphere, both amongst anglophones themselves and new immigrants (see Table 5.3).
- The role of the Québec Government within the economy and society of the province dramatically increased.
- Québec pushed (often successfully) for a right to opt out of pan-Canadian programmes in areas such as pensions and even immigration.
- Francophone Québecers increasingly focused on their identity as Québecers alone, as opposed to stressing any connection (say, as 'French Canadians') with the rest of Canada.
- Paralleling this, there was also a smaller, yet discernible, weakening in the strength and importance of Canadian identity within Canada's other provinces (Elkins & Simeon, 1980).

This emerging situation challenged the existing constitutional structure of Canada and, in particular, threatened the position of the federal government. For those attached to the latter institution, there was a need to find a centripetal force which could, especially as regards Québec, re-establish the dominance of a pan-Canadian identity and thus secure the relevance and vitality of federal Canada. A constitutional charter of rights was conceived as

Table 5.3 Development of Language Laws in Québec (1969–77)

Legislation	Key provisions
Law 63 (Law For Promoting the French Language in Québec) (1969)	• Establishes objective of making French the language of labour relations and predominant language on public signs and posters • Makes teaching of French compulsory in the Québec anglophone school system
Law 22 (Official Language Act) (1974)	• Makes French the official language of Québec • Imposes use of French on public signs and posters • Compels enterprises doing business with the Québec Government to register for francization programmes • Restricts access to English-language schools to those pupils with sufficient knowledge of English
Law 101 (Charter of the French Language) (1977)	• Imposes exclusive use of French on public signs, on posters and in commercial advertising • Extends francization programmes to all enterprises with fifty or more employees • Restricts access to English-language schools to children one of whose parents received elementary education in English in Québec (or, subject to inter-provincial agreement and reciprocation, other provinces) • Recognizes only the French version of laws as official (declared contrary to Section 133 of BNA Act and void in 1979)

Source: Stevenson (1999) and Plourde, Duval, & Georgault (2000).

just such as centripetal symbol and institution. This is apparent even in Pierre Trudeau's early writings on the subject (Trudeau [1964] 1996). From a structural perspective, the great advantage of a constitutional charter was that it would provide a 'guarantee of rights' which would 'apply equally throughout the country in a way which today's variety of legislation does not' (Canada, Government, 1969, p. 16). Moreover, this guarantee would be promulgated, interpreted, and enforced by Canadian federal institutions. Therefore, it was thought that a charter would not only ensure the future of the country as 'a single political and economic unit with a common citizenship' (Canada, Government, 1978, p. 10) but could also engender a broader identification and allegiance with federal Canada.

The charter of rights first came to the fore as a political project in late 1967. This was partially related to the elevation of Pierre Trudeau (a strong personal supporter of the project) to the position of Minister of Justice and, shortly thereafter, Prime Minister. More importantly, it was correlated with René Levesque's split with the Québec Liberals and his founding of the Mouvement Souveraineté-Association, which became the Parti Québécois the following year (Stevenson, 1999, p. 86). This founding represented the first clear institutional manifestation of the threat to federal Canada which was emanating from Québec. Despite the significant efforts of the Trudeau Government during the late 1960s and early 1970s, however, its efforts to secure new constitutionalized rights protections foundered on the rock of provincial opposition. Although remaining formally committed to the principal of a constitutional charter, the federal elite only returned to a championing of this project in the late 1970s. Again, the linkage with threatening developments in Québec was clear. Specifically, in November 1976, the Parti Québécois won power in Québec City on a platform of not only imposing a 'visage Français' on the whole of the province but also securing Québec sovereignty through the holding of a referendum on the subject. This threat to the Canadian political system prompted an even more vigorous response from the federal elite. In particular, in the wake of the defeat of the Parti Québécois's sovereignty proposals in May 1980, the federal government was provided with a strategic opportunity to push for unilateral amendment of the constitution without majority provincial support. Moreover, ultimately (and in stark contrast to the outcome in the early 1970s), a charter was imposed on Québec in the absence of its agreement. Achievement of a constitutional charter (and, ipso facto, its precise timing) clearly depended on the federal elite's investment of enormous political capital. Such an investment would have been inconceivable absent the 'threat to political stability' trigger just outlined.

5.2.2 The 'threat to political stability' trigger and the nature of the *Charter*

The dynamic unleashed by the new Québécois nationalism directly threatened the prospective power and position of the federal elite. Given that the *Charter* was devised to counter this, it follows that, in addition to any ideological factor at play, this project was strongly linked to the future-orientated rational self-interest of this group. The 'threat to political stability' trigger, therefore, contrasts significantly with the backward-looking, experiential 'aversive' trigger behind CBORA which was examined in Chapter 4. Given its clear link to self-interest, it is unsurprising that, in contrast to the situation in the late 1950s, the federal government championed a strong instrument throughout the process. More specifically, from the time of *The Constitution and the People of Canada* (1969) onwards, it promoted an instrument which not only applied to both the federal and provincial spheres of government but which was also

- constitutionally entrenched,
- supreme against all other law, and
- not subject to a CBORA-style notwithstanding clause.

Ultimately, as a *quid pro quo* for securing agreement with all the provinces bar Québec, the government proved willing to compromise on this last stipulation by agreeing to a notwithstanding provision limited to only some rights and which (in contrast to the cognate provision in CBORA) required periodic renewal at least once every five years. In other respects, however, federal Canada's vision of a strong charter of rights remained imprinted within the structure of the instrument as finally promulgated.

The 'threat to political stability' trigger also played a critical role in influencing the scope of the rights included within the *Charter*. This is most obviously reflected in the *Charter*'s minority francophone and anglophone linguistic rights. The primary aim of these provisions (and, to an extent, the *Charter* project more generally) was to re-establish within the francophone community a strong and unmediated allegiance to federal Canada.[16] This was to be achieved by demonstrating that 'the French fact existed [and could exist] throughout Canada and should not be exclusively identified with Quebec, much less with the movement for Quebec sovereignty' (Stevenson, 1999, p. 257). Tellingly, the government refused to include these provisions within the ambit of the notwithstanding clause. Nevertheless, despite its clear importance, the connection between these linguistic rights and the 'threat to political stability' trigger can be over-essentialized. To begin with, evidence of compromise is evident within these provisions.[17] More importantly, a range of other rights within the *Charter* were also intimately linked to the government's agenda, building up identities which existed on a Canada-wide, as opposed to province-specific, basis. These included the *Charter*'s promotion of a pan-Canadian, open-textured, and substantive equality (Section 15), its specific protection of multiculturalism throughout the country (Section 25), and its protection of aboriginal interests which, in many cases, straddled provincial boundaries (Section 35). The federal elite's championing of each of these provisions during the drafting process was critically linked to its overall strategic goals[18] and helps explain why, alone amongst the Westminster bills of rights, these also found a place within the *Charter*.

5.2.3 Distinguishing the 'threat to political stability' account

The elite political origin of the Canadian *Charter* has been presented in the literature as a near-perfect exemplar of the Hegemonic Preservation Thesis (HPT). According to this perspective, the *Charter* was aimed not only at maintaining and enhancing Canadian federal authority but also entrenching a neo-liberal economic structure and, most especially, promoting an 'Anglophone economic establishment and its dominant Protestant, business-orientated culture' within Québec (Hirschl, 2000a, p. 127). These claims critically misrepresent the aims and interests of the elite actors involved. It is true that the neo-nationalist project in Québec was linked to a strong belief in the power of the Québec State. This Québecé *tatism* led to renewed calls for an extreme decentralization of power within the Canadian federation, granting Québec a broad regulatory and policy-making jurisdiction. These demands threatened federal Canada and elite federal politicians did use constitutional reform to counter them. However, the alternative vision they developed was premised not on neo-liberalism but rather on the idea of a powerful Canadian state with a remit to promote economic development, reduce inequalities between Canadian citizens, and ensure the maintenance of high quality public services. This ideal was reflected not only in the various white papers produced by the Canadian Government[19] but also in a number of provisions within the *Constitution Act* (1982) itself including, most notably, the section on prompting equal opportunities and reducing regional disparities (Section 36). In other words, the conflict within elite politics represented a clash of two predominantly social-democratic state-building projects.

Secondly, notwithstanding the entrenchment of some anglophone minority linguistic rights in the *Charter*, Québec anglophone interests and, most especially, their economic interests were not uppermost in the minds of the federal framers. In fact, the *Charter* preserved all the essential elements of the restrictive language laws in Québec including most particularly its mandated francization of the economic realm (see Table 5.3). Even in the area of schooling, where the *Charter* did effect a substantive change in Québec law, its

> contribution to the welfare of Anglophones should not be overestimated. Section 23 [on minority language education rights], especially when limited in its application by Section 59 [granting Québec alone a partial opt-out], did not undo much of the damage to English-language education in Québec by Bill 101.... Enrolments in English schools did not increase significantly following the adoption of the Charter. (Stevenson, 1999, pp. 271–2)

In contrast, the principal beneficiaries of these provisions were francophone Canadians including, most especially, those who lived, or were thinking of living, in any province of Canada other than Québec. This set of people constituted the principal (and very powerful) group whom the federal elite wanted to convert to a new sense of allegiance to federal Canada. In contrast, anglophones in Québec were in direct and severe conflict with many within this group and were politically insignificant within a broader context. Given this, it is unsurprising that their needs and interests were not accorded a priority.[20]

5.3 BACKGROUND SOCIAL FORCES IN THE *CHARTER*'S GENESIS

Although the *Charter*'s immediate origins 'cannot be found in the sudden and inexplicable burst of liberal individualism' (Milne, 1982, p. 48), it was strongly aided and influenced by both the growing social salience of postmaterialist rights issues and the increased political significance of postmaterialist rights groups. This section elaborates

- the developing interest in postmaterialist rights issues and groups in Canada and their link to advocacy for a constitutional bill of rights (Section 3.1), and

- the specific role of postmaterialist rights groups in drafting the *Charter* itself (Section 3.2).

Finally, the section briefly considers the more complex role of other groups and issues within the *Charter* process including, in particular, those related to the aborigines and the economy.

5.3.1 Postmaterialism, rights, and *Charter* genesis

Subsequent to the enactment of CBORA, social support for a constitutionalized national bill of rights continued to develop. This support was tied to the same postmaterialist rights constituency which had pushed for a bill of rights prior to the 1960s. The linkage is most clearly apparent in work of the Molgat–Maguigon Special Joint Committee on the Constitution. This parliamentary committee worked between 1970 and 1972 alongside the federal–provincial negotiation process which culminated in the failed Victoria Accord. It held some 130 to 140 meetings throughout Canada and also received a

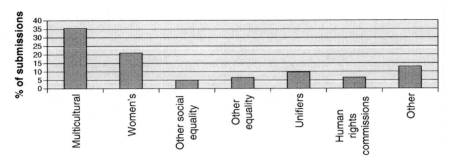

Chart 5.2 Types of group giving evidence to Hays–Joyal Special Joint Committee (1980–1) in support of an entrenched charter of rights ($n = 68$)

large number of written briefs (Tarnopolsky, 1975, p. 20). Well over 80% of those giving evidence[21] on the proposed constitutional charter of rights favoured such an instrument.[22] Moreover, as Cynthia Williams (1986) has explored, the evidence presented overwhelmingly stressed 'countercultural' rights including social equality for women, the disabled, and multicultural communities. The development of interest in these rights related to the continuing postmaterialization of Canada's socio-economic structure. Developments of importance included growing material prosperity, moves towards a service-based economic structure and, most specifically, dramatic changes in the position of women within society and the economy. Throughout the 1960s and 1970s, these new rights communities also secured, and were nurtured by, critical legislative advances. This included the comprehensive spread of anti-discrimination law, the establishment of human rights commissions federally and in all of Canada's provinces, and the federal government's adoption of an official policy of multiculturalism.

During the immediate process leading to the constitutional reforms of 1982, postmaterialist rights groups rallied behind the concept of a constitutional charter. This support was particularly forthcoming during the proceedings of the Hays–Joyal Special Joint Committee on the Constitution which sat from November 1980 through to February 1981. As Chart 5.2 outlines, of the seventy organizations which explicitly endorsed the concept of a constitutional charter of rights before the committee, over 50% (thirty-eight groups) were advocates of social equality of one stripe or another. Particularly prominent within this group were representatives of Canada's 'multicultural' community (32% of the total) and women (13% of the total). Other major supporters included the quasi-governmental human rights commissions and those representing francophone and anglophone regional minorities.

By galvanizing public support, this advocacy helped ensure the success of the *Charter* project which, in the face of severe provincial opposition, was then on a critical knife-edge. Lorraine Weinrib argues '[t]he Charter's value structure and institutional roles crystallized after weeks of nationally televised parliamentary hearings. Public interest groups came forward, representing the widest array of interests.... These hearings captured the imagination of ordinary Canadians, and across the country support for the Charter soared' (Weinrib, 2001, p. 84). Linked to these developments, throughout 1981, opinion polls demonstrated that a strong majority of Canadians favoured a constitutional bill of rights, with specific surveys placing such support at 62%,[23] 72%,[24] and even, in one case, 84%.[25] This support was utilized by the federal government in their tussle with the recalcitrant Provincial Premiers. Roy Romanov, Deputy Premier of the Province of Saskatchewan during the *Charter* negotiations argues:

> [W]hat really beat the Premiers in his period of the tug of war was that Trudeau put the Premiers in front of the television cameras in the hearings on whether or not to have a Charter.... And he was very elegant in his description of what a charter of rights would mean and what it stood for – and then he would turn to one of the Premiers and say 'OK, well you tell me why you oppose it?'. And you just couldn't win in that political battle. To the average citizen it seemed like good was on the side of the Federal Government [and] evil was on the side of these little Premiers with their grabbing every little bit of territorial jurisdiction that they could. (Interview with the author, 28 April 2005)

5.3.2 Postmaterialism, rights, and *Charter* drafting

Postmaterialist rights organizations not only mobilized behind the federal government's *Charter* but in addition, and almost as a *quid pro quo*, exerted a significant influence over its text.

The federal government's draft of the *Charter of Rights,* as released in October 1980,[26] was fundamentally influenced by

- the provisions of the CBORA (1960),
- the coming in to force of the *International Covenant on Civil and Political Rights* (ICCPR),[27]
- previous charter of rights proposals from 1969 onwards, and
- the work of the Molgat–MacGuigan Special Joint Committee.

Given that postmaterialist rights groups had participated in many of these initiatives, their imprint was already visible within the text. But other influences had also been at work. Most critically, over the summer of 1980, the *Charter* draft had been seriously weakened as a result of unsuccessful negotiations between the federal government and the provinces.

Subsequent to the government's release of its draft, postmaterialist rights groups used the Hays–Joyal Special Joint Committee process to lobby for a strengthening of the *Charter* text.[28] This process led to the following changes:

- The *Charter*'s equality provision was made more substantive by the addition of a legal right to 'equal benefit' as well as 'equal protection' of the law.[29]
- The equality provision was made open-textured and protection against discrimination on grounds of 'physical and mental disability' explicitly included.[30]
- A new clause was added requiring that the *Charter* be interpreted consistently with multiculturalism.
- The legal rights section of the *Charter* was significantly strengthened by inclusion of provisions protecting jury trial, rights against self-incrimination, and the exclusion of evidence improperly obtained.
- The clause setting out permissible limitations of rights under the *Charter* was narrowed through the deletion of the description of Canada as having a 'parliamentary system of government' and the substitution of allowing for limitations which were 'reasonable' and 'generally accepted' with the stricter standard of 'demonstrably justified'.

Even after the end of the committee process, the feminist movement successfully lobbied for further changes (Hošek, 1983, p. 288).[31] Their efforts led to a new clause (Section 28) stating that 'Notwithstanding anything in this Charter, the rights and freedoms referred to in it are guaranteed equally to male and female persons'.[32] The adoption of the 'notwithstanding' clause, agreed to by the federal government as a means of obtaining the support of a majority of Canada's provinces, came to be applied to most of these rights.[33] Whilst this eventuality was certainly not favoured by postmaterialist rights proponents, the basic structure of the *Charter* remained unchanged and was clearly indelibly marked by their advocacy.

5.3.3 Other groups and issues in the *Charter* genesis process

Alongside postmaterialist rights groups, a number of other social actors, including aborigines and economic and social organizations of both the left and the right, sought to influence the *Charter*. Compared to postmaterialists, these groups adopted a more ambiguous, or even oppositional, attitude to reform.

In stark contrast to the debate preceding the enactment of CBORA, aborigines played a visible and important role in the *Charter* drafting process. Despite their history of suffering from extensive status-based discrimination, this group generally rejected[34] conceiving their interests through a standard equality paradigm. Instead, they proposed

- entrenchment of particularized status-based rights including, most fundamentally, a right to collective self-determination, and
- protection from the possibility that other *Charter* rights (notably the right to equality) might be used to undermine special aboriginal entitlements.

Despite a suggestion in the 1978 Government White Paper that a new constitutional settlement would specifically address these aboriginal demands, the draft *Charter* as released in October 1980 failed to do so. The only specific reference to aboriginal interests was within a very weakly worded clause which, similarly to the US Constitution's Ninth Amendment, generically protected all existing non-enumerated rights.[35] During the subsequent drafting process, however, aboriginal groups were partially successful in advancing their specific agenda. As a result of the Hays–Joyal Special Joint Committee proceedings (which heavily prioritized consideration of this issue), the following was added to the *Charter* text:

- A stringently worded savings clause protecting aboriginal rights from being undermined by the other *Charter* rights.
- A new clause positively recognizing and affirming 'aboriginal and treaty rights'.

These new provisions were vigorously opposed by both the provinces, who argued that the positive rights would create serious problems around land use and appropriation,[36] and feminists (including some aboriginal feminists) who feared that the savings provision would undermine the *Charter's* protection of gender equality.[37] Additionally, despite earlier contrary indications, the proposed clauses also failed to gain the clear support of mainstream aboriginal organizations.[38] It was in this context that the protection of aboriginal interests was further weakened as a result of the addition of the limitation of 'existing' to the protection of 'aboriginal and treaty rights'.[39] In the final analysis, therefore, the final *Charter* failed to fully satisfy aborigines.[40] Nevertheless, this group was partially successful in advancing its particularized agenda. This success was due to the following factors:

- As previously noted, the protection of aboriginal rights was an extra-provincial issue which could aid the federal political elite's goal of using the *Charter* process to strengthen national unity.

- Despite its clear tension with a strict understanding of liberal rights, aboriginal calls for a recognition of their distinct needs chimed practically with the postmaterialist rights community's openness to reconceptualizing equality as about 'equality of results' as much as formal legal equality (Morton & Knopff, 2000, p. 67).

- Finally, and relatedly, aborigines benefited from widespread goodwill including, in particular, from the federal New Democratic Party (NDP) (who were a key member of the pro-*Charter* political constituency) (Romanov, Whyte, and Leeson 1984, p. 268).

Mention of this strategic position of the NDP highlights the loose, yet important, connection between the left of Canadian politics and the *Charter* project. Throughout the period of its genesis, the federal NDP was an integral member of the pro-*Charter* coalition. The party endorsed federal unilateral action when Parliament voted on the Joint Resolution in October 1980[41] and continued in its support during the following year when the government faced opposition from eight out of ten provinces.[42] The federal NDP specifically, and the left more generally, were particularly attracted to those provisions in the *Charter* which fused a basic liberal ideology with an orientation towards social change. These provisions included the equality clauses' emphasis on substantive 'equal benefit' under the law as well as its specific saving for affirmative action programmes.[43] In contrast, the Progressive Conservatives were far less supportive, seeking at times to scupper the entire initiative.[44] Progressive Conservative spokespeople were also not immune from attacking the very concept of a constitutionally entrenched charter of rights.[45] Their viewpoint was mirrored within other right-of-centre political and social forces.[46] To a significant number on the right, the *Charter* seriously threatened Canada's federal structure and traditional, conservative institutions including the family and denominational schooling.[47] Additionally, it was feared that it would result in rigid, unresponsive government,[48] undermine law and order,[49] and force the accommodation of multicultural and bilingual communities against the wishes of the majority.[50] Most of the right's rearguard attempts to ensure that the *Charter* would not have these effects were successfully repulsed.[51]

The greater support for the *Charter* project on the left as opposed to the right of Canadian politics had practical effects. Although positive socio-economic entitlements were only minimally entrenched,[52] the exclusion of any right to private property was a direct result of NDP influence. Reflecting their own left-of-centre sensibilities as well as a postmaterialist disinterest in economic liberty,[53] Trudeau and the Liberals had proved reluctant to include within the *Charter* a property rights protection similar to that instantiated in

CBORA.[54] Moreover, the proposed *Charter* released in October 1980 had entirely removed private property rights. Despite this, property right advocates benefited from the strong support of the Progressive Conservatives,[55] extensive coverage in the media,[56] and widespread civil society backing.[57] In response, the government appeared willing to re-include some such provision.[58] However, in the face of a credible threat from the federal NDP that it would withdraw from support for the *Charter* project should this eventuate, the government re-strategized and withdrew its previous offer. The failure of this initiative, therefore, was reflective not of 'fierce popular resistance' (Hirschl, 2004*a*, p. 77) but rather the left-of-centre strategic make-up of the pro-*Charter* coalition.

5.4 CONCLUSIONS

The adoption of the *Charter of Rights* in 1982 was an act of first-class constitutional importance which has indelibly shaped the nature of the Canadian regime at both a practical and symbolic level. As the PTT predicts, this adoption was the outcome of a symbiosis between a contingent political trigger and developing pressure from background social developments rooted in postmaterialism. The political origin of the *Charter* arose from the federal political elite's need to find a centripetal symbol and institution to counter the threats to the Canadian federal system emanating from a new and destabilizing form of nationalism which had emerged in the province of Québec. This 'threat to political stability' trigger determined the precise timing of change. Its formidable prospective and rationally self-interested basis also pushed the elite into supporting a strong, constitutionally entrenched model. Furthermore, the trigger's logic of countering 'centrifugal pulls on the balance' (Milne, 1986, p. 38) led to the *Charter* focusing on those rights provisions linked to building up a supra-provincial national identity. These included nationwide linguistic rights, multiculturalism and, to an extent, aboriginal rights.

Although the origins of the *Charter* depended more on a political trigger than any other bill of rights considered in this book, the project was strengthened and shaped by background social developments. The continuing postmaterialization of Canada resulted in an increasingly powerful community of civil libertarians and social equality seekers. These groups provided much needed support for the *Charter* in the face of widespread provincial government opposition. As part and parcel of such support, postmaterialists significantly influenced the framing of many of the *Charter*'s rights.

6

New Zealand and the *New Zealand Bill of Rights Act* (1990)

In 1990, eight years after Canada adopted the *Charter of Rights*, New Zealand enacted the *New Zealand Bill of Rights Act* (NZBORA). Unlike both the Canadian *Charter* and the original proposals put forward by the New Zealand Government in 1985, NZBORA in its final form was neither entrenched nor supreme against other law. Nevertheless, it was clearly influenced by its Canadian cousin and, being the first bill of rights to be adopted within the Westminster world outside of Canada, was ground-breaking. Moreover, as Palmer and Palmer (1997, p. 264) note, it has become 'one of the basic building blocks of New Zealand's constitutional arrangements'. Some thirty years prior to NZBORA, New Zealand had also engaged in a public debate on this issue which resulted in the government producing, but then promptly abandoning, a draft *New Zealand Bill of Rights Bill* in 1963. As with the five-year debate which preceded NZBORA, this (albeit stunted) development was also influenced by events in Canada (in this case, the adoption of *Canadian Bill of Rights Act* (CBORA) in 1960).

This chapter explores and explains these two different outcomes. Sections 6.1 and 6.2 briefly focus on New Zealand's first bill of rights debate. A political trigger for this debate is found in a need to re-strengthen institutional checks and balances, following abolition of the Legislative Council (New Zealand's erstwhile upper house) in 1951. However, given that this trigger failed to point directly to a bill of rights, its impact was extremely weak. As importantly, the failure to enact a bill of rights during this period related to social support for it being forthcoming only from a narrow constituency of neo-liberals; in marked contrast, civil libertarians and other postmaterialists rights groups lacked political salience and, in any case, showed no interest in furthering their concerns through a bill of rights.

Sections 6.3 and 6.4 consider in detail the genesis and lead-up to the NZBORA in 1990. The analysis is presented in schematic form in Chart 6.1 overleaf. In line with the Postmaterialist Trigger Thesis (PTT), this development was directly triggered by the left's 'aversive' reaction to a significant period of non-incumbency under the Prime Ministership of the National Party's Robert Muldoon, widely perceived as authoritarian and heavy-handed.

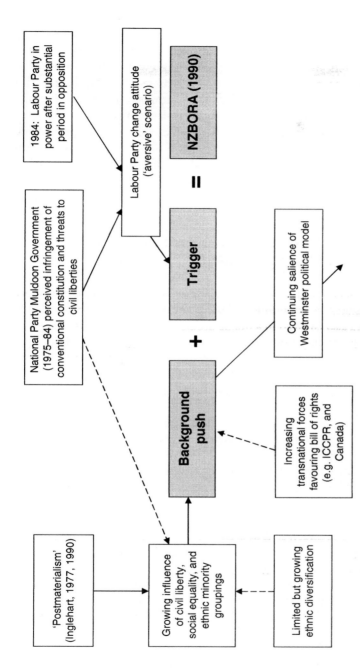

Chart 6.1 Stylized path to the *New Zealand Bill of Rights Act* (NZBORA 1990)

Alongside this, the initiative was disproportionately supported by individuals and groups associated with the civil liberty and social equality movements. Both these movements had grown in political salience and energy as a result of the postmaterialization of New Zealand society. Even within this constituency, however, opposition to a fully constitutional instrument was still strong. This opposition reflected New Zealand's resilient Westminster tradition of parliamentary sovereignty, coupled with its relative isolation from contrary transnational pressures. Allied to the tension between the bill of rights project and the Labour Party's prospective self-interest as a party of government, this pushed constitutional reformers towards advocating for a weak, statutory, and interpretative model eventually enacted as NZBORA.

6.1 CHRONOLOGY OF NEW ZEALAND'S FIRST BILL OF RIGHTS DEBATE

As detailed in Table 6.1, a heightened debate on New Zealand's constitution emerged in the wake of the abolition of the Legislative Council, New Zealand's erstwhile upper house, by the right-of-centre National Government of Sidney Holland in 1951. In that same year, the New Zealand Parliament set up a Constitutional Reform Committee to consider the future of New Zealand's

Table 6.1 New Zealand bill of rights developments (1951–64)

Date	Development
1951	Abolition of Legislative Council by National Government of Sidney Holland. Setting up of a Parliamentary Constitutional Reform Committee.
1956	*Electoral Act* entrenches the franchise, secret ballot, life of Parliament and equal electoral representation.
1957	Constitutional Society for Economic Freedom and Justice founded with goal *inter alia* of a new second chamber, written constitution, and bill of rights.
1960	National Party general election platform commits party to a bill of rights along the lines of *Canadian Bill of Rights Act* (CBORA) as well as to the investigation of the possibility of a written constitution.
1961	New Zealand Parliament's Public Petitions M to Z Committee declines to offer recommendation on Constitutional Society's petition for a written constitution incorporating a bill of rights.
1963	Draft *New Zealand Bill of Rights Bill* introduced into House of Representatives. Referred to Constitutional Reform Committee.
1964	Constitutional Reform Committee unanimously recommends that the bill not be allowed to proceed.

constitutional set-up. Five years later, the Parliament enacted a new *Electoral Act* which 'entrenched'[1] certain fundamental aspects of New Zealand's democratic system (Scott, 1962, pp. 6–7). The following year, shortly before a general election (which National lost), public debate was widened by the founding of a new pressure group, the Constitutional Society for Economic Freedom and Justice. This organization was committed to New Zealand adopting an entrenched constitution encompassing a new second chamber and a bill of rights. National exhibited significant interest in this broad agenda, agreeing in its 1960 general election manifesto to both enact a bill of rights similar to CBORA in Canada and to investigate the possibility of a written constitution (New Zealand National Party, 1960). Despite National's electoral victory that same year, however, in 1961, the Parliament's Public Petitions M to Z Committee refused to endorse any action on the Constitutional Society's public petition for an entrenched and supreme written constitution (New Zealand, Parliament, Public Petitions M to Z, 1961, p. 3).[2] Meanwhile, although the government finally introduced a watered-down version of its proposed bill of rights for parliamentary discussion in 1963, the Parliament's Constitutional Reform Committee unanimously agreed not to proceed with this the following year (New Zealand, Parliament, Constitutional Reform Committee, 1965, p. 2).

6.2 ANALYSIS OF THE FAILURE OF THE 1950s–1960s BILL OF RIGHTS CAMPAIGN

Especially given the marked contrast with Canada's adoption of CBORA in 1960, the failure of efforts during the 1950s and early 1960s to enact a national bill of rights in New Zealand merits close scrutiny. In contrast to Canada, two conditions which the PTT locates as important were absent in New Zealand at this time. Firstly, there was no political trigger which pointed particularly to the necessity of a bill of rights. Secondly, social support for a bill of rights had not developed a postmaterialist base but, rather, was confined to a narrow group of neo-liberals.

6.2.1 Political trigger behind New Zealand's first bill of rights debate

The growth of political interest in a bill of rights during the 1950s was clearly and immediately related to the National Party's abolition of the Legislative Council in 1951. This development prompted fears as regards excessive concentration of power, possible tyranny of the majority, and the potential for the proliferation of ill-considered, or even unjust, legislation. The sub-missions received by the New Zealand Parliament's Constitutional Reform Committee in 1952 all agreed that the abolition of the Council had left New Zealand with insufficient constitutional checks and balances (New Zealand, Parliament, Constitutional Reform Committee, 1952, p. 10). Reflecting this, the unanimous report of this committee stated:

> The abolition of the second Chamber in New Zealand has left the so-called 'sovereign' people with no constitutional weapons save only public opinion (which could be ignored) and an individual vote exercisable only once every three years. If the sovereignty of the people was a relatively small thing prior to 1950, it was made much smaller – in theory and in fact – by the legislation of that year and of the year 1947 which enabled the removal of the Legislative Council from the existing machinery of government. (*Ibid.*, p. 5)

It also noted with concern that 'the fate of minorities in this country is now entirely in the hands and at the mercy of any kind of single Chamber that a majority of the people elected' (*Ibid.*, p. 14).

Given this development, pressure was undoubtedly placed on the elite to enact reforms aimed at re-establishing trust in the robustness of the country's constitutional arrangements. Nevertheless, three factors limited the effect of this trigger as it related to the bill of rights question. In the first place, the trigger itself was relatively weak. This weakness was most starkly indicated by the ability of the National Government to ignore the central and unanimous recommenda-tion of the 1952 Constitutional Reform Committee, namely, that a new Senate be established to replace the Legislative Council. Secondly, in significant con-trast to the situation in Canada prior to the enactment of CBORA, this trigger never pointed to a bill of rights being especially well-suited to solving the public policy problems which had been identified. Instead, a bill of rights was discussed alongside a whole variety of other proposals including a written constitution, a new second chamber, and establishing better review mechanisms within the executive and administration. Thirdly, and finally, as the period from the actual abolition of the Legislative Council lengthened, pressure on the government to find a clear institutional replacement to it naturally reduced. Given that debate squarely on the issue of a bill of rights did not reach the public agenda until 1957, over six years later, this further dissipated the impact of this trigger.

6.2.2 Background (social) factors and New Zealand's first bill of rights debate

Proposals for a bill of rights in Canada emanated from the mid-1930s onwards from a broad constituency of civil libertarians and social equality seekers. Reflecting both the extensive postmaterialization of Canadian society and its strong cultural linkages with the bill of rights-infused United States, these groups formed a powerful constituency for a bill of rights which focused on protecting 'fundamental (and pre-economic) freedoms' such as freedom of conscience and belief (Rishworth, 1995, p. 5). By contrast, in New Zealand, a social movement campaigning for a bill of rights emerged only much later and was confined to neo-liberal activists with a very particularized agenda.

Specific social pressure to enact a bill of rights emerged in 1957, following the founding of the Constitutional Society for Economic Freedom and Justice. This vocal but narrow grouping explicitly linked the case for a bill of rights and/or a written constitution to the furtherance of a highly specific, economic vision premised on the value of free enterprise and deregulation. The Society's aims and objects published in 1957 stated:

> The principal aim and object of the society is the promotion of economic freedom and justice in New Zealand. . . . Economic freedom in this regard means that these enactments and powers must operate fairly and justly in the interests of all New Zealanders and must keep safe and secure their individual freedom, and their right to go about their several trades, business, and professions under a system of private and competitive enterprise. (Constitutional Society, 1957, p. 3)

The specific drafting of the Society's proposed constitutional bill of rights clearly reflected this ambition. Subject to only a few exceptions, Article 14 prevented the State from acquiring any right or interest in property compulsorily, with or without compensation (Constitutional Society, 1961, p. 5). Article 16's right to occupational freedom was clearly worded so as to sound the death knell to the union closed shop. Finally, and most audaciously, Article 17 purported to grant New Zealanders a right to monetary stability (*Ibid.*, p. 7).

In contrast, in basing their proposals on CBORA, supporters of a bill of rights within the National Party sought to appeal to a broader audience. Perhaps predictably, this led to reduced support from the Constitutional Society itself. In October 1962, the Society wrote in its magazine *Liberator* that '[m]embers of the Constitutional Society will not deplore any decision on the part of the Government not to proceed with the proposed Bill of Rights, because they have all along said it would not be worth the paper on which it was printed'.[3] Similarly, although the Society later endorsed the value of the proposed bill of rights before Parliament's Constitutional Reform Committee, it also stressed that 'such a Bill is no substitute for a written constitution protected by a bicameral legislature' (New Zealand, Parliament, Constitutional Reform Committee, 1965, p. 21).

Outside the narrow and economically focused confines of the Constitutional Society, there was practically no support for a bill of rights in New

Zealand. In fact, such a proposal induced widespread apprehension and fear amongst the great bulk of opinion formers. Recently opened archival sources indicate that supporters of a bill of rights within the National Government (principally Ralph Hanan) faced a barrage of criticism from within the civil service when they presented original proposals which would, similarly to the CBORA, have attempted to 'override conflicting legislation, present or future, unless its application was expressly excluded'.[4] In particular, the Permanent Head of the Prime Minister's Office stated that the bill seemed likely to be a 'seedbed of uncertainty'.[5] A similarly critical response was received from the New Zealand Department of Health.[6] Dissent continued even when the draft was significantly watered down.[7] Most tellingly, the Solicitor General A. R. C. Wild, the most senior non-partisan member of the Attorney General's Department, took the almost unprecedented step of appearing before the Constitutional Reform Committee to argue that the proposed bill was 'positively against the public interest' (New Zealand, Parliament, Constitutional Reform Committee, 1965, p. 52). These criticisms were echoed within the New Zealand academy. When informally approached by the Attorney General, Professor C. Aiken of Victoria University of Wellington stated that he saw no merit to the proposal.[8] Similarly, Professor Campbell, also of Victoria University of Wellington, advised that this legislation would be 'unnecessary, ill-advised and dangerous'.[9] All the academics who gave evidence before the Constitutional Reform Committee on the actual draft *New Zealand Bill of Rights Bill* presented a similar analysis (New Zealand, Parliament, Constitutional Reform Committee, 1965).[10] Finally, this proposal was also opposed by New Zealand's nascent civil liberty community. The Executive Committee of the New Zealand Council for Civil Liberties (NZCCL) (which had been founded in 1952) endorsed, apparently on a unanimous basis, the decision of the Public Petitions M to Z Committee that no further action be taken on the question of a bill of rights (and written constitution).[11] Similarly, its annual report of 1962 stated that it was 'difficult to see what useful purpose' could be served by any such enactment (New Zealand, Council for Civil Liberties, 1962, p. 3).

The absence of widespread social support for a national bill of rights was related to a number of factors. New Zealand's sociological make-up as a 'very small community, so homogenous in class, culture and outlook' (Scott, 1956, p. 8) tended to stunt both support for, and the development of thinking around, protecting postmaterialist rights such as civil liberty and social equality. Certainly, some of the opposition to a bill of rights was based on a clear antipathy towards such values. Within the executive, the Secretary of Labour wrote to the Minister of Immigration in 1961 arguing that a bill of rights could undermine New Zealand immigration regulations which were clearly discriminatory on the grounds of nationality and/or race.[12] Nevertheless, it is significant that supporters of immigration law reform, such as the NZCCL (*Ibid.*, p. 5), also rejected a bill of rights. This fact, together with an analysis of the textual record, indicates the critical causal importance of a widely shared cultural conception of legitimate governance. In sum, New Zealand society almost universally subscribed to a traditional Westminster understanding of democracy which prioritized the principle of a legally supreme Parliament aided and supported by a limited and apolitical judiciary. A bill of rights, broadly worded and morally, even if not legally, entrenched, was seen as anathema to such a conception. According to the New Zealand Department of Health, a bill of rights was 'a needless incursion on Parliamentary sovereignty. It savours of the day when New Zealand was a colonial dependency, the laws of which could be held invalid on the grounds that they were repugnant to an Imperial statute'.[13] Similarly, Professors D. Matheson and K. J. Keith argued that such a bill 'ignore[d] the practical, pragmatic approach of British peoples to constitutional issues including basic human rights' (New Zealand, Parliament, Constitutional Reform Committee, 1965, p. 32), whilst the Solicitor General argued explicitly that New Zealand 'should profit from the English experience and follow English methods in preserving the fundamental freedoms' (*Ibid.*, p. 35). In contrast, as Chapter 3 elucidated, Canadian attitudes were affected by a broader range of cultural influences, notably from the United States.[14]

The importance of this absence of broad social support for a bill of rights can be vividly gauged by contrasting the outcome in relation to this issue with that of the proposal to establish a Citizens Appeals Authority or an ombudsman charged with subjecting administrative decisions to scrutiny on grounds of reasonableness and fairness. This proposal also emerged as a solution to the perceived absence of constitutional checks and balances following Legislative Council abolition and was included in National's manifesto for the 1960 election (New Zealand National Party, 1960, p. 28A). The policy was strongly supported not only by the Constitutional Society,[15] but also by the NZCCL[16] and a number of influential academics who, contrawise, had strenuously opposed a bill of rights.[17] Critically, the ombudsman was seen as capable of giving new life to the principle of parliamentary sovereignty. Thus, Professor C. C. Aikman, stated that

> The Ombudsman has been described as 'Parliament's man'. He is to conduct investigations on behalf of the House of Representatives and, in appropriate cases, to place the facts before the House. It may be that rather than impairing the principle of ministerial responsibility to Parliament, the new procedures will increase its effectiveness as a method of exercising control over the executive. (Aikman, 1964, p. 416)

Given this understanding, it is unsurprising that, in contrast to the bill of rights initiative, the *Parliamentary Commissioner (Ombudsman) Act* was duly passed in September 1962 with the first Ombudsman, Sir Guy Powles, taking up his post on 1 October 1962 (*Ibid.*, p. 402).

6.2.3 Māori in New Zealand's first bill of rights debate

The stance of indigenous Māori representatives in this first debate differed from these extremely negative attitudes. In contrast to broader society, Māori concentrated on using the debate to push forward their demand, which had gathered pace from the 1920s onwards, that the Treaty of Waitangi (1840) be incorporated into New Zealand law. This Treaty, entered into by Queen Victoria (represented by Captain Hobson) and some 500 Māori chiefs, attempted to cede the governance of New Zealand to the British Crown whilst guaranteeing Māori certain rights (Orange, 1987). Whilst not necessarily endorsing the general concept of a bill of rights, the New Zealand Māori Council, the peak body representing Māori nationwide, stated before the Constitutional Reform Committee that 'the Bill would hardly be complete without some reference to the Treaty and to the obligations entered into by the Crown on that occasion' (New Zealand, Parliament, Constitutional Re-form Committee, 1965, p. 16). This demand for a reference to the Treaty was not principally prompted by a desire to counter direct discrimination against Māori. Rather, it was aimed at revisiting the land disputes of the nineteenth century and securing a greater measure of autonomy for Māori apart from the wider New Zealand society (Orange, 1987, p. 233). National's 1960 general election policy committed it to consult with Māori on the issue of Treaty incorporation (New Zealand National Party, 1960, p. 14A). Despite this, as in Canada at the same time, non-indigenous policy-makers adhered to a non-discrimination and, ultimately, assimilationist ideology which eventually undercut the logic for incorporation. On 22 June 1961, the Minister of Māori Affairs wrote to the Attorney General stating:

> The words in the proposed Bill of Rights declare the equality of Maoris before the law. Reliance upon this declaration would do away with the need for any Treaty of Waitangi Bill [formally incorporating the Treaty], once it is admitted, as it must be admitted, that the right of property recognized by the Treaty has, substantially, and in so far as it reasonably might, long since been conferred.... It can be argued that there is now nothing left in the Treaty to be acted upon, save a continuation of a right of the Maoris as British subjects.[18]

Direct reference to the Treaty was, therefore, excluded from the draft bill.[19] In sum, therefore, proposals for specifically codifying Māori Treaty rights were both supported and defeated on a substantially different basis from rest of the bill of rights. These issues and tensions would re-emerge in an even more complex form during New Zealand's second bill of rights debate in the 1980s. Nevertheless, even had the Māori proposals not been defeated on their specific merits, they would not have survived the more general difficulties which the broader bill of rights initiative encountered at this time.

6.3 CHRONOLOGY OF NEW ZEALAND'S SECOND BILL OF RIGHTS DEBATE

Throughout the rest of the 1960s and 1970s, there was bipartisan opposition to enacting a bill of rights.[20] Moreover, especially given that the Constitutional Society was wound up around 1965 (when the last issue of its magazine, *Liberator*, was produced), this issue fell off the public agenda almost entirely. Nevertheless, as Table 6.2 details, debate on a bill of rights returned to public prominence from the late 1970s when a number of public intellectuals endorsed a re-examination of the issue. Prior to the 1981 general election, the Labour Party committed itself to a bill of rights and by the time of the 1984 election, which Labour won, its policy had become both more specific and radical. Based on this policy, the new government published a white

Table 6.2 New Zealand bill of rights developments (1978–93)

Date	Development
1978–9	Sir Owen Woodhouse (President of New Zealand Court of Appeal), Professor Kenneth Keith, and Geoffrey Palmer all urge reconsideration of the bill of rights issue.
1981	Labour's manifesto commits the party to adopting a bill of rights.
1984	Labour strengthens its commitment by laying out proposals for an entrenched and supreme bill of rights which would also incorporate the Treaty of Waitangi.
1985	White paper on entrenched and supreme bill of rights published. Issue referred to Justice and Law Reform Committee.
1988	Final report of Justice and Law Reform Committee rejects entrenched and supreme bill of rights but endorses statutory, interpretative instrument.
1989	Interpretative and statutory *New Zealand Bill of Rights Bill* introduced into Parliament. No Treaty of Waitangi provisions. Referred to Justice and Law Reform Committee.
1990	Enactment of *New Zealand Bill of Rights Act* (NZBORA).

paper putting forward plans for an entrenched and supreme instrument (New Zealand, Government, 1985). In 1988, however, the Parliament's Justice and Law Reform Committee rejected this proposal, but endorsed the possibility of a statutory, interpretative instrument (New Zealand, Parliament, Justice and Law Reform Committee, 1988). The following year, such a bill was presented by the government and referred again to the Justice and Law Reform Committee. In August 1990, after some further modification by this committee, the bill was enacted, on the basis of a strict party vote (National being opposed), as the NZBORA.

6.4 ANALYSIS OF THE ORIGINS AND NATURE OF THE NZBORA

In contrast to the situation in the 1950s, the factors identified by the PTT as conducive to successful bill of rights genesis were present prior to the enactment of NZBORA. Interest in enacting a bill of rights was triggered, and structured, by an 'aversive' reaction to the perceived authoritarian rule of National's Robert Muldoon. Moreover, at a background social level, pressure to enact a bill of rights emerged from within the civil libertarian and social equality community. This development was reflective of the growing postmaterialization of New Zealand society. Nevertheless, New Zealand's second bill of rights debate was also marked by some important continuities. In particular, both the weak, experiential, and backward-looking nature of the trigger and the continued societal allegiance to a strong conception of parliamentary democracy made the achievement of a fully constitutional (i.e. supreme and entrenched) bill of rights impossible. This pushed reformers towards the more limited statutory and interpretive model eventually enacted as NZBORA.

6.4.1 'Aversive' constitutionalism and the genesis of NZBORA

The re-emergence of the bill of rights issue in the late 1970s and early 1980s was clearly prompted by an 'aversive' reaction against the activities and outlook of Robert Muldoon's National Party Government (1975–84). Substantively, the government was perceived as demonstrating a worrying disregard for traditional procedural checks and balances. A large number of its acts were thought to show disregard for the rule of law. These included the following:

- The attempt in 1976 to suspend the government's superannuation scheme by issuing a press statement in advance of legislation.[21]
- The decision in 1982 to immediately overturn a court judgment on its water-rights application relating to a dam project on the River Clyde.[22]
- The enactment of special legislation to penalize striking workers at the Marsden Point Refinery Expansion Project in 1984.[23]

More generally, the government engaged in a further centralization of political power. Of particular note

- Muldoon decided to combine the roles of both the Prime Minister and the Minister of Finance.
- In 1977, he nominated sitting National Party Cabinet Minister, Sir Keith Holyoke, as New Zealand's Governor General, ignoring both the conventional consultation with the Official Opposition on such appointments and the traditionally non-partisan nature of this office.[24]

The government's sudden and frequent implementation of various broad, and potentially draconian, initiatives was also increasingly seen as an abuse of the separation of powers, especially given that these changes were made not through Parliament but rather utilizing general statutes,[25] which granted the executive wide-ranging regulatory powers. Wage and price freezes, professional fee freezes, and rent freezes were all implemented using such powers (Rishworth, 1995, p. 11). Moreover, when the Combined State Unions successfully challenged the legal validity of a comprehensive freeze on wages and prices in 1982,[26] the government immediately saw to it that, within a few days, Parliament enacted primary legislation not only reinstating the policy but also ensuring governmental authority to pass similar measures in the future, without further recourse to Parliament (Palmer, 2004, pp. 188–9).

Secondly, and probably as importantly, the bombastic and combative *modus operandi* of Muldoon himself was alienating. Former Labour Party leader and later Prime Minister David Lange states that Muldoon had 'an extraordinary capacity to intimidate . . . a number of Labour members were genuinely afraid of him and he often had a free run. His stare alone could quell some of our front bench into inertia' (Lange, 2005, p. 122). This view is echoed by New Zealand historian James Belich who argues that Muldoon generated 'real fear and hatred in his opponents both within and without his own party' (Belich, 2001, p. 396). According to Belich, this effect had its roots in

> [a] certain mad-dog quality in Muldoon, including an inability to distinguish the significant from the trivial. He wasted his time writing insulting answers to insulting letters, and sending threatening telegrams to university lecturers who criticized him in their courses. He lashed out

at protesters (on one occasion literally), parliamentary opponents and American presidents with the same vigor and disregard of consequences. (*Ibid.*, p. 396)

The activities of the Muldoon Government ignited political concern about the status of human rights and the rule of law within New Zealand's constitutional structure. Moreover, many important public figures indicated that a bill of rights might provide a particularly well-tailored institutional mechanism for addressing this concern. Particularly important in this regard were Sir Owen Woodhouse, President of the New Zealand Court of Appeal, and Kenneth Keith, Professor of Law at Victoria University of Wellington – both of whom indicated a change of mind on the bill of rights issue in the late 1970s (Keith, 1978; Woodhouse, 1979). The new *zeitgeist* especially affected elite Labour Party politicians. Not only did these actors find themselves daily at the brunt end of Muldoon's heavy-handed and authoritarian actions, but their openness to new restrictions on executive power tended to increase as their period of non-incumbency lengthened. It was in this context that a number of key Labour MPs expressed support for a bill of rights (Hunt, interview with author, 21 June 2005; Northey, interview with author, 3 November 2006).[27] These influences had a particularly stark effect on Geoffrey Palmer, the Labour politician who provided the prime constitutional entrepreneurship behind what became NZBORA. A former law professor, Palmer's entire political career could be seen as having been 'built on opposition to Sir Robert Muldoon's method of operating the New Zealand constitution' (Palmer, 2004, p. 171). Moreover, it was experience of Muldoon which constituted the most significant factor behind his metamorphosis from a bill of rights opponent in the 1960s to being its foremost and dedicated advocate (Palmer, 1968, 1979, 1987). Speaking to the Canterbury Council on Civil Liberties in 1984, Palmer stated:

> We can no longer be confident that our fundamental rights will be protected within our system of Government. Ten years ago I shared that confidence when I myself argued against the adoption of a Bill of Rights in New Zealand. However, times have changed. Since then we have seen inroads made into our traditional rights and freedoms through the abuse of Executive power.[28]

After being elected to Parliament in 1979, Palmer played a critical role as Secretary of the Labour Party's Policy Council in ensuring that a commitment to a bill of rights became a part of Labour's policy programme (Palmer, interview with author, 16 November 2004). Moreover, when elevated to the position of Prime Minister in 1989, Palmer specifically retained responsibility for the bill of rights policy in order to ensure that no attempt was made to drop it (Palmer, 1992, p. 58). This action was significant in helping to ensure that the 'aversive' trigger which had prompted elite interest in a bill of rights culminated in concrete reform.

In addition to determining the timing of bill of rights genesis, this trigger critically affected both the strength and scope of NZBORA. Relative to strength, the 'aversive' trigger was fairly weak since it was principally grounded in backward-looking experiences, as opposed to perceived prospective self-interest. On return to government, a number of prominent Labour politicians including Mike Moore, later briefly to become Prime Minister himself, expressed the traditional fears of a party of government that a bill of rights would be proved 'unduly restrictive of the freedom of the government to act nimbly' and 'could result in rights being ossified' (Northey, interview with author, 3 November 2006). More generally, there was an absence of 'enthusiasm' for the bill of rights policy either amongst members of the Labour Government or backbenchers (Palmer, 1992, pp. 58, 62). Indeed, Northey argues that only about eight people within the Labour caucus were actually committed to the original white paper proposals (Northey, interview with author, 3 November 2006). Coupled with the strong societal allegiance to a traditional Westminster conception of parliamentary democracy (discussed below), the relative weakness of this trigger made achievement of a fully constitutional bill of rights impossible. This pushed supporters towards the more limited statutory and interpretative model eventually enacted as NZBORA.[29] Relative to the scope of reform, NZBORA focused on protecting 'procedural' rights, which had been threatened and undermined by Muldoon.[30] This reflected the particular 'process'-based understanding of bills of rights[31] shared by the NZBORA framers. The 1985 bill of rights extensively protected rights associated with the democratic arena (e.g. freedom of speech, association, and the right to vote), as well as the courts (e.g. the right to counsel) (New Zealand, Government, 1985, p. 28). In contrast, as Professor Keith, a key adviser to the government on the bill of rights project noted, rights seen as more substantive were downgraded:

> The draft New Zealand Bill places major emphasis on the processes of government – writ large and small. There is consequently less emphasis on . . . substantive rights than is to be seen in some instruments. That is to say, substantive rights are left rather more to the political processes, processes which are protected and enhanced by some of the provisions. (Keith, 1985, p. 312)

In particular, rather than providing an open-textured equal protection and benefit provision (as under the Canadian *Charter*), only a narrower and close-textured non-discrimination protection was included. This was originally limited to matters connected to race (including colour and ethnic or national origins), sex, and religious belief. Similarly, rights to privacy and family life were excluded on the basis that they 'would seem to be concepts which are too vague to be included in the bill of rights'.[32]

6.4.2 Background social forces and the genesis of NZBORA

In contrast to the earlier debate, social support for a bill of rights in the late 1970s and 1980s came from civil libertarians and social equality seekers. Within the civil libertarian community, alongside the conversion of Professor Kenneth Keith, other supporters included Dr. Jerome Elkind, Anthony Shaw,[33] and Tim McBride.[34] Elkind and Shaw were high profile academics and joint authors of *A Standard for Justice: A Critical Commentary on the Proposed Bill of Rights for New Zealand* (1986). Meanwhile, McBride was a long-time member of the NZCCL and editor of the *New Zealand Handbook of Civil Liberties*. Organizational support was also forthcoming from Amnesty International in New Zealand,[35] as well as the quasi-governmental Human Rights Commission (New Zealand, Human Rights Commission, 1986).[36] Similarly, 65% of the thirteen submissions received from social equality seekers during the original parliamentary inquiry into a constitutional bill of rights were supportive of such an instrument.[37] This contrasted markedly with the global figure of 27% support from all of the 334 submissions received.

In significant respects, the scope of NZBORA reflected the outlook and preferences of these groups. At a general level, the NZBORA focused entirely on ensuring greater protection for civil liberties and against discrimination. More specifically, although the NZBORA framers tended to emphasize procedural civil liberty rights (see above), pressure from social equality seekers ensured that

- the anti-discrimination grounds within NZBORA mirrored the existing legal protections against private discrimination,[38] and
- a specific provision exempting good faith, affirmative action activities was included.[39]

The linkage of NZBORA's anti-discrimination clause to existing private law protections not only resulted in the immediate addition of 'marital status' as a ground of non-discrimination, but also had wider indirect effects. When these latter provisions were expanded via the *Human Rights Act* (HRA 1993) to include seven additional grounds,[40] NZBORA was also updated. This 'undercut . . . significantly, the difference between the [closed-textured] non-discrimination [provision in NZBORA] and a[n] [open] guarantee of equality' as in the Canadian *Charter* (Taggart, 1998, p. 279).

The central role of civil liberty and social equality in shaping NZBORA was the product of a number of factors. First and foremost, it reflected a general increase in the salience of postmaterialist themes and issues within New Zealand society. As Belich documents, the period from 1960 onwards saw fundamental change within the New Zealand economy and society. In particular, there was a dramatic rise in the number of tertiary educated citizens: 'The number of New Zealand university graduates in 1959 had been estimated at a mere 10,000. By 1980, there were 170,000' (Belich, 2001, p. 509). These new graduates constituted themselves at the centre of a growing postmaterialist middle-class constituency deeply concerned with issues connected with human rights and social equality. In particular, parts of this new grouping formed the core of New Zealand's burgeoning women's liberation movement; the first women's liberation conference and feminist magazine *Broadsheet* were both launched in 1972 (Belich, 2001, p. 497), and a gay liberation movement emerged at approximately the same time (Auckland Lesbian and Gay Lawyers, 1994, pp. 93–6). The new emphasis on social equality was given a further impetus by an, albeit limited, diversification of inward immigration patterns from the 1960s onwards to include not only Europeans but also significant numbers of Pacific islanders (Belich, 2001, p. 533).[41] Alongside these basic structural changes, two other factors made the civil liberty and social equality community more internally supportive of protecting rights through a bill of rights. Firstly, the Muldoon Government's seemingly unbridled ability to undermine procedural civil liberties made many within the civil libertarian community painfully aware of the inadequacy of traditional political mechanisms for protecting human rights within the constitution. Secondly, transnational pressure to adopt a more formalized protection of human rights also exerted a limited effect. The *International Covenant on Civil and Political Rights* (ICCPR), which came into international effect in 1976, specifically urged states to 'develop the possibilities of judicial remedy' (Article 2.3.b) with regard to the protection of civil and political rights. New Zealand ratified this Covenant in 1978, and during its first report to the UN Human Rights Committee (a body set up to oversee compliance) faced criticism for failing to develop such remedies through a bill of rights (New Zealand, Government, 1984, p. 7). The subsequent drafting of NZBORA was influenced by the provisions of this instrument. Beyond this, a broader 'demonstration effect' from other Western countries, notably Canada, was of significance for some actors (Cooke interviewed in Sturgess & Chubb, 1988, pp. 375–6).

Notwithstanding the positive advocacy of a number of civil libertarians and social equality seekers, the second bill of rights debate in New Zealand was also marked by significant social opposition to an entrenched and supreme bill of rights as proposed by the white paper. Not only did the National Party oppose it,[42] but the oral and written submissions gathered in 1985 and 1986 by the travelling Justice and Law Reform Committee of the New Zealand Parliament mirrored this disquiet. Of the relevant briefs submitted, 241 (or 73%) were totally opposed to the initiative, whilst only 91 (27%) expressed broad support (New Zealand Government, 1987, p. 4).[43] Though less vocally opposed, the general public was also not enthusiastic. A poll conducted during the general election of 1987 found that only 52% of Labour voters supported the bill of rights proposal, while 58% of National voters were opposed. In addition, polls taken during both the 1984 and 1987 general elections found that a bill of rights was not identified by a statistically significant number of respondents as an issue of particular importance to them personally (Levine, 1991, p. 342). Undoubtedly, the most vociferous opposition was forthcoming from social conservatives.[44] Nevertheless, apathy and even outright opposition to the white paper extended well beyond this constituency, encompassing even a number of civil liberty and social equality groupings including the NZCCL and the Women's Electoral Lobby (Wellington).[45] The proposals were also attacked by many within the New Zealand legal establishment including Sir Clifford Richmond,[46] President of the New Zealand Court of Appeal between 1976 and 1981, and the leaders of the New Zealand Law Society, the central body of the legal profession. At the root of this opposition was certainly not agreement on particular discrete policy perspectives, such as that which united social conservatives. Instead, these contributors were strongly committed to a democracy which placed its trust in the ability of discrete decisions made by a democratically elected Parliament to resolve all political disputes fairly. For example, the chairman of NZCCL, Rob Murfitt, argued against a bill of rights on the basis that it would allow judges, who are 'not subject to public pressure, nor do they stand for election' to rule on 'issues that should be decided much more democratically'.[47] Similarly, the New Zealand Law Society argued that it was 'odd to suggest that important issues of policy should be determined by the lottery of adversary litigation'.[48] More colourfully, one of its vice-presidents described the white paper draft as amounting to 'legisla[tion] by bumper sticker'[49] and reflecting the 'monstrously anti-democratic assumption that the ordinary New Zealand voter cannot be trusted to know what is good for him'.[50] Finally, the Women's Electoral Lobby (Wellington) argued:

The whole concept of a Bill of Rights with the final arbiters being the Judges and not an elected body of Representatives is itself a matter of concern. An elected body of Representatives can be dismissed after three years. . . . Their views are known and on public record, if we don't like their views we can dismiss them after three years. That is democracy.[51]

This Westminster-descended conception of democracy, whilst less completely and fervently adhered to than during the first bill of rights debate, reflected New Zealand's particularly strong affiliation with traditional British legal and political norms and practices. In formal law, until the passage of the *Supreme Court Act* (2003), New Zealand's highest court remained the Privy Council in London.[52] Moreover, similarly to the United Kingdom, a pragmatic political culture had developed which was inhospitable to the codification of constitutional guarantees (Cleveland, *c.*1979; Wilson, interview with author, 11 November 2004). Finally, although present, contrary transnational influences were extremely weak; certainly, any 'soft law' pressure from the ICCPR system was different in kind from that of the much more formalized *European Convention on Human Rights* (ECHR) system in the United Kingdom itself.[53] Alongside the relatively weak nature of the political trigger behind reform (discussed above), this societal opposition and distrust ensured that the original white paper proposal could not immediately proceed in any form. Indeed, the opposition of the New Zealand Law Society alone has been described as 'perhaps the most significant in ringing the death knell of the White Paper proposal' (Rishworth, 1995, p. 19).[54] The near-total abandonment of the white paper not only delayed the enactment of any bill of rights but, more importantly, pushed constitutional reformers towards supporting the limited statutory and interpretative model which came to be enacted as NZBORA.

6.4.3 Specific issues in the genesis of NZBORA

Part of the second bill of rights debate centred on the suggested inclusion of both socio-economic and aboriginal rights within the instrument. Eventually, neither of these types of rights found a place within NZBORA. This reflected a number of complex factors, including that the groups pushing for such rights were not in full agreement with the postmaterialist rights philosophy which was at the heart of the project.

Regarding the socio-economic aspect, theorists associated with the Hegemonic Preservation Thesis (HPT) have argued that '[t]he driving force behind the 1990 constitutionalization of rights in New Zealand was provided by a coalition of economic actors who were pushing for neoliberal economic reforms' (Hirschl, 2000*c*, p. 83). This is incorrect. It is true that, whilst coming from a left-of-centre tradition, the Labour Government which enacted NZBORA had in significant measure abandoned this for the pursuit of market-based economic reforms. However, Labour's new economic policy emerged as a result of pressures from very different constituencies within the party. Whilst economic policy was developed by Finance Minister Roger Douglas and Associate Minister of Finance Richard Prebble (both of whom did have strong neo-liberal connections), the bill of rights project was associated with Geoffrey Palmer and his political allies including Bill Dillon (later Chair of the Justice and Law Reform Committee). Palmer had strong links with postmaterialist rights groupings but, contrawise, did not want his project associated with the economic agenda of Douglas and Prebble.[55] From the beginning, Palmer stressed that economic rights and, in particular, neo-liberal rights should be excluded from any bill of rights. Indeed, he specifically emphasized to his officials that there should be '[n]o reference to economic matters, taxation [or] property rights'.[56] The absence of neo-liberal rights ensured that, far from offering their support, neo-liberal economic actors vociferously attacked the bill of rights policy. For example, the Hon. George Gair, National's spokesperson on labour and industrial relations, stated:

> Nowhere in the New Zealand draft bill of rights is there any equivalent of the United Nations tenet that 'no one may be compelled to belong to an association.' My question is, Why? . . . By this nefarious device the Government seeks to insulate its supportive unions from the need to face up to the challenge of changing times. . . . If ever there were a wish to kiss the union boot, what could be more craven?[57]

Similarly, during the 1985–6 consultation on the white paper proposals, some 18% of opposed submissions cited negatively the lack of protection for private property or voluntary unionism.[58] Pressure for including these rights continued strongly right up to the enactment of NZBORA in 1990.[59] This pressure, however, was rebuffed.

In 1988, Parliament's Justice and Law Committee mooted the possibility of including a range of social and economic rights within what was now intended to be an unentrenched and interpretative bill of rights instrument. Its proposal suggested mixing 'right-wing' rights to private property with 'left-wing' rights such as a right to an adequate standard of living and the right to work (New Zealand, Parliament, Justice and Law Reform Committee, 1988, p. 10). Not being central to the postmaterialist rights philosophy which underpinned the whole project, the proposed legalization of this wider range of rights was successfully opposed[60] by many associated with NZBORA including civil liberties lawyer Tim McBride[61] and Geoffrey Palmer.[62]

NZBORA's aboriginal rights debate raised issues of even greater complexity than the socio-economic dimension just considered. Following on from the Labour Party's Open Government policy, the 1985 white paper proposed that the rights of the Māori people under the Treaty of Waitangi should be 'recognized and affirmed' within any new bill of rights. The proposed legal entrenchment of these provisions was clearly designed to appeal to the increasingly politically salient Māori community which had long been associated with Labour.[63] Certainly, many non-Māori Pakeha New Zealanders expressed fear that the change would result in Māori interests being inappropriately prioritized and uncertainly in the law thereby created. For example, Paul East MP, the National Party's spokesperson on constitutional affairs argued that the clause would 'lif[t] the lid on pandora's box' and 'create expectations the Government cannot fulfil'.[64] The proposal was also significantly more radical than the Māori Council's suggestion in 1963, then rejected, that the proposed statutory bill of rights should include 'some reference' to the Treaty (New Zealand, Parliament, Constitutional Reform Committee, 1965, p. 16). Despite this, Māori generally (although far from universally[65]) came out against the proposed Treaty clause. Māori criticized the fact that the clause did not make referral to the Waitangi Tribunal (a quasi-judicial advisory body set up in 1975 with substantial Māori representation) mandatory, that the 'reasonable limitations' provision could be applied to their detriment, and that the entire clause could be changed or repealed through the ordinary amendment process, possibly without the support of Māori themselves (Kelsey, 1990, p. 54). Most fundamentally, it was argued that to include the Treaty within any enactment mainly dealing with other matters would demean its *mana*, or status, and *tapu*, or sacred nature.[66] Instead, it was suggested that the Treaty be entrenched on its own and given absolute supremacy.[67] Such a proposal, however, was clearly politically impossible, not least given the widespread concerns which had been expressed about the entrenchment generally and the potential for inappropriate prioritization of Māori interests more specifically. Faced with this chorus of opposition from all quarters, the 1988 report of the Justice and Law Reform Committee recommended that the Treaty clause be dropped. The majority of members (i.e. Labour) emphasized that, given that Māori opposition had focused on the dangers of the Treaty clause being subject to repeal, it was untenable to place it within what was now proposed to be a completely unentrenched statute (New Zealand, Parliament, Justice and Law Reform Committee, 1988, p. 4).

Māori failure to rally behind the Treaty clause was clearly significant in its demise and deserves a specific explanation, especially given its surprising contrast with the earlier debates of the 1960s. At root, this changing orientation resulted from a political radicalization and alienation of Māori which developed in the wake of that community's increase not only in size,[68] but also urbanization[69] and awareness of new racial ideologies such as the Black Power movement in the United States. Although urbanization was correlated with improved socio-economic opportunities, the greater *de facto* integration which it spawned was associated with a greater sense of relative deprivation and new threats to the integrity of the Māori language and culture. Radicalization developed strongly, following the economic downturn of the mid-1970s onwards and led to a politics of confrontational direct action and protest as seen in Parliament's grounds in 1975, Bastion Point in 1977–8, and annually between 1971 and 1998 at every commemoration of the Treaty signing at Waitangi. Concomitantly, this mode of politics was ill-equipped to engage constructively in debates of negotiation and compromise such as that necessitated by the 1985 white paper. Additionally, and relatedly, Māori underestimated the potential benefit to them of the proposed Treaty clause. For example, many were unaware that the Treaty, at that time, had no formal status in New Zealand law[70] and that the clause would have given it some (perhaps imperfect) status. Additionally, the New Zealand judiciary may have been perceived to be more opposed to the Māori agenda than was accurate.[71]

6.5 CONCLUSION

Over the past fifty years, New Zealand engaged in two prolonged periods of debate over whether or not to adopt a national bill of rights. The first debate, which resulted in no change, occurred in the late 1950s and early 1960s. It was triggered politically by a felt need to strengthen checks and balances within New Zealand's governance arrangements following the abolition of New Zealand's upper house, the Legislative Council, in 1951. However, a bill of rights never appeared especially suited to mending the institutional deficiencies which abolition of the Legislative Council had helped create and expose. Social support for it was confined to a narrow section of neo-liberal actors centred on the Constitutional Society. The draft bill of rights which this society produced reflected its ideological presuppositions. Moreover, despite the Minister of Justice Ralph Hanan's decision to ground his policy on the rather differently phrased CBORA, civil society and governmental rejection of the proposal was near-universal. This rejection reflected the weakness of postmaterialist rights constituencies in New Zealand society at this time coupled with its overwhelming adherence to a traditional Westminster understanding of governance based on parliamentary sovereignty and a limited, apolitical judiciary.

In a number of respects, New Zealand's second debate of the late 1970s and 1980s was quite different. Here, interest in enacting a bill of rights emerged as part of an 'aversive' reaction against the perceived violations of the rule of law and the authoritarian and heavy-handed actions of National's Robert Muldoon. To many elite policy-makers, including Geoffrey Palmer and Professor Kenneth Keith (both opposed to reform in the 1960s), a bill of rights was especially well-suited to protecting against a future repeat of these experiences. Additionally, the social constituency favouring such an instrument was far more wide-ranging than in the earlier period. Reflecting their growing political importance and increased exposure to new transnational forces, a number of individuals and groups within the civil libertarian and social equality community provided critical support for this initiative. The input of these postmaterialist rights constituencies also impacted on NZBORA's drafting, ensuring that it concentrated not on entrenching neo-liberal liberties but rather on securing non-economic civil and political rights. Alongside this, the imprint of the 'aversive' political trigger was reflected in the NZBORA's emphasis on 'process'-based rights which had been most threatened during the Muldoon era. Notwithstanding these differences, however, there remained a significant tension in the second debate between a strong bill of rights and not only the prospective, rational self-interest of Labour as a party of government but also a traditional Westminster conception of democracy which remained fairly well-entrenched throughout New Zealand society. This ensured that the original proposal for a fully constitutionalized instrument proved impossible. This fact not only delayed the enactment of the bill, but also pushed constitutional reformers towards supporting a limited statutory and interpretative model eventually enacted as NZBORA in 1990.

7

The United Kingdom and the
Human Rights Act (1998)

Following thirty years of public debate, in 1998, the United Kingdom enacted the *Human Rights Act* (HRA), thereby acquiring a modern bill of rights. The HRA was not entrenched, did not grant the judiciary a power to strike down incompatible legislation, and, at a formal level, only gave a domestic legal status to rights which were already binding on the United Kingdom transnationally through the *European Convention on Human Rights* (ECHR). Nevertheless, the direct applicability of HRA combined with the absence at the national level of the limiting 'margin of appreciation' doctrine pointed to the Act exerting deep and systematic effects going well beyond the United Kingdom's transnational human rights obligations. Three aspects – a more unequivocal requirement that other law be interpreted in conformity with the Act where possible (Section 3), a formalized provision for the higher courts to issue a non-binding Declaration of Incompatibility where such interpretation was not possible (Section 4), and a specific judicial remedies section (Section 8) – made it stronger than the *New Zealand Bill of Rights Act* (NZBORA) considered in Chapter 6. Given this, it is unsurprising that, from the beginning, the Act was widely hailed as being of fundamental constitutional significance. Lord Lester, who had favoured a bill of rights since at least the late 1960s, stated that it 'will exercise a magnetic force over the entire political and legal system, and is an Act of fundamental constitutional importance' (Lester, 2000, p. 89). Similarly, opponent Keith Ewing described it as 'the most significant formal redistribution of power in this country since 1911, and perhaps since 1688' (Ewing, 1999, p. 79). These understandings were mirrored in the press. Francis Gibb of *The Times* argued in October 1998 that the Act would be 'the biggest legal and constitutional reform to take place in Britain since the Bill of Rights of 1689'.[1] Meanwhile, an editorial in *The Guardian* from October 2000, when the HRA actually came into legal effect in England and Wales, stated that it was 'a civic innovation on a par with devolution' then being implemented within both Scotland and Wales.[2]

This chapter explains the origins of this important enactment. Additionally, it situates this explanation within a broader analysis of the United Kingdom's public debate on a bill of rights over time. Following Section 7.1's brief chronological summary, Section 7.2 explores the growth of background forces favouring bill of rights genesis. It demonstrates that, since the late 1960s, a politically salient postmaterialist rights lobby, composed of civil libertarians and social equality seekers, not only developed strongly but disproportionately supported a bill of rights. Alongside this, the United Kingdom's participation in the transnational ECHR system also encouraged bill of rights genesis. As Chart 7.1 schematizes, both factors provided critical background support behind what became the HRA; moreover, the imprints of both types of force are reflected in its final form. In contrast to the gradual and generally secular development of civil society pressure for a bill of rights, elite political debate has been marked by an ebb and flow of interest. Section 7.3 argues that this phenomenon relates to this book's broader political trigger perspective. Political interest in enacting a bill of rights first emerged in the mid-1970s and was linked to the strategic position of the smaller parties in Parliament who, given both their postmaterialist rights ideology and general exclusion from traditional political power frameworks, were naturally attracted to power-diffusing constitutional reforms. Nevertheless, the influence of these parties remained highly constrained and, therefore, reform was unsuccessful during this period. In contrast, some twenty years later, an 'aversive' political trigger did clearly develop within the Labour Party and the left more generally. The trigger was rooted in Labour's experience of seventeen years out of power under a Conservative Government which, especially under Thatcher, was widely perceived to be illiberal and authoritarian. As shown in Chart 7.1, this trigger provided a political context within which enactment of a bill of rights became possible. However, given that the backward-looking, experiential nature of the trigger was both weak and conflicted with Labour's prospective self-interest as a party of government, only a limited, statutory bill of rights (the HRA) proved achievable. The last part of Section 7.3 tentatively considers the implications of this analysis for exploring the renewed elite political interest in a more indigenous bill of rights which has developed in the United Kingdom post-2006. Finally, Section 7.4 draws the various strands of argument together and demonstrates how they link to the broader Postmaterialist Trigger Thesis (PTT) perspective forwarded in this book.

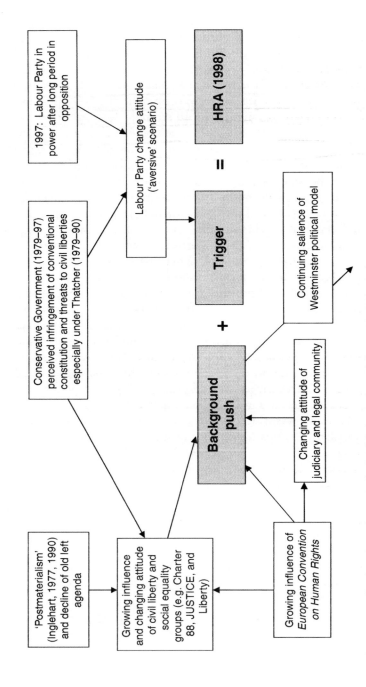

Chart 7.1 Stylized path to the United Kingdom's *Human Rights Act* (HRA 1998)

7.1 BACKGROUND AND CHRONOLOGY

The United Kingdom's contemporary bill of rights debate may be linked back to hundreds of years of constitutional development within the British Isles. Any such analysis would encompass consideration of *Magna Carta* (1215), the *Petition of Right* (1628), the *Habeas Corpus Act* (1679), and the *Bill of Rights* (1688). Developments which were to exert a direct influence on this debate, however, only emerged in the post-Second World War period. As Table 7.1 elaborates, the first such incident came in 1951 when the United Kingdom ratified the ECHR, a human rights framework which was legally binding at the transnational level. Nevertheless, it was not until 1966 that the United Kingdom recognized the compulsory jurisdiction of the European Court of Human Rights and allowed individuals to directly petition the European supervisory institutions. Shortly after this, a public debate on whether to adopt a domestic bill of rights also began, with figures from across the political spectrum endorsing such a move (Hailsham, 1969; Lester, 1969; Macdonald, 1969). This proposal found a political home within the Liberal Party (which, after 1988, merged with the Social Democrats to become the Liberal Democrats). Civil liberty groups also expressed an interest including JUSTICE from 1970 onwards and the National Council for Civil Liberties (NCCL) from 1977. In contrast, broader political support for such a change was episodic. In particular, whilst party political support for a bill of rights was largely confined to the Liberal Party in the early 1970s, the latter part of this decade saw the emergence of interest in such a reform amongst members of both the Labour and Conservative parties. No change, however, was forthcoming and interest then receded during much of the 1980s, only to re-emerge in a more sustained and focused form within the Labour Party and left more generally towards the end of this decade. It was this development which led to the enactment of the HRA, a statutory instrument based on the *European Convention*, in 1998. The latter 1990s, however, saw an increasingly negative attitude towards such reforms within the Labour Party; moreover, this negativity was equally mirrored on the Conservative benches. Finally, however, the period since 2006 has been marked by a renewed interest within all the political parties in the possibility of enacting a truly indigenous British bill of rights which would replace, modify, or complement existing HRA provisions.

Delegating Rights Protection

Table 7.1 British bill of rights developments

Date	Development
1951	United Kingdom accedes to the *European Convention on Human Rights* (ECHR).
1966	United Kingdom adopts individual petition to European supervisory mechanisms and compulsory jurisdiction of European Court of Human Rights.
1968–9	Case for a domestic bill of rights put forward by range of figures from across political spectrum.
1970	Achievement of a bill of rights becomes Liberal Party policy.
1970	Chairman of JUSTICE urges adoption of a bill of rights.
1974	Lord Justice Scarman urges adoption of an entrenched bill of rights.
1975	Conservative MP Sir Keith Joseph supports adoption of a bill of rights.
1976	Labour Party National Executive Committee Human Rights Subcommittee urges adoption of a 'Charter of Rights'.
1977	National Council for Civil Liberties (NCCL) urges domestic incorporation of *European Convention.*
1979	Conservative's general election manifesto commits party to holding all-party talks on a bill of rights.
1979–83	Conservative Government fails to convene all-party talks on a bill of rights.
1987	Conservative and Labour front bench oppose parliamentary attempt to enact a bill of rights based on the *European Convention.*
1988	Founding of Charter 88, a constitutional reform pressure group whose first demand was for a bill of rights.
1990–1	Institute of Public Policy Research (IPPR) and Liberty (formally NCCL) publish draft British bills of rights.
1991	Labour Party commits to enacting a bill of rights
1993	Labour Party endorses policy of incorporating *European Convention* (stage one), followed by the enactment of an indigenous bill of rights (stage two).
1996	Labour Party drops commitment to any second stage of reform.
1997	Labour Party general election manifesto includes commitment to the incorporation of the *European Convention.*
1998	Enactment of the *Human Rights Act* (HRA) and cognate announcement of the creation of the Joint Parliamentary Committee on Human Rights.
2000	HRA comes into full force.
2001	Conservative Party leader argues for HRA repeal.
2003	Home Secretary announces that he is 'fed up' with the judicial use of the HRA.
2005	Conservative Party general election manifesto commits to 'reform or repeal' the HRA.
2006	Conservative Party leader argues for an entrenched 'British bill of rights' to replace the HRA.
2007–8	Labour Government moots possibility of British Bill of Rights and Duties but states no reform will take place until after general election.

7.2 BACKGROUND PRESSURES IN THE BRITISH BILL OF RIGHTS DEBATE

Background pressures to enact a bill of rights developed steadily from at least the late 1960s onwards. Social and economic change led to the growth of a politically powerful postmaterialist rights lobby. This group not only provided important general backing for the concept of a bill of rights but also its conceptualization of how rights should be protected exerted a significant influence on the final shape of the HRA. In addition, the United Kingdom's increasing involvement in the transnational ECHR system pushed forward the domestic bill of rights debate and critically influenced the final shape of the HRA.

7.2.1 Social and ideological origins of the United Kingdom's bill of rights debate

As the theory of postmaterialization predicts, 'the new affluence and mobility of the post-war era' prompted 'a radical dislocation in social attitudes' which by the late 1960s had led to the beginnings of what was termed a 'permissive society' (King, 2007, p. 66). This society

> permitted the previously impermissible: abortion, conspicuous cohabitation, nudity in films and on stage and homosexual relations among consenting adults. Interracial marriage became more common, traditional gender roles became increasingly blurred as women took up jobs previously reserved for men, both sexes' dress styles grew increasingly classless, many traditional dress codes disappeared altogether, and there were radical changes in forms of address with the traditional 'Guv'nor', 'Sir', and 'Madam' giving way to a culture in which even total strangers were permitted to address each other by their first names (which, in turn, were no longer 'Christian' but 'given' names). (*Ibid.*, p. 66)

These societal changes sounded the death knell for the 'old social and political deference' (*Ibid.*, p. 66) and spawned a commitment to a large-scale reform of the law in the area of civil liberties and social equality. The emergence at the same time of social interest in enacting a bill of rights was strongly linked to these developments. Anthony Lester's Fabian Tract of 1969 decried the law's disproportionate restrictions in relation to immigration, the careless delegation of power to officials, and unjust denials of freedom of movement, belief, and expression. Lester argued a bill of rights could ameliorate these problems by 'direct[ing] attention more insistently and systematically than at present to issues of principle involving the individual and the State' (Lester, 1969, p. 14). In a similar vein, the Liberal lawyers group which recommended a bill of rights in the same year linked this to efforts to counter intolerance towards racial and religious minorities, threats to privacy, and the concentration of power in Whitehall, industry, and the mass media (Macdonald, 1969).

As the debate matured and developed, this linkage between support for a bill of rights and a postmaterialist social liberal ideology continued to dominate. Relative to civil society

- In 1970, the Chairman of JUSTICE, Lord Shawcross, endorsed the need for a bill of rights.[3] JUSTICE is a human rights lawyers' association set up in 1957 and, since 1958, also the British Section of the International Commission of Jurists. Amongst its founders was Peter Beneson who later went on to instigate Amnesty International (Madsen, 2004, p. 69).

- In 1977, the National Council for Civil Liberties endorsed incorporating the ECHR into domestic law.

- By the mid-1980s, the campaign for a bill of rights launched by the Constitutional Reform Centre, a loose grouping founded by the Liberal politician Richard Holme, had gained the support of a formidable array of civil liberty and social equality groups including Article 19 (a free speech campaign group), the British Institute of Human Rights, the Campaign Against Censorship, the Disablement Income Group, the Howard League for Penal Reform, Index on Censorship, the Joint Council for the Welfare of Immigrants, the Prison Reform Trust, the Scottish Council for Civil Liberties, and the Spastics Society.[4]

- In 1988, a new and higher-profile constitutional campaign group, Charter 88, was founded with a primary aim of securing a bill of rights. Survey work carried out in the early 1990s demonstrated that the vast majority of Charter 88 members, at all levels of the movement, shared 'postmaterialist' policy preferences.[5]

- Finally, in the early 1990s, the NCCL (now renamed Liberty) conducted a high-profile campaign for a bill of rights which involved a number of social equality groups including the Anti-Racist Alliance, the British Council of Organizations of Disabled People, the Fawcett Society (the United Kingdom's main women's equality group), and Stonewall (the United Kingdom's leading gay rights group) (Foley, 1994, p. 5).

Similarly, core party political support for a bill of rights was concentrated amongst postmaterialist social liberals. In particular

- Achievement of a bill of rights became official Liberal (later Liberal Democrat) policy in 1970 and, with the exception of the shortened manifesto for the second general election of 1974, every Liberal/Liberal Democrat manifesto issued between 1970 and 1997 included a commitment to this (Dale, 2000, *passim*).

- Members of the Liberal Democrats and its founding parties, the Liberal Party and the Social Democratic Party, were directly responsible for twelve out of the seventeen attempts to introduce a bill of rights into either the House of Commons or House of Lords (see Table 7.2).

Table 7.2 Parliamentary attempts at a UK-wide bill of rights prior to *Human Rights Act* (HRA)

Year(s)	Sponsor (and chamber)	Political party	Substantive basis of bill
1969	Viscount Lambton (Commons)	Conservative	*Canadian Bill of Rights Act* (CBORA) (with additional clauses)
1969	Emelyn Hooson QC (Commons)	Liberal	Macdonald (1969) proposals
1970	Earl of Arran (Lords)	Liberal	CBORA (with additional clauses)
1975	James Kilfedder (Commons)	Democratic Unionist	CBORA (preferred)
1975	Alan Beith (Commons)	Liberal	*European Convention*
1976	Lord Wade (Lords)	Liberal	*European Convention*
1977 and 1978	Lord Wade (Lords)	Liberal	*European Convention*
1979*	Lord Wade (Lords)	Liberal	*European Convention*
1980 and 1981*	Lord Wade (Lords)	Liberal	*European Convention*
1981	Alan Beith (Commons)	Liberal	*European Convention* (follow on from Wade's 1980–1 effort)
1981	Robert Maclennan (Commons)	Social Democratic	*European Convention*
1985 and 1986*	Lord Broxbourne (Lords)	Conservative	*European Convention*
1987	Sir Edward Gardner (Commons)	Conservative	*European Convention* (follow on from Broxbourne's 1985–6 effort)
1990	Lord Holme of Cheltenham (Lords)	Liberal Democrats	*European Convention* (no specific bill)
1992	Robert Maclennan (Commons)	Liberal Democrats	*European Convention* (no specific bill)
1994	Graham Allen (Commons)	Labour	*European Convention* plus indigenous rights additions
1995*	Lord Lester of Herne Hill (Lords)	Liberal Democrats	*European Convention*

* All three readings completed.

- A large proportion of the small number of politicians in the two other main parties who championed a bill of rights were also associated with post-materialist social liberalism.[6]

As in the cases of Canada and New Zealand, support for a bill of rights has at times also proved appealing to those advocating a more economically focused, libertarian or neo-liberal vision of human rights. In the late 1960s, the Society for Individual Freedom (SIF) supported and helped draft the bill of rights put forward by Viscount Lambton.[7] Founded in 1942 as the Society of Individualists, SIF 'challenged collectivism' and 'campaigned for the extension and protection of personal freedom, for less State control (including less taxation), and for genuinely free enterprise in place of protected State and private monopolies' (Myddelton, 1994, p. 1). Meanwhile, in the mid to late 1970s, some Conservatives argued that it might be possible to draft a bill of rights that directly furthered an economically libertarian agenda by, for example, limiting the level of taxation and severely curtailing the encroachment of planning laws on private property (Joseph, 1975, pp. 10–12). Despite this, advocacy from neo-liberals was only sporadic in nature and decreased significantly from the late 1970s onwards. These groups played no direct role at all in movement for, and framing of, what became the HRA. In both these respects, the contrast with postmaterialist rights groups was stark.[8] Finally, although not particularly well-organized, much of the opposition to a bill of rights has come from traditionalist conservative forces concerned that the modern ideology of human rights critically undermines traditional institutions including the nation state, the nuclear family, and the Church.[9] During the enactment of the HRA in 1998, peers concerned about these latter two institutions managed, in the House of Lords, to pass an amendment to the then bill which shielded from its impact actions by a person taken 'in pursuance of a manifestation of religious belief in accordance with the historic teaching and practices of a Christian or other principal religious tradition represented in Great Britain' (Great Britain, Parliament, House of Lords, *Debates,* 5 February 1998, col. 788). Although the government managed later to get this amendment overturned, it was forced to add a special interpretative provision requiring the courts to have 'particular regard' to the importance of the 'right to freedom of thought, conscience and religion' in certain circumstances (Section 13, HRA).[10]

Notwithstanding their support for a bill of rights, postmaterialist rights groups in the United Kingdom have proved particularly concerned to ensure that this does not detract from the democratic involvement of the people through Parliament. This concern was a product both of a political culture which prioritized resolving disputes through Parliament and a diffuse fear about the 'reactionary' nature of parts of the British judiciary.[11] Reflecting this, in the early 1990s, the NCCL developed a 'democratic entrenchment' model of bill of rights (Klug, 1991). This complex model suggested:

- Combining elements of parliamentary and judicial finality through dividing rights between principally 'due process' guarantees which would be subject to full judicial review and a range of broader rights subject to a greater degree of parliamentary control.
- Setting up a quasi-independent human rights scrutiny committee within Parliament with responsibility for vetting bills for compatibility with the bill of rights.
- Setting up a human rights commission with a remit to promote democratic deliberation and cultural support for human rights.

This 'democratic entrenchment' model impacted (albeit in a highly watered-down form) on drafting of the HRA.[12] It was reflected in the following:

- The HRA's 'declarations of incompatibility' provision, which allowed the judiciary to signal inconsistently between the HRA and other primary legislation without effecting any formal legal change.[13]
- The setting up of a parliamentary Joint Committee on Human Rights (JCHR) announced at the same time as the HRA's enactment.
- The eventual establishment of a Human Rights and Equality Commission.[14]

7.2.2 The ECHR

The United Kingdom's participation in the transnational ECHR system exerted an important independent effect both in encouraging bill of rights genesis and influencing its shape. In contrast to the Universal Declaration of Human Rights (UDHR 1948) upon which it was partially based, the ECHR was designed to be legally binding. Moreover, a specific institution, the European Court of Human Rights,[15] was set up to issue judgments in particular cases. Despite misgivings about this structure (Marston, 1993), the Attlee Labour Government adopted the ECHR in 1950. Nevertheless, only some sixteen years later did the Wilson Labour Government accept the right of individual petition to, and compulsory jurisdiction of, the European Court of Human Rights in particular cases (Great Britain, House of Commons, *Debates*, 7 December 1965, col. 235). Although largely unanticipated at the time, this change had an important, albeit gradual effect on the legal and political order. By 1989, the court had found the United Kingdom in violation of the

Convention some twenty-three times, the highest within Europe (Jackson, 1997, p. 17). Many of these findings were far-reaching and, in each case, the government responded by changing the law.[16] Meanwhile, the British courts increasingly used the Convention and the court's case law 'as sources of principles or standards of public policy' when domestic law was ambiguous, when the common law was undeveloped, and when determining the manner in which judicial discretion should be exercised (Lester & Beattie, 2007, p. 65).[17]

These developments encouraged moves towards a domestic bill of rights and structured that debate around incorporating rights already found in the Convention. More specifically:

- The successful role of the European Court of Human Rights in finding and correcting rights 'violations' against the United Kingdom encouraged civil liberty and cognate organizations to see value in legalizing human rights protections domestically. It also provided these groups with a powerful 'litmus test' (Brazier, 1998, p. 145), handy for demonstrating that there was a systematic weakness in the domestic protection of human rights.

- As the right of individuals under the ECHR to access the European Court of Human Rights became *de facto* entrenched, the costs to the political elite of conceding a cognate domestic bill of rights appeared to significantly reduce, especially if this instrument was confined to protection of the same rights as in the Convention.

- The increasing consciousness that United Kingdom courts could be, in effect, overruled by the European Court of Human Rights whilst being themselves unable to take the ECHR fully into account in their reasoning, encouraged a shift in judicial and legal elite thinking from scepticism and even hostility to a bill of rights in the 1970s to widespread support in the 1990s.[18]

Some analyses have even argued that the United Kingdom's engagement with the ECHR fundamentally determined the trajectory of the United Kingdom's bill of rights debate prior to the enactment of the HRA.[19] A number of separate, yet converging, facts demonstrate this to be an overstatement. Firstly, not all the bill of rights proposals given a serious public airing since the late 1960s have been based on the ECHR.[20] Additionally, at the time of the HRA's enactment, the European Court of Human Rights had never argued that giving such a domestic effect to Convention rights was amongst the international obligations taken on by state parties as a result of the ECHR. Furthermore, it has been argued by a number who were intimately involved in the drafting of the HRA that it reflected far more than a desire to 'bring home' existing ECHR rights.[21] On the other hand, despite the presence of the HRA, the number of violations of the ECHR found against the United

Kingdom by the European Court appears to have continued to increase, indicating the importance of factors other than non-incorporation in any explanation of this.[22] Finally, neither the postmaterialization processes explored at the beginning of this section nor the development of gradual pressures from the *European Convention* can explain the elite politics of Britain's bill of rights debate. It is to this critical issue that Section 7.3 turns.

7.3 POLITICAL TRIGGERS, THE HRA, AND THE UNITED KINGDOM BILL OF RIGHTS DEBATE

In contrast to the gradual emergence of civil society and transnational pressures for a bill of rights, strong elite political interest in such a project has tended to be episodic as opposed to developmental in nature. This section argues that these ebbs and flows within the elite political debate are best explained through recourse to the political trigger perspective developed throughout this book.

7.3.1 The elite politics of the United Kingdom's late 1970s bill of rights debate

The elite bill of rights debate first developed momentum in the late 1970s when key individuals and groups within the Labour and Conservative parties called for the enactment of an indigenously framed bill of rights and/or incorporation of the ECHR into United Kingdom law. These included, from the Conservative side, Sir Keith Joseph (1975), party spokesperson on policy and research, Lord Hailsham (1976), Shadow Lord Chancellor and the Rights Committee of the Society of Conservative Lawyers (1976). From the Labour side, just retired Home Secretary Roy Jenkins[23] and the Labour Party National Executive Committee's Human Rights Committee (1976) voiced a similar opinion. In early 1977, the Conservatives even (unsuccessfully) moved amendments to include a bill of rights based on the ECHR in the Scottish devolution legislation then going through Parliament.[24] Later, they committed in their general election manifesto to convening all-party talks on a national bill of rights (Conservative Party (Great Britain), 1979).

These developments were prompted by the weakness of the two main parties and concomitantly the strategic position of the Liberals within politics at the time. Following the election of a hung Parliament in February 1974, a second general election in the October resulted in a majority of only three for

Labour. By 1976, even this slender majority had been eliminated as a result of by-elections. This precarious and unstable situation granted unprecedented power to the Liberal Party and to the (Scottish and Welsh) nationalists who also supported a domestic bill of rights at this time.[25] Between March 1977 and July 1978, the influence of the Liberal Party on the framing of government policy was even formalized through the Lib–Lab Pact (Marsh, 1990).

Notwithstanding its ability to influence the political agenda, however, the proactive power of the Liberal Party was distinctly bounded. Writing on the Lib–Lab pact, Ian Marsh (*Ibid.*, p. 309) notes that '[w]hilst the Liberals can be seen to have successfully exerted their veto power and to have achieved modification of government proposals, their failure to advance their own agenda is clear'. In any event, none of the specific experiences of this time pointed clearly to the need for a bill of rights. It is notable that, on the constitutional front, even the Liberals focused most of their energy on other goals including pushing forward plans for devolution in Scotland and Wales and direct elections to the European Parliament based on proportional representation (*Ibid.*, p. 309). This constrained influence, combined with a certain disinterestedness in the bill of rights issue, ensured that neither of the two main parties was presented with a clear impetus to back reform. Therefore, no fully fledged trigger for a bill of rights solidified at this time. Moves within the Labour Party to push for a bill of rights were vociferously opposed, and eventually clearly defeated, by traditionalist forces (Minkin, 1992, p. 216). Meanwhile, whilst the Conservatives did agree to convene all-party talks on a bill of rights, this commitment was soon forgotten once the general election in 1979 had returned them to power with a clear majority.

7.3.2 Labour, 'aversive' constitutionalism and the HRA (1998)

In the 1980s, the leadership of both main political parties returned to opposing a bill of rights. During a House of Commons debate in February 1987 on a *Bill of Rights Bill* introduced by back-bencher Sir Edward Gardner (Conservative MP for Fylde and Chairman of the Commons Select Committee on Home Affairs), the Solicitor General Sir Ian Percival stated: 'Because the Government believe that the underpinning of liberty by law is best achieved by a free Parliament and an independent judiciary in the political climate and tradition of this country, I cannot commend the Bill to the House' (Great Britain, House of Commons, *Debates*, 6 February 1987, col. 1275). Similarly, responding for the Labour front bench, Nicholas Brown argued: 'To allow the courts to question legislation would be to undermine the separation of powers and place the formulation of legislation in the hands of unelected and politically unaccountable persons. If the judges were to determine the legality of legislation, it would transform the role of judges and bring them further into the political arena' (*Ibid.*, p. 1276).

Despite this, from the late 1980s onwards, political interest in enacting a bill of rights re-emerged on the left of British politics including within the Labour Party itself. This interest paved the way for the enactment of the HRA in 1998. Similarly to the origins of the NZBORA analysed in Chapter 6, this was engendered by an 'aversive' trigger formed in reaction to Labour's negative political experiences during a long period of opposition.

One of the simplest factors which engendered this trigger was that Labour experienced an unprecedented, seventeen-year period out of power. This eroded the executive-minded, power-hoarding mentality that had, in modern times, been central to Labour's thinking as a party of government (Bogdanor, 2001, p. 155). Combined with this ideational shift, it also led to fears of a permanent Conservative hegemony which, in turn, encouraged new forms of cooperation between Labour and the Liberal Democrats (renamed from the Liberals after merging with the Social Democrats in the later 1980s). Similarly to the 1970s, this openness led to Liberal Democratic involvement in the formulation of policy advice. For example, the Institute of Public Policy Research (IPPR), which had been founded in 1988 by figures close to the Labour leadership as a 'progressive' alternative to neo-liberal think tanks such as the Adam Smith Institute, appointed William Goodhart, Jeffrey Jowell, and Anthony Lester – all prominent Liberal Democrats – to a committee charged with drawing up a draft bill of rights, and even invited the latter to act as its chair (Lester, Cornford, & Dworkin, 1990). Formalized institutional links peaked in October 1996 with the setting up of a Joint Labour–Liberal Democrat Committee on constitutional reform. However, informal linkages proved as relevant. For example, Lester argues that he played a critical role in converting former Shadow Lord Chancellor Derry Irvine to supporting a bill of rights and that Irvine, in turn, helped convert former Labour leader John Smith (Lester, interview with author, 18 May 2005).[26]

As importantly, ideational support for a bill of rights and a more codified constitution was directly galvanized by concrete experience of what was perceived as the Conservative Government's authoritarian policies and disregard for traditional checks and balances, especially under Margaret Thatcher (1979–90). With regard to checks and balances, the Greater London Council and the other five metropolitan authorities – all Labour-dominated – were simply abolished through the *Local Government Act* (1986). More specifically, the Conservatives became associated with a range of policies which were seen as hostile to civil liberties and social equality. Take, for example, those related to freedom of expression. Here, Thatcher invoked the *Official Secrets Act* to pursue vigorous and vociferous legal action against the divulging of information by Clive Ponting in relation to the Falklands War and Peter Wright in relation to the operation of the intelligence services (Ewing & Gearty, 1990, pp. 143–69). Additionally, 1988 saw the Home Secretary announce a broadcasting ban on interviews with Northern Irish terrorists and their supporters. Implemented without notice, it included within its reach the political wing of the Irish Republican Army, Sinn Fein, whose membership included fifty-six councillors and one MP.[27] That same year, restrictions on freedom of expression were imposed on local authorities with new provisions preventing their involvement in the 'promotion of homosexuality' or the 'teaching in any maintained school of the acceptability of homosexuality as a pretended family relationship'.[28]

More generally, the Conservatives' bellicose and belligerent style of government appeared to underpin a dismissive attitude towards democratic constraints. David Beetham (1989, p. 274) argued, with some hyperbole, that the Conservatives had engaged in a 'ruthless and single-minded use of state power to neutralise opposition, to undermine the autonomy of any agencies that might hinder the project', thus transforming Britain into a 'leadership state' (*Ibid.*, p. 279). Similarly, Paul Hirst (1989, p. 279) stated '[f]or Mrs Thatcher democracy means no more than a periodic plebiscite which selects who should rule; it has little or nothing to do with how they should rule'.

Many opponents of Thatcher, including Beetham and Hirst, argued that her *modus operandi* was only possible 'because of the unique and unreformed character of the British constitution' (Beetham, 1989, p. 275). From this analysis was spawned a surge of interest within the intellectual circles of the centre left in new formalized constitutional protections, including a bill of rights. Most notably, in November 1988, Charter 88 was launched by the left–liberal journal, the *New Statesman and Society*.[29] Meanwhile, both the IPPR and the NCCL produced draft bills of rights in the early 1990s.[30] The IPPR's links with Labour have already been noted. Meanwhile, NCCL also had a clear left orientation; it had been founded in response to civil liberties abuses associated with the Labour movement's hunger marches of the 1930s and continued to have 'strong trade unions links' (Klug, 2000, p. 147).[31] Reflecting their power-maximizing ambitions as a party of government, the Labour Party itself was initially much more sceptical of this new constitutional agenda.[32] Nevertheless, in 1991, shortly after Margaret Thatcher departed 10 Downing Street, it finally committed to enacting some form of bill of rights, thereby becoming the first major political party to do so.[33] In 1993, following a fourth general election loss the previous year, Labour committed to a more far-reaching two-stage process. This encompassed the initial incorporation of the ECHR, followed by the drafting and then entrenching of an indigenous bill of rights (Labour Party, 1993).

Analysis of the thinking of elite Labour politicians at this time demonstrates the 'aversive' roots of this new policy. For example, Paul Boetang, then Shadow Parliamentary Secretary for the Lord Chancellor's Department, stated that the new commitment to a bill of rights was 'Labour's unequivocal response to the Conservative Party's abuses of authority and abdications of responsibility during fourteen years in office'.[34] Similarly, Liberal Democrat politician Robert Maclennan (who jointly chaired the Labour–Liberal Democrat joint consultative committee in 1996–7) argued that in relation to constitutional reform generally

> eighteen years of Conservative government with substantial majorities, and the impregnable certainty of their right to do what they liked with power so long as they had it, conditioned the thinking of the two excluded parties. Judicial review of executive action, particularly of the action of successive Conservative Home Secretaries, had come to seem like the only effective check on an overreaching government. The centralization of power was the over-arching concern of the Labour and Liberal Democrat politicians who worked out the common programme of reform. (Maclennan, 2005, p. 16)

It was this 'aversive' trigger which paved the way for the enactment of the HRA shortly after the Labour Party returned to government in 1997. Nevertheless, its principally backward-looking, experiential nature made it relatively weak in comparison to the prospective self-interest of Labour as a party aspiring to government. As with NZBORA in New Zealand and CBORA in Canada, this fact came to limit the strength of reform. In 1996, following clear signs that its prospects of holding sole executive power in the near future had fundamentally improved, Labour abandoned all commitment to a second stage of bill of rights reform and argued only for a partial incorporation of the ECHR (Labour Party, 1996). Reflecting this, the HRA as finally enacted in 1998 is not entrenched and grants Convention rights only an interpretative legal status vis-à-vis other primary law (Section 3, HRA (1998)). It was also adopted with little of the public involvement and consultation generally associated with an overarching 'higher law'.[35] Nevertheless, especially as a result of the inclusion of Section 4, which allows the judiciary to formally signal incompatibility between HRA rights and other primary legislation, the Act does grant the judiciary an unprecedented role and influence. It therefore poses a significant (albeit somewhat implicit) challenge to the Westminster principle of parliamentary sovereignty which, particularly in light of the wide reach of the legislation, is genuinely path-breaking.[36] Finally, given that the

HRA was almost completely derived from the wording of the ECHR, the 'aversive' nature of the trigger which prompted it did not have a direct effect on the drafting of its rights protections. Nevertheless, the ECHR itself is a highly proceduralist instrument with a relatively narrow scope of rights protection very similar to that of both NZBORA and CBORA (cf. Moravcsik, 2000, pp. 234–5). The scope of the HRA, therefore, mirrors that predicted by the nature of the 'aversive' trigger.

7.3.3 Britain's contemporary bill of rights debate (2007–present): some first thoughts

During its enactment in 1998, the Conservative Party expressed grave reservations about the HRA and even (unsuccessfully) moved an amendment in the House of Commons declining to give it a second reading (Great Britain, Parliament, House of Commons, *Debates*, 16 February 1998, col. 781). In 2001, shortly after 9/11, the Conservative leader, Iain Duncan Smith, committed the party to repealing the HRA when next in office.[37] Meanwhile, the Labour Government's own commitment to the HRA discernibly weakened, especially following its coming into full force in October 2000. Despite this, since the 2005 general election, Britain's bill of rights has both intensified and become somewhat less negative. In particular, in June 2006, the new Conservative leader David Cameron (2006, p. 161) rejected his party's old policy of outright repeal and argued instead that the HRA should be replaced by an entrenched British bill of rights setting out 'the core value which give us an identity as a free nation'. Meanwhile, the following year, the Labour Party's *Governance White Paper* also mooted the possibility of expanding the list of rights and obligations included in the HRA so as to produce a genuinely British bill of rights (Great Britain, Government, Ministry of Justice, 2007). Finally, the Liberal Democrats remained officially committed to enacting an entrenched British bill of rights which would complement and build upon the existing HRA.

Behind the apparent unanimous support for a British bill of rights, however, lay a reality of indecision, ambiguity and incoherence.[38] The Labour Party's approach variously emphasized the importance of new rights especially in the socio-economic realm, the need to stress responsibilities as opposed to rights and the continuing overriding importance of parliamentary sovereignty. Ultimately, the party failed to implement any reform prior to the 2010 general election or even include mention of a British bill of rights in their general election manifesto.[39] This outcome dovetailed with a widespread, cabinet-level revolt against plans for further bill of rights genesis, with Labour ministers, including allegedly the former Home Secretary Jacqui Smith, citing concern that such a change would 'strengthen the hand of the judiciary over parliament'.[40] Meanwhile, the Conservatives variously presented the rubric of a British bill of rights as a vehicle for strengthening constitutionalized rights protections and for removing, or at least weakening, the existing protections of the HRA. Thus, Cameron stated in 2006 that the HRA was remiss in failing entirely to protect the right to jury trial and in not adequately protecting freedom of expression. This element of his speech reflected a more jaundiced attitude to discretionary government which became evident in the wake of the Conservatives' experience of a near decade out of power. At the same time, however, he also argued that the HRA was inappropriately generous in its rights provisions, thereby undermining the fight against crime and terrorism. This very different strand of thinking reflected a continuing strong feeling amongst many within the party that the contemporary human rights agenda conflicts with Conservative values around law and order and a limited state. In the lead-up to the 2010 general election these latter concerns came to be expressed in more vigorous language. Thus, in late 2008, the then Shadow Minister for Justice Nick Herbert (2008, p. 10) frontally attacked the HRA stating that the contemporary emphasis on rights had led to 'a skewed regard for the rights of those who shout the loudest' as well as misguided, 'negative' and 'expensive' attempts to 'drive better performance in public services' (*Ibid,* p. 11). He also stated that the Act has eroded the principles of parliamentary sovereignty, the separation of powers and even democracy itself. Meanwhile, notwithstanding the Liberal Democrats theoretical support for a strong indigenous bill of rights, they invested relatively little political capital in this, preferring instead to mount a vigorous defence of the existing HRA.

In the wake of the formation of the unprecedented Conservative-Liberal Democratic Coalition Administration in May 2010, the new Government has announced the formation of a Bill of Rights Commission to recommend further reform in this area.[41] However, the joint policy which may emerge from this new approach remains deeply unclear. Whilst the Liberal Demo-crat's position and some of the Conservative's rhetoric in opposition may point to a case for further positive bill of rights development, powerful forces within the Conservative Party remain committed to legislation which rows back on existing protections. Given this, it may be argued that significant change in the level of bill of rights institutionalization in the UK appears unlikely in the short- to medium-term. Instead, reform is more likely to alter the precise content of the protection whilst leaving the overall level of institutionalization substantially unchanged.

7.4 CONCLUSIONS

The United Kingdom's bill of rights debate in general and the genesis of the HRA in particular follow the broad logic of the Postmaterialist Trigger Thesis (PTT). Both have been structured not only by developmental background factors but also episodic trigger ones. Relative to background factors, interest in enacting a national bill of rights first emerged in the late 1960s; it was linked to the emergence of a postmaterialist rights lobby concerned with civil liberties and social equality. Although proposals for a bill of rights have been forthcoming from a variety of quarters over subsequent decades, this post-materialist, or social liberal, rights constituency has continued to provide the most consistent and important support for such a reform. Organizations which played a critical role not only in advocating generally for a bill of rights but also helping to structure the final form of the HRA include Charter 88, the National Council on Civil Liberties, and JUSTICE. In addition to this postmaterialist rights factor, the United Kingdom's participation in the trans-national ECHR system encouraged a formalization of human rights domesti-cally. It also strongly influenced the substantive content of the HRA.

Notwithstanding the importance of these background forces, however, the sporadic nature of political interest in bill of rights genesis is largely reflective of trigger factors operating especially at the elite political level. Whilst the Liberal Party (later Liberal Democrats) has consistently supported bill of rights genesis since 1970, both main parties have usually adopted a wary attitude towards this idea, especially when in government. This wariness reflects the power interest of both Labour and Conservative as parties of government, given that bills of rights constrain the power and discretion of the executive by transferring scarce policy-making rights to the courts. During certain periods, however, the attitude of one or other of the main parties has been at least partially transformed. In the late 1970s, the rise of the Liberal Party to a position of strategic influence led to both Labour and the Con-servatives hinting at the possibility of a bill of rights. Despite this, Liberal influence on the policy agenda remained highly constrained. Therefore, neither of the main parties was confronted with an immediate rationale for change and no reform was forthcoming. In contrast, during the 1990s, a clear political trigger did develop on the left of British politics including in the Labour Party. Seventeen years in the political wilderness under a Conservative Government widely perceived to be illiberal and authoritarian saw Labour grow closer to the Liberals (now renamed the Liberal Democrats), and finally embrace the need for greater checks and balances on the executive including through a bill of rights. Whilst Labour's interest in substantial change did dissipate as it drew closer to the reins of executive power, the momentum of this 'aversive' dynamic still ensured the passage of a watered-down, but nevertheless, unprecedented statutory bill of rights (the HRA) soon after Labour returned to government in 1997.

8

Australia and the failure of national
bill of rights genesis

Despite over thirty years of public debate, Australia has not adopted a national bill of rights. This contrasts with the adoption of such an instrument throughout the rest of the Western democratic world including in the three other Westminster systems examined in the previous chapters. This chapter demonstrates the capacity for the Postmaterialist Trigger Thesis (PTT) to explain this puzzling and unusual outcome. Following a chronological outline in Section 8.1, Section 8.2 analyses the origins and nature of the Australian bill of rights debate. The section explores the social and ideological locus of support for the bill of rights initiatives which have been forwarded. It demonstrates that interest in an Australian bill of rights arose alongside the development of a postmaterialist civil liberties and social equality lobby and has been strongly championed, and shaped, by such forces throughout subsequent decades. In Section 8.3, attention shifts to explaining the failure of these initiatives. The hypothesis that an inherent weakness of social demand for a bill of rights can explain this outcome is considered. This hypothesis is rejected in the light of evidence demonstrating that civil liberty and social equality forces have not been less developed in Australia compared with other Westminster democracies. Instead, the section argues that the failure is best explained by factors which have retarded the elite political supply of a national bill of rights. Firstly, the strong institutional fragmentation of the political system has made it harder for the political elite to successfully champion such a (quasi-)constitutional reform. However, this fragmentation is no more severe than in Canada where, as Chapters 4 and 5 demonstrated, national bill of rights institutionalization (BORI) is well-advanced. More importantly, there has been a lack of in appropriately powerful political trigger, providing political actors with an impetus for reform, during the historical periods when political forces close to the postmaterialist rights lobby have held power. In each case, the absence of such a trigger sounded the death knell for the various bill of rights initiatives which had been forwarded.

8.1 BACKGROUND AND CHRONOLOGY

Despite its failure to enact any concrete reform, Australia has periodically debated adopting a national bill of rights. Table 8.1 summarizes key events which relate to this. An important precursor to the modern debate is found in the late nineteenth century when the British colonies of Australasia were discussing the terms on which they might federate. The Australian Constitution did finally include limited rights relating to religious non-establishment and free exercise of religion (binding only at the federal level), a right in criminal proceedings to trial by jury (binding only at the federal level and only 'on indictment'), a right to non-discrimination on the sole ground of state

Table 8.1 Australian bill of rights developments

Date	Development
1901	*Constitution of Australia* creates the Commonwealth of Australia. Some limited rights protections included, but both general equal protection clause and a bill of rights excluded.
1944	Dr Herbert Evatt, Attorney General in ALP Curtin Government ties proposal for extension of federal government's economic and regulatory powers to new constitutional protections for free speech and religion. Defeated at referendum.
1959	Australian Parliament's Joint Committee on Constitutional Review unanimously rejects proposal for a bill of rights.
1969	Australian Labor Party (ALP) commits to securing a constitutional bill of rights.
1973–4	Statutory *Human Rights Bill* introduced by ALP Whitlam Government. Abandoned in lead-up to 1974 general election.
1984	Gareth Evans, Attorney General in new ALP Hawke Government produces draft *Australian Bill of Rights Bill*. Leaked during 1984 general election and abandoned.
1985	Australian Senate's Legal and Constitutional Affairs Committee conducts inquiry into bill of rights issue.
1985–6	New Attorney General, Lionel Bowen, introduces weakened *Australian Bill of Rights Bill*. Passes House of Representatives but not the Senate. Abandoned August 1986.
1988	*Constitution Alteration Acts* propose entrenchment of further limited rights in the constitution. Defeated at referenda.
2008	Robert McClelland, Attorney General in new ALP Rudd Government, sets up National Human Rights Consultation Committee charged with producing proposals on a national bill of rights.
2009	National Human Rights Consultation Committee's report recommends statutory *Human Rights Act* binding at federal level only.
2010	ALP Rudd Government rejects a statutory *Human Rights Act*, backing only limited parliamentary and administrative human rights measures.

residence (binding at both the state and federal level), and a provision which empowered the acquiring of property by federal Australia but only on 'just terms'. Generally speaking, however, Australia rejected the constitutionalization of rights protections (Williams, 1999).

The first sign of any change of approach came in 1944 when the Curtin Government tied its proposals to maintain federal powers over employment and production into the post-Second World War period to the inclusion to new constitutional protections protecting freedom of expression and freedom of religion at the state and federal level.[1] This initiative, however, was defeated at referenda (Galligan, 1990*a*). Labor subsequently returned to its previous distrust of legalized rights protections; this can be seen most clearly in the unanimous rejection of a bill of rights by the Australian Parliament's Joint Committee on Constitutional Review in 1959 (Australia, Parliament, Joint Committee on Constitutional Review, 1959, p. 47).[2] Nevertheless, support for a bill of rights grew throughout the subsequent decade leading in 1969 to the non-parliamentary wing of the Labor Party formally committing to 'provide for the protection of fundamental Civil Rights and Liberties' within the Constitution (Galligan, 1990*a*, p. 355). Given that the right-of-centre Liberal–National coalition has continued to clearly oppose (often strenuously) any suggestion of a bill of rights, this change established a division between the two main blocs in Australian politics, which has continued into the present.

All four subsequent federal Labor administrations have made some attempt to enact a bill of rights; moreover, excluding the special case of the 1988 referendum, the various initiatives have all been based primarily on the *International Covenant on Civil and Political Rights* (ICCPR). During the Whitlam Government (1972–4), a statutory bill of rights supreme against all other law and, through recourse to the federal external affairs power (Section 51 (xxxix), *Constitution of Australia*), binding at both the federal and state level was introduced into Parliament (Australia, Parliament, Senate, *Debates*, 21 November 1973);[3] it was subsequently abandoned. A similarly structured bill of rights was drafted by Attorney General Gareth Evans when Labor returned to power under Bob Hawke in 1983. This proposal, however, failed to gain the clear backing of the Cabinet's Administrative and Legal Sub-Committee (Scott, 1999, p. 155). Having been leaked during the 1984 general election, it was scrapped and Evans removed from his portfolio. The new Attorney General, Lionel Bowen, drafted a weaker statutory bill which was not to be justiciable against State action. This was passed by the House of Representatives (Australia, Parliament, House of Representatives, *Debates*, 15 November 1985) but, after becoming stuck in the Senate, was finally abandoned in late 1986.[4] Despite continuing in power until 1996, the Labor Government made no further attempt to enact a bill of rights.[5] However, the Constitutional

Commission[6] – a body set up by the government in December 1985 to formulate recommendations for the updating of the constitution in time for the bicentenary of British settlement of Australia in 1988 – continued its work. In 1988, the government gave its formal backing to the commission's initial recommendation[7] that a limited set of additional rights be entrenched in the constitution.[8] These proposals were put to referendum in September 1988 but, along with the other recommendations[9] which emerged out of the commission's work, were defeated (Galligan, 1990*b*).

During the early 1990s, the Australian High Court adopted a more activist approach to rights issues in the area of Aboriginal title, implied rights under the Australian Constitution and the role of international human rights law in the delimitation of administrative discretion. For some, it appeared that Australia was close to acquiring a '*de facto* bill of rights' through the back door.[10] However, outside the area of Aboriginal affairs, these rights were almost exclusively confined to the narrow area of freedom of political communication.[11] In any case, from the mid-1990s, the High Court pulled back on its new activist agenda issuing a number of decisions which underscored the limitations of its approach (Gelber, 2005).

Labor returned to power under Kevin Rudd in 2007. The following year, the new Attorney General, Robert McClelland, established a National Human Rights Consultation Committee with a remit to examine the future of federal human rights protection. The report of the committee, finalized in September 2009, recommended *inter alia* that Australia enact of a statutory bill of rights/ human rights act, binding at the federal level only (Australia, National Human Rights Consultation Committee, 2009). In April 2004, however, the government rejected this proposal, agreeing only to some of the more limited parliamentary and administrative measures also suggested in the report (Australia, Government, 2010).

8.2 ORIGINS AND NATURE OF AUSTRALIA'S BILL OF RIGHTS DEBATE

Australia's bill of rights debate emerged out of the post-Second World War growth of a postmaterialist rights constituency. This grouping, which from the mid-1960s became associated with the ALP (and the Australian left more generally), has provided core support for the bill of rights initiatives over the subsequent decades. In contrast, a strong opposition has been forthcoming from the principal opponents of postmaterialist rights, namely, religious and 'family values' campaigners, nationalist Australians, and States' rights proponents.

Neo-liberal economic groupings have also conspicuously failed to support the various proposals which have been put forward.

Before directly analysing these matters, it is useful to return to a consideration of the constitutional debate at the time of the Australian founding. Here, the rejection of the formalized rights protections was motivated by at least two distinct beliefs. Firstly, the founders conceptualized Australia as a British community and, therefore, drew ideological strength from a British (or more specifically English) legal tradition which prioritized the role of Parliament and distrusted the value of abstract rights declarations. In particular, as Haig Patapan (1997a, p. 243) notes: 'Dicey's rejection of entrenched rights and his theory of parliamentary sovereignty and the rule of law were to have a major influence on the founders. He provided the arguments that would justify the retention of traditional English remedies while being wary of any attempts to entrench rights in the constitution.' Secondly, many profoundly feared that legalized human rights guarantees would undermine valued discriminatory practices relating, in particular, to the treatment of people of Asian descent and also Aboriginal people.[12] As John La Nauze (1972, p. 232), the leading historian of this period has stated: '[s]ome of the opponents of [legalized rights] guarantees were thinking of specific and existing discrimination which they would have been prepared to defend'. These beliefs exercised a magnetic hold over the Australian imagination during the first half of the twentieth century. However, they began to be significantly undermined after the Second World War. The 1944 constitutional rights proposal represented a limited precursor to this development. This unsuccessful initiative was almost exclusively associated with the then Attorney General Dr Herbert Evatt, 'a man of liberal convictions' who was 'deeply involved in the international movements of his day' including the new human rights movement of the United Nations and the Atlantic Charter (Galligan, 1990a, p. 348). In general, however, it was not until the 1960s that a reorientation of values became clearly visible. Spawned principally by Australia's social and economic development, this period saw the rise of a large, young, middle-class, and university-educated 'New Left':

> This younger generation of Australians were better educated than their parents, much larger in number than the small number of pre-war elite, more progressive in outlook than their conservative forebears, and sensitive to the broad forces affecting Australia and the rest of the world. They entered adult and public life with a strong desire to improve social and political conditions in Australia, and with the capacity to implement their own political policies and programs. (Tavan, 2005, p. 115)

Spearheaded by the outlook and energy of this new social constituency, it was in the 1960s and early 1970s that Australian society began to reject some of the discriminatory and homogenizing aspects of its traditional culture. Tavan again notes: 'Sexism, racism, conformism, Puritanism, and materialism were increasingly rejected, replaced by values such as individualism, hedonism, anti-authoritarianism, permissiveness, and quality-of-life issues' (*Ibid.*, p. 168).

These developments had their origins outside party politics. However, throughout the 1960s, this new postmaterialist constituency became increasingly associated with the ALP. This new alliance was rooted not only in a shared commitment to 'social change in an egalitarian direction' (Inglehart, 1990, p. 293), but also in a desire on the left to reach out to new groups to counteract the effects of the declining political importance of its traditional working-class base. This new development spawned a significant shift in the policy of the party. It was also linked to a change in personnel culminating in 1967 with the replacement as party leader of Arthur Calwell, an aged, old-style nationalist, staunch Catholic, and strong defender of the White Australia policy, with Gough Whitlam, a young, reformist, internationalist lawyer (Galligan, 1990*a*, p. 353; Hocking, 1997, p. 71; Scott, 1999, p. 59). Returning to policy, in 1963, Labor established a civil liberties section within its platform, which called for a national civil liberties committee and for federal and state civil liberties acts. Two years later, this section was expanded and support for a 'White Australia' immigration policy formally abandoned.[13] Finally, in 1969, the ALP's racist past was clearly repudiated and a strong commitment made to tackle discrimination not only on the grounds of race but also sex (Galligan, 1990*a*). At the same time, and in a linked move, a pledge to include a bill of rights within the Australian Constitution was included within the civil liberties section (*Ibid.*, p. 355). Throughout the rest of the 1970s, Labor's new bill of rights policy was strongly linked to the promotion of these emerging postmaterialist civil liberty and social equality concerns. In 1972, Lionel Murphy, another of Labor's internationalist, 'New Left', lawyers and then Attorney General in the Whitlam Labor Government, defended the need to move beyond responsible government and the common law in the following terms:

> The common law and our system of responsible government do not stop any Australian government that feels so inclined discriminating against whomsoever it pleases, so long as those discriminated against are in the minority or are politically powerless. Ask Aborigines, particularly in Queensland, and many women what equality before the law and equal protection of the law means to them. Whatever Sir Robert Menzies may think of the United States Supreme Court it cannot be denied it has worked an immeasurable service to the nation in the whole field of race relations. And whatever he may think of the capacity and wisdom of our founding fathers, a reading of the pre-Federation Convention debates would oblige him to concede that they rejected a Bill of Rights for

> Australia not just because of their faith in parliamentary democracy, but
> because of their fear that an 'equal protection' guarantee would rule out
> discriminatory legislation against Australian Chinese. This is the legacy
> we must now try to live down. (Murphy, 1974, p. 7)

Murphy's bill of rights initiative received support from postmaterialist rights
groups including the Council for Civil Liberties in New South Wales.[14] In
contrast, the core rivals of this new agenda, namely, 'family values' religious
campaigners[15] and law and order proponents,[16] strongly opposed the idea.

Support for a bill of rights from postmaterialist rights groups was even
stronger during the 1980s. Analysis of the submissions received by the Senate
Standing Committee on Constitutional and Legal Affairs, which conducted
an inquiry on a bill of rights in 1985, indicates that Councils for Civil Liberties
in four out of six of Australia's states wrote in support of the idea.[17] Even more
strikingly, 100% of the submissions received from social equality seekers
supported it,[18] including groups representing ethnic and religious minorities,[19] women,[20] sexual minorities,[21] and the unemployed.[22] In contrast, well
over half the submissions received in opposition were from individuals and
groups with a conservative 'family values' or religious philosophy. These
opponents of postmaterialist rights argued that a bill of rights would undermine Australia's Christian heritage, grant rights which were contrary to the
Bible, and usurp parental authority. Similarly, a number of nationalist Australian organizations argued that moves to enact a bill of rights were part of
'an internationalist conspiracy proved by the fact that only the Warsaw pact
countries [had] adopted the International Covenant'.[23] Finally, reflecting the
distinction between a postmaterialist rights ideology and economic liberalism, neo-liberal groups argued that the type of bill of rights being proposed
would prove harmful, given its failure to entrench private property rights or
an explicit right not to join a trade union. In particular, Chris Cullen,
President of the Australian Chamber of Commerce, labelled Bowen's *Bill of
Rights Bill* (1986) 'a dangerous piece of social engineering that will do little to
protect individual human rights'.[24]

This core locus of ideological support and opposition was also mirrored at
the political level. In particular, a bill of rights was strongly promoted by
Senator Gareth Evans, an internationalist civil liberties lawyer. Additionally,
the Australian Democrats, a small postmaterialist, left–liberal party founded
in 1977, advocated for a strong bill of rights which would bind both the state
and federal level of government.[25] Political supporters of these initiatives
emphasized that a bill of rights would promote social equality ensuring that
the 'treatment meted out to groups and minorities such as Aborigines, homosexuals, single parents, Members of the Communist Party [and] migrants'

corresponded with the central aspects of Australia's 'liberal democratic trad-ition' (Mr Hand, Labour MP for Melbourne, Australia, Parliament, House of Representatives, *Debates*, 14 November 1985, p. 2847). In contrast, the core political opponents of the bill, who were concentrated within the Liberal and National parties, based their opposition on the belief that the bill would 'not confer on the family the widest possible protection which many would believe is the natural and fundamental privilege entitled to families' (John Spender MP, Shadow Attorney General, Australia, Parliament, House of Representatives, *Debates*, 14 November 1985, p. 2747). Instead, it 'reflect[ed] only the values of a self-proclaimed, self-serving cultural elite' (Senator Knowles (Western Australia), Australia, Parliament, Senate, *Debates*, 17 February 1986, p. 461). Additionally, they argued that the enactment of a national bill of rights, especially if carried out through invocation of the federal external affairs power, threatened the federal basis of the country by effecting 'a massive, unprecedented shift in the balance of power from the States to the Federal Government' (John Spender MP, Shadow Attorney General, Australia, Parlia-ment, House of Representatives, *Debates*, 14 November 1985, p. 2746).

8.3 EXPLAINING NATIONAL BILL OF RIGHTS FAILURE IN AUSTRALIA

The social locus of support for and opposition to a bill of rights genesis in Australia has clearly mirrored that found in Canada, New Zealand, and the United Kingdom. It therefore confirms the broader postmaterialist rights logic forwarded in this book. Nevertheless, the contrast in outcome with these other countries presents an important puzzle. Two types of explanation for it appear possible. Firstly, it has been suggested that overall social support for bill of rights genesis has been weaker in Australia than in other Westmin-ster democracies and that this can explain the failure of the various initiatives. Secondly, and alternatively, it may be that particular elite political factors including, most especially, the absence of a relevant political trigger have blocked otherwise achievable reform. This section first considers, and then rejects, the inherent weak demand perspective. The second part of the section then analyses how an elite 'blockage' perspective better elucidates the Austra-lian outcome. Most importantly, it argues that the various bill of rights initiatives which have been forwarded have foundered on the absence of a strong political trigger for reform.

8.3.1 Inherent demand and the Australian bill of rights debate

A dominant perspective within social science regarding Australia's failure to enact a national bill of rights argues that this has resulted from social and other inherent forces favouring such an instrument being weaker in Australia compared with other Westminster democracies. In this vein, Brian Galligan states that 'the Australian situation is quite different from the Canadian where Prime Minister Trudeau was able to tap strong popular support for the Charter of Rights and Freedoms'. In contrast to the Canadian situation, Galligan argues that 'Australia does not have a rights culture' and there has been 'an antagonism or indifference to a bill of rights among the general public' (Galligan 1990*a*, p. 365).

There is evidence which appears to favour this inherent weak demand perspective. During the mid-1980s' debate on the *Australian Bill of Rights Bill* (1985), a good deal of vocal, grass-roots opposition was forthcoming. As Senator Macklin, the Democrat Senator for Queensland and a prominent bill of rights supporter, stated during these debates: 'I and other senators have received hundreds – in fact, in my case, thousands – of letters [against the bill]' (Australia, Parliament, Senate, *Debates*, 14 February 1986, p. 472). Later that decade, proposals for the constitutional entrenchment of a limited range of rights were also rejected at referenda. Additionally, at least some of the inherent pressures or demands on political elites which are present in Canada and the United Kingdom have been absent in Australia. Australia has lacked anything comparable to the linguistic bifurcation which, as Chapter 5 eluci-dated, has been linked to strong and stable social support for rights entrench-ment in Canada in recent times. Turning to the United Kingdom comparison, formal transnational legal pressure on the elite to enact a bill of rights has been weaker in Australia compared to the situation in Britain, following that country's involvement in the *European Convention on Human Rights* (ECHR) system. In contrast to the situation in the United Kingdom post-1966, Australia has found it easy to ignore findings from the ICCPR Human Rights Committee since this committee is not a court and, therefore, cannot issue legally binding decisions (Hovell, 2003*a*). This situation has continued after acceptance in 1991 of an optional protocol allowing for individual petition to this committee (Charlesworth, 1991; Hovell, 2003*b*).

Despite this, the core claims of the inherent weak demand thesis are contradicted by more powerful and significant empirical evidence. Therefore, this thesis must be rejected. Turning to public opinion survey results during the period of the 1980s and early 1990s, a representative section of the public in all four Westminster democracies were questioned about their attitude towards a bill of rights. As outlined in previous chapters, in Canada, during the lead-up to the *Charter*, evidence suggests that approximately 70% of the public supported the idea of a constitutional bill of rights.[26] Similarly, surveys conducted during 1991 in the United Kingdom[27] and during 1991–2 in Australia[28] both suggest that approximately 70% supported the idea of a bill of rights (whether constitutional or merely statutory). In contrast, the only relevant poll on this subject in New Zealand, conducted during the lead-up to the 1987 general election, found that those in favour of a bill of rights were outnumbered by those opposed, undecided, uniformed, or indifferent (Levine, 1991, p. 342). These surveys suffer from deficiencies. Neither the question posed nor the precise model of bill of rights assumed is identical. Moreover, the public's knowledge and interest in such issues may also be limited, casting particular doubt on the extremely high percentages expressing support for such instruments across these cases (Leane, 2004, p. 181).[29] Nevertheless, at the least, the results strongly suggest that popular support for a bill of rights in Australia has been at a minimum comparable with that in the United Kingdom and seemingly significantly higher than in New Zealand.

These findings in relation to the Australia/New Zealand comparison also correlate with an analysis of relevant submissions made to official committees on this topic. As previously noted, during the 1980s, inquiries on the merit of enacting a bill of rights broadly based on the ICCPR were undertaken by parliamentary committees in both Australia and New Zealand. In each case, an open call was made to both individuals and civil society groups to submit their views. In New Zealand, the Parliamentary Justice and Law Reform Committee organized two official inquiries on this subject. Whilst one held in 1985–6 consulted on a fully constitutional (i.e. supreme and entrenched) model as originally suggested in the 1985 white paper, the 1989 inquiry related to the watered-down proposals for a non-entrenched and merely interpretative instrument eventually enacted as the New Zealand Bill of Rights Act (NZBOR). In Australia, the Senate Standing Committee on Constitutional and Legal Affairs organized a similar inquiry in 1985. Although officially not wedded to any particular form of bill of rights, in practice, the committee focused on a model which, whilst not entrenched, was to be supreme against all other law. This model (put forward by Gareth Evans when Attorney General in the early 1980s) constituted a midway point between the two extremes considered in New Zealand. Therefore, in analysing public and civil society support for a bill of rights in relation to these inquiries, it is appropriate to compare figures compiled from this Senate inquiry with a composite average figure of support for the two different models consulted on in New Zealand. Approximately 40% of the 129 relevant submissions received were supportive of a pro-'bill of rights' position in Australia (Australia, Parliament, Senate,

Standing Committee on Constitutional and Legal Affairs, 1985). In contrast, compositing the figures from the two inquiries in New Zealand indicates little over 30% of the 302 submissions provided a similar degree of support (New Zealand, Parliament, Justice and Law Reform Committee, 1985–6, 1989–90).[30]

A third source of evidence relates to the absolute and comparative strength of the social equality community. In Australia, the political importance of this group has been augmented by a sizeable 'multicultural' migrant community which developed as a result of peculiarly large and diverse migration from the end of the Second World War onwards.[31] Again, comparison with New Zealand is instructive. In both cases, a proxy measure of the size of the 'multicultural' immigrant community can be constructed by taking the proportion of the population born overseas and then excluding individuals born within those parts of the industrialized world – the United Kingdom and Ireland, Canada, the United States, and Australasia – which share a common language and substantially common culture with Australia/New Zealand.[32] Figures compiled for 1986 (a year when the bill of rights debate was on the public agenda in both countries) and 1991 (just after the passage of the NZBOR) indicate that the 'multicultural' immigrant community was approximately twice as large in Australia as in New Zealand. Whereas this group comprised 12.2% of the Australian population in 1986 and 13.6% in 1991, the relevant figures for New Zealand are just 5.3% and 6.7%, respectively (Australia, Australian Bureau of Statistics, 1994, p. 18; New Zealand, Statistics New Zealand, 1998, pp. 27–30). Of course, it is true that the indigenous Māori population in New Zealand is much larger than the Aboriginal population in Australia. However, as Chapter 6 elucidated, in contrast to 'multicultural' immigrant communities, Māori actually reacted rather negatively to the bill of rights proposals in New Zealand. This divergence appears to have been rooted in the rather different outlook of this group compared to social equality actors.[33]

Comparison with the United Kingdom presents a similar picture. Although figures including Northern Ireland[34] are not available, data from the 1991 census of Great Britain suggests that the 'multicultural' immigrant community comprised only 5.2% of the population (Great Britain, Office of Population, Censuses and Surveys, 1993, p. 162). Finally, analysis of the 1991 Canadian census provides a figure of some 12.4% (Canada, Statistics Canada, 1992, pp. 8–34) which, whilst clearly significant, is still not as high as Australia. In sum, therefore, as Chart 8.1 indicates, this evidence demonstrates that at least one important social grouping – the 'multicultural' community – strongly associated with support for a bill of rights has actually been peculiarly developed in the Australian case compared at least with New Zealand and the United Kingdom.

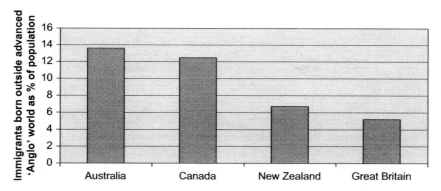

Chart 8.1 Comparative strength of the 'multicultural' community in Australia, Canada, New Zealand, and Great Britain (1991)

Sources: Australian Bureau of Statistics (1994); Canada, Statistics Canada (1992); New Zealand, Statistics New Zealand (1998); Great Britain, Office of Population, Censuses and Surveys (1993).

Overall, comparative evidence does not support the hypothesis that the inherent pressures on the political elite to enact a bill of rights have been lower in Australia than in the United Kingdom or New Zealand. At most, the inherent weak demand thesis helps explain why a constitutional bill of rights along Canadian lines has not been forthcoming. It cannot explain Australia's failure to enact a more limited statutory bill of rights along the lines of NZBOR or the HRA.

8.3.2 Elite political blockages and the Australian bill of rights debate

Exploring factors which have retarded the elite political supply of a national bill of rights does provide an explanation for the failure of Australian bill of rights initiatives. Two such factors have relevance. Firstly, the significant institutional fragmentation of the Australian political system has raised the bar which a bill of rights initiative has to surmount in order to become law. Nevertheless, the similar features of the Canadian political system demonstrate that these barriers can be overcome, given sufficient political momentum. Secondly, and more importantly, in contrast to Canada, New Zealand, and the United Kingdom, the Australian political elites have not been confronted with a sufficiently powerful political trigger, providing an immediate impetus for a bill of rights. This fact ultimately explains the absence of a bill of rights. Its central causal effect comports with the book's broader PTT explanation of how a bill of rights project can successfully be engendered.

Institutional fragmentation

The design of the Australian political system includes heavy and deliberate institutional fragmentation. The *Constitution of Australia* (1901) restricts the sovereignty of federal institutions by apportioning powers vertically between the federal and state levels of government. Recent court decisions have reduced the legal importance of these restrictions, at least as they relate to human rights concerns. Most importantly, in *Tasmanian Dam* (1983), the High Court found that, if federal Australia was a party to an international treaty, then its external affairs power (Section 51 (xxix), *Constitution of Australia*) allowed it to legislate for the states even if the treaty did not cover a subject matter which had the quality of being of international concern.[35] The decision confirmed the capacity of federal Australia to enact a bill of rights, binding at both the federal and state levels, so long as this was linked to the implementation of an international treaty such as the ICCPR. Nevertheless, the recently disbanded National Human Rights Consultation Committee still found that these provisions significantly limited the type of federal statutory bill of rights which would be legal. In particular, the committee's report stated that, at a procedural level, this instrument could not require State courts to interpret State laws consistently with protected rights, nor require State ministers to provide statements of compatibility when introducing legislation (Australia, National Human Rights Consultation Committee, 2009, p. 304). Its ability to require that States establish parliamentary committees to scrutinize bills for compatibility with the protected rights was also considered doubtful (*Ibid.*, p. 305). More substantively, the committee noted, at least if reliance was placed on the external affairs power, no such bill of rights could bind the States to standards more exacting than those required by Australia's obligations under international law (*Ibid.*, p. 303). In any case, cultural allegiance to a strictly applied vertical federalism remains salient within a powerful section of the Australian community; the High Court's centralizing jurisprudence in the area of human rights has been the subject of substantial and sustained criticism (Craven, 1999). Secondly, the constitution fragments power horizontally within the federal sphere itself. This document defines the jurisdiction of the Australian High Court, and the court system more generally, as extending to the exercise of 'judicial power' over legal 'matters' (Chapter III, *Constitution of Australia*). At the same time as empowering and protecting the courts, however, this provision is also constraining. The Solicitor General recently advised the National Human Rights Consultation Committee that court enforcement of broad socio-economic rights such as the right to health, education, and adequate housing would 'not be compatible with Ch III of the Constitution' (*Ibid.*, Appendix E, p. 26).[36] Furthermore, he also argued that any provision requiring that legislation be interpreted compatibly with rights set out in a bill of rights might raise constitutional issues 'if courts in Australia were expected to redraft legislation in a way that courts in the United Kingdom have been willing to do in the light of similar language in the *Human Rights Act* 1998' (*Ibid.*, Appendix E, p. 6). Additionally, a number of legal authorities have also argued that any requirement that courts issue declarations of incompatibility may, given its lack of direct legal consequences for the parties in the litigation, also fail to be validly linked to an exercise of judicial power (McHugh, 2009).[37] In addition to defining the nature of the judicial power, the constitution also establishes an elected upper chamber, the Senate, with virtually coequal powers to the lower house of Representatives from which the government is principally drawn (Galligan, 1995, p. 75). The Senate has acted as a major block on legal change, especially after the replacement in 1949 of a plurality-based system of election to the Senate with a single transferable vote system of proportional representation. This change has ensured that the governing party is usually deprived of a controlling majority within the upper house (Galligan, 1995, p. 89). Finally, formal amendment of the Australian Constitution remains onerous requiring not only the agreement of both houses of Parliament, but also a national referendum carried by both an overall national majority and a state-wide majority in a majority of states (Section 128, *Constitution of Australia*). A survey of thirty democracies completed by Donald Lutz in 1992 found that only two countries (the United States and Yugoslavia) had a constitution more difficult to amend than Australia's (Lutz, 1995, p. 261). Similarly, in a study of thirty-six constitutions in force during the period 1945–96, Arend Lijphart (1999) places the Australian Constitution within the highest category of constitutional rigidity alongside only four others.

This institutional fragmentation has certainly hindered the ability of Labor to implement a bill of rights on its own terms. During the 1970s, implementation of Labor's bill of rights was harmed by both strenuous opposition claims that it represented an unwarranted assault on State autonomy[38] and, according to Whitlam, fears that it might be held unconstitutional by the High Court.[39] Although these legal concerns later receded somewhat, in the 1980s, Labor's bill of rights policy was similarly attacked as a violation of state autonomy and, in addition, ultimately became bogged down in the Senate. During this time, the Senate was controlled not by Labor, but rather by an opposition divided between strong federalists opposed to a bill of rights in principle (notably the Liberal–National coalition) and another group unwilling to settle for a weak bill which, in particular, did not extend its reach to cover the states (the Australian Democrats). Finally, the current blocking majority control of the Coalition and Family First, both traditional opponents of a bill of rights, certainly constituted a formidable barrier against any attempt by the Rudd Government to introduce a *Human Rights Act* as proposed by the National Human Rights Consultation.[40]

This level of institutional fragmentation has not confronted governments seeking to enact a bill of rights in either New Zealand or the United Kingdom. Neither country has an entrenched (or even codified) constitution and they respectively have either no or, in the case of the British House of Lords,[41] a much weaker second chamber. Therefore, in contrast to the situation in Australia, the 1980s Labour Government in New Zealand did not face any federalism concerns and, as a result of the unicameral and then first past the post nature of the New Zealand Parliament, was able to dictate the precise terms of the NZBOR which was then duly enacted on the basis of a strict party vote. In the United Kingdom case, the institutional constraints on the government in relation to what became the *Human Rights Act* (HRA) were also much weaker. It is true that elements of the original bill opposition in the House of Lords and an amendment unacceptable to the government was passed severely restricting the scope of the bill should it conflict with traditional religious practices (Great Britain, Parliament, House of Lords, *Debates*, 5 February 1998, col. 788). Nevertheless, the government was able to overturn this amendment by agreeing to a much weaker special interpretative provision on freedom of thought, conscience, and religion (this became Section 13, HRA (1998)). Ultimately, and in stark contrast to the Australian situation, it was known on both sides that the government could have recourse to the *Parliament Act* (1949) which would have allowed it to override the House of Lords following a delay of approximately one year.

Nevertheless, the relatively high level of BORI in Canada vividly indicates the limited importance of institutional fragmentation as an explanation for the failure of bill of rights genesis in Australia. The Canadian Senate is somewhat less powerful than its Australian counterpart.[42] However, its federal system is generally considered even more decentralized than Australia's. Prior to 1982, federal Canada's ability to bind both the provincial and federal spheres to a common bill of rights was much more restrained since it lacked any cognate to federal Australia's expansive external affairs power. Moreover, even prior to 1982, the formal amendment process under the Canadian Constitution was also onerous. Examining the period 1945–96, Lijphart places the Canadian Constitution alongside the Australian in the highest category of constitutional rigidity (Lijphart, 1999, p. 220).

Contingent political triggers

Far more so than institutional fragmentation, the failure of bill of rights initiatives in Australia has resulted from the absence of an appropriate political trigger, providing elites with an immediate impetus for change. As previously noted, from the late 1960s onwards, postmaterialist rights groups formed a loose alliance with the ALP, leading the non-parliamentary wing of that party to formally commit to the goal of a bill of rights as early as 1969. However, despite constituting one of the two major political blocks in Australian politics since 1950, Labor has only held power nationally for around twenty years, which is only approximately half the number of years during which the right-of-centre Liberal–National coalition has governed. Most importantly, with the possible exception of the period since the re-election of Labor in 2007, the periods in which the party has held power have not been contingently suited to sustaining political support for a national bill of rights project.

Bill of rights initiative in the Whitlam era (1972–5)

No period in Australian history has seen anything similar to the 'threat to political stability' dynamic which underpinned the genesis of the *Charter of Rights* in Canada. Unlike Canada, Australia has not developed significant regionally based ethnic or linguistic divisions, which might threaten the fundamental stability of the federal political system. On the other hand, the context surrounding the victory of Labor in 1972 relates more closely to the 'aversive' trigger dynamic which played such a potent role in the genesis of bills of rights in Canada (1960), New Zealand (1990), and the United Kingdom (1998). In particular, Labor had experienced a long twenty-three-year period of opposition which, as Chapter 7 stressed, naturally encourages an attitude more open to legal constraints on executive power. Additionally, Gough Whitlam was replacing a Liberal-led government that was widely seen as reactionary in its social and moral attitudes (Horne, 1965, p. 157). Nevertheless, aside perhaps from the difficult issue of Vietnam conscription (Macintyre, 1999, p. 226), this government did not have a recent reputation for strong government, authoritarianism, or disregard of civil liberties. By the early 1970s, its controversial 1950s attempt to ban the Communist Party had ceased to be a live policy concern. Indeed, as early as 1965, Donald Horne (1965, p. 153) found that, under the Liberals, there was 'less practical concern with [counter-acting] domestic Communists than there was under Chifley [Labor Prime Minister 1945–9]'.

In a number of other respects, the political situation was disastrous for a bill of rights project. To begin with, the postmaterialist rights constituencies supporting it were still fairly new and ill-developed. Radical reforms linked to these groups were, therefore, never likely to be easy to implement. Anthony Mason, former Chief Justice of the High Court, stated: 'I don't think that there was any strong support for a bill of rights until the 1980s and I'm not sure how strong the support for the bill of rights was even then' (Mason, interview, Sydney, 12 January 2004). Secondly, the government's period of office – a mere three years – was an exceedingly short one for getting legislation of such constitutional importance enacted, especially given the institutional fragmentation of the Australian political system noted above. Finally, and most importantly, the Whitlam years were 'the most turbulent and crisis-ridden since the depression' (Manne, 1999, p. 198). The developing economic, financial, and political crisis naturally came to consume the energies of the administration, drowning out commitment to engage in what was considered somewhat cerebral law reform. This crisis eventually reached a dénouement on 11 November 1975 when, following the coalition-controlled Senate's ongoing refusal to grant the government supply, the Governor General Sir John Kerr dismissed Whitlam as Prime Minister.

Bill of rights initiatives in the Hawke and Keating era (1983–96)

By the time Labor returned to power in 1983, aspects of the socio-political environment appeared more promising. Labor ruled for a much longer period of some thirteen years. Moreover, cultural and legislative change linked to a postmaterialist rights agenda had had time to bed down within sections of the Australian community.[43] Despite this, even more so than in the early 1970s, there was no political trigger which provided the Labor leadership with an immediate impetus for reform.

More specifically, there was a marked absence of those factors necessary for an 'aversive' trigger as developed in both the United Kingdom and New Zealand. Firstly, Labor had only experienced eight years out of power which was a rather short period within the context of that party's history. Secondly, whilst Labor's experience of the crisis of 1975 undoubtedly reshaped the party's constitutional outlook – leading, amongst other things, to clear advocacy for an Australian Republic (Whitlam, 1979, p. 185) – the political lessons learnt pointed away from, not towards, support for greater checks and balances. Thus, the events leading up to the debacle of November 1975 were widely perceived on the left as resulting from the deliberate blocking by the Senate and, later, Governor General Kerr of the democratically mandated 'range of options of an elected government fighting for its survival' (Whitlam, 1979, p. xii). More specifically related to the bill of rights issue, the judicial system was implicated in this not only by Kerr's own judicial background (he was a former Chief Justice of New South Wales), but also by the 'improper advice' (*Ibid.*, p. 83) which the Chief Justice of Australia, Sir Garfield Barwick, gave to Kerr, namely, that 'the course upon which Your Excellency has determined is consistent with your constitutional authority and duty' (*Ibid.*, p. 1). Thirdly, and most crucially, the previous Liberal–National Government under Malcolm Fraser was quite different in both tone and substance to that of, for example, Muldoon in New Zealand or Thatcher in the United Kingdom. In stark contrast to both these individuals, Fraser had acquired a reputation for consensual leadership and for showing a 'very strong liberal or progressive vein' in both his thought and action (Ayres, 1987, p. 83). The Fraser Government had also continued with many aspects of the postmaterialist rights agenda of the Whitlam era. In particular, this government had set up both the Commonwealth Ombudsman in 1977 and a Human Rights Commission in 1980, naming Peter Bailey, a prominent legal activist in the former Whitlam administration, as the latter institution's first head (Bailey, 1990, p. 112). Fraser also drove forward the recognition of Aboriginal land rights in the Northern Territory (Ayres, 1987, pp. 371–2) and, in relation to women's equality, established a National Women's Advisory Council (Ramsay, 2007, p. 257), ratified the *UN Convention on the Elimination of All Forms of Discrimination Against Women* (CEDAW), and began the drafting of federal legislation on sex discrimination (Evans Case, 2004, p. 169). Additionally, the government strongly promoted the social equality of Australia's burgeoning ethnic minorities. This was achieved through 'the absorption of the multicultural ethos into the organs of government' (Kelly, 2000, p. 370), encouraging the establishment of ethnic associations to assist migrants, founding the Australian Institute of Multicultural Affairs in 1978, and developing ethnic media output in the wake of the establishment of the Special Broadcasting Service in 1980 (*Ibid.*, p. 370).[44]

From 1984 onwards, the Australian Democrats came to hold the balance of power in the Senate. Founded in 1977 as a small party with strong grass-roots origins, the Democrats had a highly developed non-executive power orientation, vividly symbolized in their strapline motto 'keeping the bastards honest'. Additionally, they were ideologically left–liberal. As with the Liberals/Liberal Democrats in the United Kingdom, both these factors encouraged a strong commitment to a bill of rights. Nevertheless, similarly to the experience of the British Liberals in the late 1970s (when they formally held the balance of power), the Democrats found it possible to exercise a veto over what they saw as an inadequate Labor proposal on a bill of rights but impossible to forward their own stronger model.

Fundamentally, the trajectory of the bill of rights initiative was driven not by the Democrats but rather by Labor's half-hearted attitude which, in turn, was rooted in the absence of a political trigger for reform. Labor completely abandoned its statutory *Australian Bill of Rights Bill* in 1986, despite clear indications that the Democrats would pass the bill if it were appropriately strengthened.[45] Almost no members of the Labor Government were willing to publicly support the work of the Constitutional Commission or vocally back its 1988 rights referenda recommendation even when these were subject to vitriolic attack from the Liberal–National coalition. The lack of elite Labor support for the bill of rights initiative has been noted by Gareth Evans, the minister put in charge of the original proposals, as the 'huge problem' he faced (Evans, 1992 quoted in Scott, 1999, p. 155). Similarly, Michael Tate, a Labor Senator during the 1980s, doubted whether there was a 'wholehearted' support for the initiative amongst Labor MPs, stated that the whole initiative was a rather 'artificial exercise', and even expressed his own personal opposition to this reform (Tate, interview with author, 1 May 2005). Given that Tate was being described in mid-1980s newspaper reportage as 'one of the strongest supporters of the Bill of Rights' in the Labor caucus,[46] this represents particularly clear evidence of the lack of elite Labor support for change at this time. Finally, following the abandonment of these various initiatives in the latter half of the 1980s, no further attempt to introduce a bill of rights was made by Labor. Instead, after Paul Keating replaced Bob Hawke as Prime Minister in December 1991, Labor's constitutional agenda turned to an unsuccessful attempt to make Australia a republic in time for its centenary of nationhood in 2001. Arguably, this initiative was originally designed to appeal to a similar postmaterialist constituency as Labor's erstwhile bill of rights policy (Betts, 1999). Nevertheless, in critical contrast to it, republicanism, at least in the 'minimalist' form in which it was formulated (Australia, Republic Advisory Committee, 1993), posed no threat to the power of the existing political elite.[47]

Bill of rights initiative in Rudd era (2007–present)

In 1996, the Keating Labor Government was replaced by a Liberal–National coalition under Prime Minister John Howard. Howard had a history of strong opposition to a bill of rights, having been a principal Liberal spokesperson against the various Labor initiatives of the 1980s.[48] Moreover, in significant contrast to Fraser, the Howard Government was linked to a number of policies which were strongly opposed by civil liberty and social equality interests. Areas of conflict included the government's treatment of asylum seekers (Marr & Wilkinson, 2003), aborigines (Rundle, 2001), and gays and lesbians (Johnson, 2003), as well as new security measures enacted in response to a perceived increased threat of terrorism (Williams, 2004, pp. 27–37).

These experiences did prompt a mild 'aversive' reaction within the ALP and amongst the opponents of Howard more generally. Thus, in 2002 the then Shadow Attorney-General, Robert McClelland, linked his call for a bill of rights to criticisms of Howard's anti-terrorism policies.[49] Moreover, the year following Labor's federal election victory of 2007, McClelland as the new Attorney-General set up a national human rights consultation committee charged with considering the question of adopting a national bill of rights alongside other human rights issues. The committee, chaired by Jesuit priest and human rights activist Frank Brennan, received a number of submissions criticizing key elements of Howard's human rights policies (Australia, National Human Rights Consultation Comittee, 2009, p. 15) and urging adoption of a bill of rights (*Ibid*, p. 264). In September 2009, the committee's report recommended adoption of a bill of rights/human rights act, albeit drafted in a statutory and interpretative manner and only applicable to the federal sphere (*Ibid*).

Despite these developments, however, the nature of this trigger was ultimately far too weak to catalyze change. First and foremost, in contrast to political figures such as Thatcher in the United Kingdom and Muldoon in New Zealand, the style of Howard's political leadership did not galvanize concern about the misuse of political power. In fact, far from being abrasively over-reaching, even Howards critics noted that he generally wore the 'face of mildness and unassuming dignity' (Craven, 2003, p. v) and promoted 'an idea of government not as leadership, but as stewardship—that the governor, as the ship's pilot, has no influence on where the ship of state is going, but merely plots a course according to the needs of the passengers' (Rundle, 2001, pp. 54–5). Second and relatedly, many of the concerns about human rights policies under Howard were shared by only a small section of the Australian population. Thus, whereas some 70 per cent of the relevant submission to the National Human Rights Consultation Committee argued that human rights were not adequately protected in Australia, survey research commissioned by the committee suggested that only 7 per cent of the general public shared this understanding (Australia, National Human Rights Consultation, 2009, p. 349).[50] It was also relevant that the Rudd Government does not intend to dismantle a number of the policies which were concretely criticized by the human rights lobby including, for example, the ethnically targeted emergency response to the problem of child sexual abuse in remote Aboriginal communities in the Northern Teritory. Compounding this weakness, any attempt to implement the bill of rights recommendation raised the problem of getting this through a Senate controlled by political forces unsympathetic to the broad ideological thrust of the committee's outlook.

Given this, it is unsurprising that both the ALP cabinet[51] and the parliamentary caucus[52] reacted testily towards the committee's recommendations including, most particularly, the idea of a bill of rights. Although McClelland was slated to provide a government response to the committee's report in December 2009, this was postponed.[53] Finally, however, in April 2010, McClelland announced that the government would not introduce a bill of rights. Instead, the government has adopted some of the more limited suggestions of the committee including more money for human rights educations, the executive vetting of legislation for compatibility with core United Nations human rights treaties, and the setting up of a dedicated Parliamentary Committee on Human Rights. This new framework will not be subjected to review until 2014 (Australia, Government, 2010). Given this, it is clear that there is no prospect of a national bill of rights in Australia emerging in the short to medium term.

8.4 CONCLUSIONS

This chapter has demonstrated the capacity of the PTT to explain both Australia's lack of a bill of rights and the more general contours of its debate on this subject over the past thirty years. As in Canada, New Zealand, and the United Kingdom, proposals for a bill of rights have been championed and shaped by a constituency of civil liberty and social equality seekers, and given added political saliency by the postmaterialization of advanced industrialized democracy. In contrast, other groups including neo-liberals and social conservatives have generally opposed these proposals and seen their interests marginalized within their frameworks. For example, to the chagrin of neo-liberals, all the statutory bills of rights put forward since the early 1970s have either excluded mention of private property rights or explicitly excluded corporations from their protections.

Explanations of the failure of Australia's bill of rights initiatives have generally focused on the alleged special weakness of social forces demanding a bill of rights in this country compared to other similar democracies. However, as Section 8.2 elaborated, a wealth of evidence indicates that the inherent demand for a bill of rights has not been lower in Australia than in other Westminster democracies, notably New Zealand and the United Kingdom, where a bill of rights has been forthcoming. In fact, statistical evidence demonstrates that the 'multicultural' community, a key group within the social equality constituency, has actually been stronger in the Australian case even than in Canada. In contrast to the focus on inherent demand, this chapter has demonstrated that Australia's anomalous position is explained by political factors which have 'blocked' the supply of a bill of rights. To begin with, the extensive institutionalization fragmentation of the Australian political system has raised the bar which elite supporters of a bill of rights have to surpass in order to bring this project to fruition. However, as the Canadian case demonstrates, these barriers can be overcome given appropriate political momentum. More importantly, during critical periods of its history, Australia has lacked an appropriately strong political trigger, providing elites with an immediate impetus for change. In contrast, whether rooted in a 'threat to political stability' or in an 'aversive' response to negative experiences during a long period in opposition, such a dynamic has been critical to national bill of rights genesis in all the other cases considered in this book.

Part III

Conclusions

9

Postmaterialist forces and political triggers

The book has explored bill of rights outcomes in four Westminster democracies with a combined population of a little over one hundred million persons. Notwithstanding this, the Postmaterialist Trigger Thesis (PTT) constructed here connects to, and has important implications for, understanding developments well outside this setting. This chapter examines some of the most relevant connections. Section 9.1 briefly recapitulates the most salient features of the PTT. Following this, Section 9.2 argues that, beyond the Westminster world itself, the thesis has direct applicability to instances of deliberate bill of rights institutionalization (BORI) in internally stable, advanced democracies. The adoption of the Israeli Basic Laws on human rights in 1992 is briefly outlined as an exemplar case. The final, and most tentative, section explores the broader relevance of the thesis considering, in turn, both its political trigger and postmaterialist aspects.

9.1 RISING TIDES AND POLITICAL TRIGGERS: THE PTT

9.1.1 Rising tides

Postmaterialization has constituted the most important background factor behind BORI projects in countries such as Canada, the United Kingdom, New Zealand, and Australia. Ever greater material prosperity, increased cognitive mobilization, and a more individualized economy and society have led to a growing number of people placing a new emphasis on non-economic values and priorities including self-expression, equality, and the quality of life. These individuals have provided backing, either directly as activists or more diffusely as mere supporters, for civil liberty and social equality groupings. In turn, these groupings have pushed for adoption of a bill of rights. Their advocacy has also exerted an important influence on the content of bills of rights. Reflecting the priorities of civil libertarians and social equality seekers, all the government-sponsored bills of rights enacted or proposed within Westminster democracies have included nine core legal procedural rights, five core civil rights, and a right to equality or non-discrimination (see Appendix A).

Despite the centrality of postmaterialist pressures, the PTT stresses that this factor interacts with a range of others which may have either a positive or negative effect. For example, as has recently been stressed within the post-materialist literature more generally (Inglehart & Welzel, 2005), long-term cultural traditions continue to systematically structure political attitudes and outcomes. In the case of the Westminster democracies, British-descended norms of parliamentary sovereignty and an apolitical judiciary have damp-ened demand for a strongly constitutionalized bill of rights. Additionally, transnational forces, such as the *European Convention on Human Rights* (ECHR), have also exerted an independent effect on both the strength and structure of bills of rights. It is the combined impact of all these factors which determines the extent and nature of pressure for BORI.

9.1.2 Political triggers

Notwithstanding the critical role of postmaterialization and other back-ground forces, these pressures are insufficient on their own to prompt a successful national bill of rights project. Additionally, a contingent political trigger which provides actors with a clear and immediate impetus for change is also required. Given that bills of rights work by transferring powers from powerful ordinary political institutions such as the executive to the judiciary, the institutional position of incumbents generally ensures that, even if linked to social interests that favour a bill of rights, they will not whole-heartedly support it. Nevertheless, a sufficiently strong triggering event or dynamic leads not only to the question of bill of rights adoption rising to the top of the political agenda but also to elite political backing for this reform. Given the critical position of incumbents within the policy-making process, such a conversion is essential if reform is to be successful. This conversion may be galvanized by a strategically placed political entrepreneur with a strong normative commitment to reform. John G. Diefenbaker in the case of the *Canadian Bill of Rights Act* (CBORA), Pierre Elliot Trudeau in the case of Canadian the *Charter,* and Geoffrey Palmer in the case of the *New Zealand Bill of Rights* all exemplify such a constitutional entrepreneur. Although it is more difficult to locate such a figure in the British case, John Smith, as Labour's leader, clearly played an important role in constructing that party's bill of rights policy in the period prior to the *Human Rights Act* (HRA).

Notwithstanding the critical role of political triggers in bill of rights adoption, the PTT departs from the strategic understanding of this process by arguing that the political trigger behind reform need not be rooted in clear prospective self-interest. Instead, a trigger may be engendered principally by an experiential reaction against past negative political experiences. Turning to specifics, this book has located two triggers which prompt bill of rights genesis:

- Firstly, under the 'threat to political stability' trigger, a bill of rights emerges as part of a centripetal response to growing centrifugal threats to the continuing stability of a country's political regime. This trigger is predominantly strategic although it is also marked by a normative commitment to a certain conception of the political community.

- Alternatively, under the 'aversive' trigger, a bill of rights emerges as part of a reaction against the prior experience of a substantial period in opposition under a government perceived to be illiberal and heavy-handed. Critically, this trigger is not principally prospective and strategic in nature but, contrawise, is predominantly rooted in a backward-looking and experiential dynamic.

Alongside determining the precise timing of any successful project, the political trigger underpinning change will also effect the nature of the bill of rights proposed. More particularly:

- The type of trigger may effect which rights are suggested for protection. In an effort to shore up political unity, a 'threat to political stability' bill of rights project will generally emphasize a set of substantive values and understandings shared by citizens. In contrast, reacting against the overreaching of power by a previous government, an 'aversive' bill of rights project will tend to emphasize a narrower range of procedural civil liberty and democratic rights.

- The nature of the trigger will also impact on the strength of the bill of rights. In particular, the 'threat to political stability' trigger, which is substantially prospective and self-interested in nature, will tend to engender elite political support for a fully constitutionalized instrument. In contrast, the 'aversive' trigger, which is rooted in reactions to past experience and may, in fact, conflict with prospective self-interest, will be associated with support for more limited, generally statutory, developments.

Chart 9.1 provides a schematic summary of the core attributes of the PTT including the relationship between its various elements.

	BACKGROUND PUSH		POLITICAL TRIGGER		BILL OF RIGHTS INSTITUTIONALIZATION (BORI)
		+		=	
General nature	Long-term process which increases pressure for reform. Operates especially at the social and civil society level.		Short-term and specific event or dynamic. Operates especially at the elite political level.		Reform requires both political trigger and adequate development of background factors. Strength and nature depend on the combined impact of both types of factor.
Most salient features	Postmaterialist value change which increases the political importance of civil liberty and social equality interests.		Contingent change in political environment providing an immediate impetus for a bill of rights.		Level of BORI depends on (a) status of instrument, (b) rigidity of instrument, and (c) scope of rights protection.
Other factors of importance	Transnational pressure for human rights formalization. Background culture (which may promote or inhibit change).		Political entrepreneurship by a strategically placed actor may further encourage change.		Critical details include (a) exact nature of rights included in instrument and (b) exact relationship envisaged between the executive, parliament, and the courts.
Role/impact	Influences strength and scope of bill of rights.		Directs catalyser of change and determines its precise timing. Influences strength and scope of bill of rights.		Alters institutional, political, and legal environment. Extent ranges from 'moderate' (very low BORI), through to 'radical' (high BORI).

Chart 9.1 Bill of rights institutionalization (BORI) according to the Postmaterialist Trigger Thesis (PTT)

9.2 DIRECT APPLICABILITY OF THE PTT:
ISRAEL AS AN EXEMPLAR CASE

The PTT has a broader relevance which stretches well beyond the four Westminster countries from whose experience it was developed. Nevertheless, it is clearly a bounded or middle-range theory.[1] It is only directly applicable to other cases of advanced and internally stable industrialized democracies engaging in a deliberate and public debate as to whether to adopt a bill of rights. This section briefly considers which countries might fall within this rubric. The case of Israel's adoption of Basic Laws on human rights in 1992 is then outlined as an exemplar of the broader applicability of the PTT.

In discussing the shape of bill of rights outcomes in the democratic world, Chapter 2 listed fifteen democracies where any bill of rights currently in force was adopted in a non-transition context. These countries, together with their current BORI score, are relisted in Table 9.1. Given that this listing was derived from a partial sample of democracies assembled by Lijphart (1999), the number of such cases is likely to be significantly larger than fifteen. This suggests the PTT may be directly applicable to a far from negligible range of other cases. Nevertheless, not all the countries listed in the table fit within the

Table 9.1 Bill of rights institutionalization (BORI) in non-transition cases

Country	BORI level
Finland	3.67
Colombia	3.33
Venezuela	3.33
Canada	3.00
Switzerland	2.83
Denmark	2.75
France	2.58
Trinidad and Tobago	2.58
Ireland	2.50
Sweden	2.50
The Netherlands	2.17
United Kingdom	1.50
New Zealand	1.17
Israel	1.08
Australia	0.00

rubric laid out at the beginning of this section. To begin with, although all are formally designated as democratic, some (e.g. Venezuela) are not advanced industrialized countries. Secondly, in a few cases (e.g. Trinidad and Tobago), the current bill of rights replaced a previous instrument which was adopted at a moment of political transition. Finally, in yet other cases, the shift towards a bill of rights resulted not from a deliberate legislative act but rather from a decision of the judiciary which had not been predicted politically. For example, in France, this development resulted from the *Associations Law* decision of 1971, which found that the human rights preamble to the 1946 French Constitution was justiciable (Bell, 1994, p. 138). In these cases, therefore, the PTT would be only partially applicable.[2]

Ultimately, it is beyond the scope of this book to systematically analyse the reach of the PTT. Given this, the wider applicability of the thesis will merely be indicated by demonstrating its capacity to help explain one further case, namely, Israel's adoption of its first Basic Laws on human rights in the early 1990s.

9.2.1 Socio-politics of the Israeli Basic Laws

The linkage between the adoption of the Israeli human rights Basic Laws and a postmaterialist rights agenda are clear and striking. Although a bill of rights had been periodically proposed from the founding of Israel in 1948 onwards, the immediate origins of these Basic Laws are traceable to activities of Member of the Knesset (MK) Professor Amnon Rubinstein. Rubinstein not only spearheaded the enactment of an integrated Basic Law on Human Rights throughout the 1980s but, when this proved unachievable, unbundled its various aspects into four separate Basic Laws, two of which were successfully enacted in 1992. As an academic and, from 1977, both the founder and a leading politician of Shinui (Change), Rubinstein has a forty-year long record of supporting postmaterialist rights causes including the separation of religion and State, civil marriage, and social equality. For example, in the early 1990s, he coupled his initiative on a bill of rights with a successful attempt to repeal military regulations which discriminated against gay and lesbian Israelis.[3] The broader locus of political support for, and opposition to, the reforms also betrays a strong cleavage around support for, or opposition to, postmaterialist rights positions. Table 9.2 tabulates the final vote in the Knesset on *Basic Law: Human Dignity and Liberty*, the more important and far-reaching of the two Basic Laws.[4]

The parliamentary representatives of four parties – Shinui, Ratz, Mapan, and Hadesh – voted without exception for this law. As outlined below, their

Table 9.2 Final vote on Israel *Basic Law on Human Dignity and Liberty* (1992)

Support for law	
Political party	Votes (as % of seats)
Hadesh	3 (100)
Mapan (Meretz)	3 (100)
Ratz (Meretz)	5 (100)
Shinui (Meretz)	2 (100)
Likud	11 (30)
Labor	7 (18)
Mafdal	1 (20)
Total	**32**

Registered abstention	
Political party	Votes (as % of seats)
Mafdal	1 (20)

Opposition to law	
Political party	Votes (as % of seats)
Black Panthers	1 (100)
Degel Hatorah	2 (100)
Geulat Yisrael	1 (100)
Tehiya	3 (100)
Moldet	2 (100)
Moriah	1 (100)
Shas	5 (100)
Agudat Yisrael	3 (60)
Mafdal	1 (20)
Likud	2 (5)
Total	**21**

only commonality was commitment to a postmaterialist or 'left–liberal' ideology. The political interests of Shinui in the separation of religion and State, civil marriage, and social equality have already been mentioned. This party was also a prominent member of Liberal International. Ratz, also known as the Movement for Civil Rights and Peace, combined a similar domestic agenda with commitment to the defence of the rights of the Palestinians including an Israeli withdrawal from the Occupied Territories.[5]

Meanwhile, whilst both Hadesh and Mapan hailed from the traditional (and in Hadesh's case, extreme) left, both had a more recent history of engagement with postmaterialist and human rights issues. Thus, Hadesh, which defines itself as a non-Zionist party, was and is a strong advocate for the equal rights of Arabs within Israel (including the right of return or compensation for Palestinian refugees). It also supports a complete withdrawal from all of the Occupied Territories. Similarly, Mapan had emerged as a major proponent for a new approach to the Palestinian conflict including direct talks with the Palestine Liberation Organization (PLO)(Lochery, 1997, p. 166).

Enactment of the law also depended upon support from within the two major political blocs of the time in Israel, namely, the Labor and Likud parties. Despite only a small minority of its Knesset members actually casting a vote at the final reading, Labor was, in principle, almost universally supportive of the human rights Basic Laws. In fact, during the first reading on *Basic Law: Human Dignity and Liberty* in April 1991 some 61% of Labor MKs voted for the law; meanwhile, at no point in the process (including third reading) did any Labor MK oppose the law or even formally abstain. This reality reflected the growth during the 1970s and 1980s of powerful new groupings within Labor (namely, Mashov and Kfar HaYarok) who were strongly postmaterialist in their values and extremely close to both Shinui and Ratz (Rynhold, 2007). Although the right-of-centre Likud was ideologically split on the issue (with a number of MKs, notably Michael Eitan, eventually voicing their explicit opposition), the key politicians who pushed for human rights Basic Laws within this party also shared a postmaterialist policy outlook. For example, Dan Meridor, the Likud Justice Minister who promoted for a Basic Law on human rights throughout the late 1980s and early 1990s, has been a strong advocate of the values of civil liberties and social equality throughout his political career. Thus, Hashem Mahameed, an Arab MK representing Hadesh at the time of the enactment of the Basic Laws, stated that he thought Meridor was 'known as a very straight, good man', that 'people liked and loved him', and that if a poll was conducted amongst the Arab population it would be found that 'Meridor is one from the main politicians that we might be in favour of' (Mahameed, interview with author, 9 November 2009). Meanwhile, opposition to the law was forthcoming from right-wing opponents of a postmaterialist rights ideology.[6] These included MKs from both the small ultra-religious parties, namely, Degel Hatorah, Geulat Yisrael, Moriah, Shas, Agudat Yisrael, and Mafdal, as well as MKs of a more secular right-wing persuasion from Moldet and Tehiya. Irrespective of their origins in Ashkenazi, Sephardi, Haredi, or Mizrahi Judaism, ultra-religious MKs argued that the new laws would threaten both the religiously Jewish nature of the Israeli State and, in particular, discriminatory religious practices (especially as regards civil status and divorce) within the legal system. MKs from the secular right feared that the laws would undermine the security of the Israeli State and threaten the organic growth of its Jewish nationalist basis.[7] As outlined below, during the process of enacting these Basic Laws, some important compromises were made in response to these concerns. Despite this, the laws retained their potent postmaterialist rights core. This can be seen in their emphasis on rights linked to the intrinsic, personal worth of each individual including protection against arbitrary arrest or imprisonment, invasions of privacy, and failure to respect human life, body, and dignity.[8] Also reflecting a postmaterialist outlook, the laws conceive the State not only as a potential violator but also necessary and active protector of human rights.[9] Finally, in transferring more responsibility over human rights to the courts, the law intentionally empowered an institution which had a historical track record of prioritizing postmaterialist rights such as social equality and freedom of expression.[10] This aspect was stressed throughout the debate by MKs representing a wide variety of political preferences.[11]

Israeli society has been subject to a number of cross-cutting sociological processes over recent years. One of these, however, has undoubtedly been an increase in postmaterialist sentiment amongst many Israelis. For example, in some contrast to earlier studies (Gottlieb & Yuchtman-Ya'ar, 1983), recent analysis has found that 'Israel's relatively advanced level of industrial and economic development has apparently been conductive to the inculcation of post-materialist values to its citizens' (Yuchtman-Ya'ar, 2002, p. 363). Based on a representative survey of some 1,119 Israel Jews, Yuchtman-Ya'ar places Israel alongside Belgium, France, and Austria as regards the self-expression aspects of postmaterialization and alongside the Netherlands, Switzerland, and Finland as regards its secular-rational aspect. Perhaps surprisingly, he finds Israel more secular-rational than both the United Kingdom and Canada and Israelis more tolerant of both abortion and homosexuality than their general socio-economic position would predict (*Ibid.*, p. 357).[12] Polling carried out between 1975 and 1987 also confirmed growing Israeli public support for core civil liberty values, namely, procedural protection against arbitrary searches and arrests and protection against interferences with personal privacy (Simon & Landis, 1990). At the same, the public also increasingly supported a more active role for the courts and litigation in resolving social and political problems (Barzilai, 1999).

These changes led both to the growth of political forces explicitly representing postmaterialist priorities and to concrete policy changes which reflected the same. The period from the late 1970s through at least to the 1999 general election was marked by an increase in the parliamentary representation of explicitly postmaterialist parties such as Ratz and Shinui.[13] In 1992, just after the enactment of the Basic Laws on human rights, these two parties merged with Mapan to form a new centre–left, liberal party, Meretz. This party went on to win twelve seats and a place of unprecedented influence within the thirteenth Knesset. At the same time, the proportion of postmaterialists entering the Israeli Labour Party also increased dramatically. Jonathan Rynhold (2007, pp. 428–9) finds that 'in the 1988 election [which immediately preceded enactment of the Basic Laws on human rights], eight out of the nine Labour MKs were drawn from Kfar HaYarok [one of the two main postmaterialist factions within the party at this time]. Their success was linked to the introduction of wider democratic procedures for the selection of candidates, thereby reflecting their popularity among Labour's mass membership' (*Ibid.*, pp. 428–9). The increased influence of this new socio-political grouping was linked not only to the enactment of the Basic Laws on human rights but also other 'left–liberal' or postmaterialist policy changes including the decriminalization of homosexuality in 1988, the inclusion of protection against sexual orientation discrimination in employment in 1992,[14] and, most momentously, the Oslo Accord of 1993 whereby the Israeli Government attempted to make (albeit eventually unsuccessfully) important anti-realist compromises with the Palestinians in an effort to secure a comprehensive peace (*Ibid.*).

9.2.2 Political triggers and the elite politics of the Israeli Basic Laws

Although the gradual increase in postmaterialist pressure constituted a significant factor behind the enactment of the Basic Laws on human rights, it can provide no answer to three important questions:

- Firstly, why did politicians prove uniquely willing to implement such a deliberate restriction on their political discretion during the period of the Twelfth Knesset (1988–92)?
- Secondly, why did significant compromises prove necessary?
- Thirdly, why could the laws only be enacted near the end of the Knesset term and on the basis on a free vote, backbench initiative featuring only limited participation from the two main parties?

As in the Westminster cases, answers to such questions depends on a deeper analysis of the elite political environment during this period. As the rest of this section demonstrates, the timing, and even the possibility, of the Basic Laws on human rights depended on the emergence during the late 1980s and early 1990s of a political trigger, cognate to the 'threat to political stability' trigger prior to the Canadian *Charter*. It was this trigger which provided key political elites with an immediate impetus for constitutional reform including a bill of rights. On the other hand, the continuing strategic position of opponents of reform ensured not only that those who hoped to cooperate with such figures within government proved reluctant to publicly back the new measure but, as importantly, that key compromises proved necessary.

From the late 1970s onwards, Israeli politics became more centrifugal. This fact was symbolized most clearly in the defeat of the Labor-led government in 1977, a first since Israel's founding in 1948. As a result, the small political parties found it increasingly possible to impose their demands upon others within the political system (Lowy, 1989, p. 134). Specifically, in the context of the escalation of the ethno-religious conflict within Israel, a variety of small right-wing and, most especially, ultra-religious parties came to exert a growing and disproportionate influence over the formulation of public policy. This influence was particularly problematic given that, at a sociological level, support for postmaterialization and secularization had actually increased, rather than reduced, within broader Israeli society (Edelman, 2000). As Hanna Lerner states:

> Politically, the religious parties obtained growing power as the bearers of the balance of power ever since 1977, when the Labour party lost its first election since the founding of the state. Whilst the power of the religious parties was ascending, Israeli secular society was increasingly shifting towards the values of liberal individualism. The secular-religious divisions became further pronounced by the increasing unity of the religious bloc. (Lerner, 2004, p. 242)

The structure of the constitutional system, based as it was on proportional representation and *de facto* parliamentary sovereignty, was more and more located as a prime enabler of this dysfunctional fissiparity. This fuelled a very substantial decline in public loyalty towards the Israeli political system. Survey evidence indicated that, between 1973 and 1990, the proportion of Israelis who had a negative perception of 'politics in Israel' increased from 30% (1973) to 56% (1984) to 77% (1990) (Mandel, 1999, p. 277).[15] A growing sense of constitutional crisis came to a head during the period of the Twelfth Knesset (1988–92). Reflecting a further polarization of the Israeli electorate, the 1988 election had resulted in the ultra-religious right parties – Shas, Agudat Yisrael, Mafdal, and Degel Hatorah – increasing their Knesset seats from ten to eighteen. Forging an alliance with the right-of-centre Likud (which had secured one more seat (40) than the rival Labor Party (39)), these parties were originally offered not only positions within the government but also Likud support for legislation restricting conversion to Judaism (with major concomitant implications for civic status and rights to important State benefits). Although this offer was withdrawn following the decision to form a Likud-led government of national unity (which included Labor), the mooting of such a change fuelled the fears of postmaterialist and largely secular sections of Israeli politics as to the disproportionate power of these parties and their potential capacity to impose illiberal and restrictive policies on the rest of the country. Increasingly, intellectual and political figures associated with a postmaterialist politics linked their criticism of this development with a demand for centripetal constitutional change. The reforms most commonly suggested were changing the voting system so as to directly reduce the influence of the small religious parties and enacting a bill of rights, thereby empowering the Supreme Court to enforce the evolving fundamental human rights values of the Israeli nation against the contrary factional forces of religious and/or nationalist illiberalism. For example, in 1989, Marina Lowy argued in her defence of a written constitution instantiating both these changes not only that '[i]n Israel, it is the secular majority that most commonly requires protection from religious dogma imposed by the religious minority' (Lowy, 1989, p. 127) but also that it was '[r]ising impatience with the electoral system, lack of agreement on basic political-social issues, and a static constitutional scheme [which] combine to demand broad reform' (*Ibid.*, p. 135). These perceptions were further accentuated by the so-called stinking manoeuvre which followed the demise of the national unity government in 1990. This affair was prompted by Labor MK Shimon Peres's attempt to fashion a new Labor-led administration by offering Aryeh Deri, leader of the ultra-religious party Shas, a number of key positions within a new government. In the event, the scheming failed since the hawkish grass roots of Shas forced Deri to back a Likud-led government from which Labor was excluded. Nevertheless, both the ability of the small religious parties to exert such power over government formation and the generally underhand and secret nature of the negotiations forced the issue of constitutional change to the top of political agenda (Meridor, interview with author, 20 October 2009; Rubinstein, interview with author, 19 October 2009). Additionally, the new government which was formed suffered from a low level of authority and was relatively non-cohesive (*Ibid.*). This provided an ideal 'policy window' within which constitutional entrepreneurs such as Amnon Rubinstein and Dan Meridor could push forward their agenda.

Much of the impetus behind constitutional reform centred on attempts to directly reduce the fissiparity of the Israeli political system, most particularly, through electing the prime minister separately from the proportionally elected Knesset.[16] Relatedly, this environment nurtured new proposals to entrench fundamental rights against the vagaries of ordinary electoral politics.[17] In April

1989, Minister of Justice Dan Meridor put forward a draft Basic Law on human rights. Opposition from the ultra-religious forces of the by then highly unstable national unity government, however, forced abandonment of the bill. Nevertheless, later that year, Amnon Rubinstein forwarded the same proposal as a backbench initiative. Garnering support from the Labour, Likud, and the small left–liberal parties, this proposal passed first reading 53–19.[18] Again, however, opposition from ultra-religious parties within the government led to Likud assurances that the proposal would not get past the Knesset's Constitution Committee (which was controlled by Likud member Uriel Lynn).[19]

The political origins of these proposals were pushed forward by a potent prospective logic to institutionally reduce the power of the ultra-religious (and other cultural right-wing) parties through a bill of rights. This encouraged support for a strong bill of rights. In this vein, the Meridor/Rubinstein proposals of the late 1980s proposed a fairly comprehensive entrenchment of civil and political rights (including equality rights) as a constitutional Basic Law.[20] Cutting across this, however, the continuing strategic influence of the ultra-religious parties made compromises essential. This also explains why so few members of the two main parties were willing to actively support the idea, at least until near the end of the Knesset term. Even the original Meridor/Rubinstein proposals were subject to significant limitations which reflected this strategic environment.[21] After their demise, however, more drastic changes were proposed. Specifically, in the spring of 1991, Rubinstein agreed to abandon attempts to entrench an explicit right to equality and an explicit right to freedom of religion. The other aspects of his proposal were then broken down into four discrete Basic Laws. The proposed Basic Laws on freedom of expression and freedom of assembly did not progress beyond a preliminary reading. By contrast, *Basic Law: Human Dignity and Liberty* (which protected a wide range of civil rights whilst excluding explicit coverage of the most controversial) together with *Basic Law: Freedom of Occupation* (which protected a narrower right to freedom of vocation) did secure subsequent legislative consideration. Although the former was subject to further limitations during its parliamentary passage,[22] both these Basic Laws were successfully enacted in March 1992. Israel thereby acquired its first bill of rights.

9.2.3 Final summary of Israeli case

Similarly to the Westminster cases considered in detail in this book, the origins of the Israeli Basic Laws on human rights depended on two factors. Over the long term, the gradual postmaterialization of Israeli society led to the growth of socio-political groups who had as a key *raison d'être* the promotion of 'left–liberal' causes, notably as related to human rights. These groups, which included the new political parties Shinui and Ratz as well as factions internal to the Labor Party, championed this reform. Notwithstanding the importance of this ideological or social factor, the actual genesis of the Basic Laws on human rights also depended on a political trigger which provided elites with an immediate impetus for change. This trigger emerged out of the increasing fissiparity of Israeli politics which tended to expand the influence of small and unrepresentative ultra-religious parties. As in Canada prior to the *Charter*, centripetal constitutional reform was located as an important mechanism for countering these trends. Galvanized by constitutional entrepreneurship forthcoming especially from Amnon Rubinstein and Dan Meridor, this trigger paved the way for the enactment of *Basic Law: Human Dignity and Liberty* and *Basic Law: Freedom of Occupation*. Despite this, the continuing strategic position of the ultra-religious parties reduced the extent of explicit support from members of the two main parties, delayed enactment until the dying days of the Knesset term and, most importantly, limited both their strength and scope.

9.3 BROADER RELEVANCE OF THE PTT

Relating the PTT to developments outside its direct domain of applicability is inevitably fraught with difficulty; it is also somewhat speculative. Nevertheless, both the political trigger and, even more especially, postmaterialist elements of the thesis do connect with events and processes operating within a significantly broader context. Reflecting this, the final section tentatively links the PTT to wider debates concerning, firstly, the role of political transition and political triggers in bill of rights genesis and, secondly, the changing nature of rights and bills of rights in a postmaterialist setting.

9.3.1 Political transition, political triggers, and bill of rights genesis

One important fact which this book has systematized through the BORI variable is that bills of rights vary importantly in terms of their designed strength. Speaking generally, the broader human rights literature has associated strong bills of rights with political transition (Darrow & Alston, 2000). This association was also confirmed in the quantitative regressions presented in Chapter 2. Such a correlation has been related to:

- A pressing ideational need to distinguish new governing arrangements from the arbitrariness of a previous, and now rejected, regime (Scheppele, 2000).
- The strategic need, in a situation of high uncertainty and fluidity, for political actors to 'insure' themselves against possible negative future eventualities (Ginsburg, 2003).

The PTT was developed as an explanation for the origins of bills of rights in stable, advanced industrialized democracies. It is, therefore, unable to speak directly to this literature. Nevertheless, the thesis' claim that an immediate political trigger is required to catalyse change, importantly chimes with it. Similarly to the role of political transition in these other cases, a political trigger provides elites with an immediate rationale for change. Despite this, political triggers in internally stable democracies are generally much weaker in nature than a regime-level change such as political transition. This fact helps explain why bill of rights genesis in these former cases is usually relatively weak. Finally, the PTT indicates that in a non-transition context, a political trigger may be either predominately strategic/rationally self-interested or, by contrast, rooted primarily in a backward-looking experiential dynamic. This suggests that both ideational and strategic factors are also likely to matter in transition contexts.

Notwithstanding the importance of political transition and political triggers, the broader cultural and social context also matters. For example, as the results in Chapter 2 demonstrated, whether or not a country has a British heritage is highly significant. In sum, a British heritage is systematically correlated with lower BORI in both transition and non-transition contexts. As the case study chapters emphasized, Westminster democracies have been much more deeply influenced by British legal and political culture than any other set of countries; the suppressing effect of this heritage is, therefore, especially apparent. Even here, however, powerful social factors have encouraged development of a bill of rights. Most particularly, as in other stable, advanced democracies, the growth of postmaterialist rights constituencies has played a vital role in facilitating, and structuring, BORI. The rest of this section turns to an analysis of the broader social and political implications of this association between postmaterialism and many modern bills of rights.

9.3.2 Rights and bills of rights in a postmaterialist setting

Bills of rights are structurally and philosophically liberal instruments, primarily designed to provide rights for the individual against the State. More specifically, the long-term historical roots of these instruments can be linked to a defence of economic liberalism against the forces of 'faction' which might undermine a system of free enterprise. In the period leading up to the first national bill of rights, enacted in the United States in 1791, the defence of private property was granted a critical, even pivotal, position. During this period, 'there was no right more changeless and timeless than the right to property' (Reid, 1986, p. 27); the deprivation of this right was clearly seen as a deprivation of human liberty. Reflective of this, James Ely finds that '[t]he Fifth Amendment [included within the *US Bill of Rights*] explicitly incorporated into the Constitution the Lockean conception that protection of property is a chief aim of government' (Ely, 1992, p. 54). Throughout the nineteenth and into the early twentieth century, a desire to protect and promote economic liberty strongly influenced both the origins and interpretation of bills of rights and similar constitutional rights provisions. At a textual level, bills of rights enacted during the period tended to prioritize private property. These protections were often included alongside only a relatively short list of rights. Furthermore, they were generally stated in a particularly stringent form whereby interferences with property could be justified only in the context of a clear public purpose and with full compensation. Similarly, despite rejecting an overarching constitutional bill of rights, private property was also protected within the new *Constitution of Australia* enacted in 1901. At the level of advocacy and rhetoric, leading proponents of economic *laissez-faire* deprecated the principle of parliamentary sovereignty, proposing a legal and political order in which property protections were constitutionally entrenched. For example, Herbert Spencer argued not only that 'the assumed divine right of parliaments, and the implied divive rights of majorities are superstitions' ([1884] 1982, p. 161) but that 'as true Liberalism in the past disputed the assumptions of a monarch's unlimited authority, so true Liberalism in the present will dispute the assumption of unlimited parliamentary authority' (*Ibid.*, p. 26). Finally, in judicial interpretation, private property was also often granted a particular precedence. Most notably, in the United States, the private property protections in the *US Bill of Rights* were amongst the first to be directly applied against sub-national State action (Ely, 1992, p. 7); the late nineteenth century also saw the judiciary expand the reach of these protections, particularly as regards which governmental actions constituted a 'taking' of property (*Ibid.*, p. 91).[23]

A number of prominent socio-legal theorists, notably Michael Mandel and Ran Hirschl, have argued that the post-war enactment of bills of rights in stable, advanced democracies has been similarly motivated by an overriding desire to entrench economic liberalism and free enterprise. By contrast, however, the PTT advances a different perspective. It argues that these instruments have been supported, and shaped, by actors principally concerned not with economic liberalism but rather with a conception of citizenship which prioritizes democratic and personal civil rights and the equality of socially disadvantaged groups. This 'cultural left' conception of rights can be seen clearly in the drafting of the various bills of rights analysed in this book's case studies. All give emphasis to protecting rights linked to democratic processes (e.g. freedom of expression and assembly), legal processes (e.g. the right to a fair trial), and equality/non-discrimination. The constituency of actors who strongly value these types of rights has increased as a result of cultural changes prompted by growing material prosperity, more cognitively challenging work patterns, and greater individualization within society. This new postmaterialist cohort has therefore formed a vanguard behind the push for BORI. Given this, the relationship between these modern bills of rights and the old constitutionalist agenda of economic liberalism should be seen as one of agnosticism. This agnosticism is most clearly reflected in the complete absence of a right to private property in four out of the seven bills of rights enacted or proposed by Westminster governments since 1945 (Appendix A). Even in the three cases where such property rights have been included, they have been drafted in a manner significantly less demanding than that recognized, for example, in the Fifth Amendment of the United States Constitution. For example, the provision in the United Kingdom's HRA not only fails to explicitly guarantee a right to fair compensation in the event of expropriation but also includes an extremely broad and highly discretionary limiting provision which severely reduces the scope of the right.[24]

Alongside defending private property, the general limitation of State power was also of concern for classic liberalism. In contrast, postmaterialist bills of rights adopt a position of some ambivalence as regards the reach and limitation of the State. Undoubtedly, they can operate as a shield against an allegedly overreaching State. For example, the protection of freedom of expression in the *New Zealand Bill of Rights Act* (NZBORA) led to the overturning of a criminal conviction for flag-burning at a political demonstration; meanwhile, the freedom of religion provisions in the Canadian *Charter* led to the striking down of the *Lords Day Act*'s restrictions on otherwise lawful activities pursued on a Sunday.[25] At the same time, however, a presumption of State non-interference, even in relation to civil rights, has often been rejected. In a number of cases, the bills of rights examined in this book have been explicitly worded so as to stress that the State has important positive responsibilities which it must carry out. The Canadian *Charter* requires that the State ensure that individuals enjoy not only the equal protection but also 'equal benefit' of the law without discrimination (Section 15 (1)), specifically allows for affirmative action or reverse discrimination programmes (Section 15 (2)) and also requires that the State protect aboriginal or native interests (Section 35). Secondly, a number of provisions have placed an increased resource burden on the State. Under the

HRA, it has been held that free legal assistance must be provided by the State in a range of both civil and criminal cases where the interests of justice are held to require this.[26] Furthermore, it has been found that a failure to provide social security support may breach a positive duty by the State to prevent inhuman or degrading treatment in some cases.[27] Similarly, the Canadian *Charter*'s equality provision has been found to require that the British Columbia Government fund sign language interpreters for deaf British Columbian health-care users.[28] Finally, provisions in a postmaterialist bill of rights have even been found to require, or at least shore up the legitimacy of, State action explicitly designed to limit private activity. In the United Kingdom, the HRA protection of private and family life has been used to create a legal right of privacy directly enforceable against other private parties.[29] Somewhat similarly, the Canadian *Charter*'s equality and multiculturalism provisions have provided legal support for Canada's hate speech and obscenity laws when faced with a freedom of expression challenge.[30]

This relationship of ambivalence is reflective of more general tension amongst postmaterialists as regards the role of the State. On the one hand, the individualized and self-expressive outlook of postmaterialists encourages a growing emphasis on the value of each individual. This may also lead to a reduced support for traditional hierarchical organizations, including many State institutions (Dalton, 2004, p. 105). At the same time, in contrast to classic liberalism's emphasis on securing the formal availability of rights and equality for all, postmaterialists tend to emphasize ensuring substantive rights outcomes and an 'equality of results' for vulnerable populations and those suffering social discrimination (Morton & Knopff, 2000, p. 67). Securing such 'radical social change' (Inglehart, 1971, p. 992) generally necessitates State action. It, therefore, encourages a reorientation of human rights so as to accommodate, and even on occasion require it.[31] Thus, as Van Deth (1995, p. 3) has stressed, postmaterialization is associated with 'increasing pressures on governments to deal with all manner of problems'. Finally, and perhaps most significantly, individualization in postmaterialist society can leave citizens feeling more exposed and vulnerable. Especially in the context of a weakening of informal mechanisms for responding to risk, this development has encouraged growing demands that the State take on the responsibility for supervising, auditing, and certifying both itself and others so as to ensure an increasingly 'risk-free' society. At the extreme, and despite their very different long-term historical origins, postmaterialist bills of rights may become co-opted into the State-directed audit and risk management explosion which has become a hallmark of advanced industrialized society (Power, 1997; O'Neill, 2002). In this vein, reviewing the practical effect of the United Kingdom's HRA on government-funded adult social care in England, Kathryn Ellis finds a:

predominantly defensive response to the HRA which is variously described as a 'weapon of litigation' that threatens to engender a 'compensation culture' and 'swamp' social services with dubious legal challenges.
The 'compensation culture', moreover, is interpreted as a further privil-
eging of managerial over expert performance indicators. The combination of risk management procedures and greater formalisation of practice
which . . . is required to avoid or defend challenges [has] led to fears that
professional flexibility and discretion would be curtailed still further.
(Ellis, 2004, p. 335)

Overall, Ellis argues that '[t]he danger in the UK is that if audit governance is
reinforced by the anticipatory responses of social services departments seeking to avoid litigation under the HRA, then front-line practice could become
yet more defensive' (*Ibid.*, p. 337).

The complex and multifaceted political, cultural, and legal relationships
between State power and bills of rights with a postmaterialist origin are
certain to continue to develop and evolve over the coming decades. Above
all, this complexity is rooted in the general ambivalence regarding the role of
the State displayed by postmaterialist rights advocates more generally. This
issue is clearly one of the most important facing modern democracies. In the
final analysis, it is broader connections such as these which make study of bills
of rights and their origins both endlessly fascinating and of significance to the
future health of our society.

Rights protected in government-sponsored bills of rights enacted or proposed in Westminster democracies

Legal and due process rights

	Canadian Bill of Rights Act (1960)	New Zealand Bill of Rights Bill (1963)	Australian Bill of Rights Bill (1973)	Canadian Charter of Rights and Freedoms (1982)	Australian Bill of Rights Bill (1985)	New Zealand Bill of Rights Act (1990)	Human Rights Act (UK) (1998)
Right to life	✓ (Clause 1)	✓ (Clause 2.a)	✓ (Article 30)	✓ (Clause 7)	✓ (Article 18)	✓ (Clause 8)	✓ (Article 2 & Protocol 6, Articles 1 & 2)
Prohibition of torture etc.	✓ (Clause 2.b)	✓ (Clause 2.a)	✓ (Article 28 & 29)	✓ (Clause 12)	✓ (Article 30 & 31)	✓ (Clause 9 & 23.5)	✓ (Article 3)
Habeas corpus	✓ (Clause 2.c.iii)	✓ (Clause 3.ii)	✓ (Article 20.10)	✓ (Clause 10.c)	✓ (Article 23)	✓ (Clause 23.c)	✓ (Article 5.4–5)
Fair and public hearing	✓ (Clause 2.f)	✓ (Clause 3.d)	✓ (Article 25)	✓ (Clause 11.d)	✓ (Article 25)	✓ (Clause 25.a)	✓ (Article 5.1)
Presumption of innocence	✓ (Clause 2.f)	✓ (Clause 2.f)	✓ (Article 23 & Article 25.1.e)	✓ (Clause 11.d)	✓ (Article 24)	✓ (Clause 25.c)	✓ (Article 5.2)
Right to be notified of reasons for arrest or charge	✓ (Clause 2.c.i)	✓ (Clause 3.c)	✓ (Article 20.5)	✓ (Clause 10.a)	✓ (Article 20)	✓ (Clause 24.a)	✓ (Article 6.3.a)
Right to counsel	✓ (Clause 2.c.ii)	✓ (Clause 3.c.ii)	✓ (Article 21.a)	✓ (Clause 10.b)	(Article 26.a–b)	✓ (Clause 24)	✓ (Article 6.3.c)

(continued)

	Canadian Bill of Rights Act (1960)	New Zealand Bill of Rights Bill (1963)	Australian Bill of Rights Bill (1973)	Canadian Charter of Rights and Freedoms (1982)	Australian Bill of Rights Bill (1985)	New Zealand Bill of Rights Act (1990)	Human Rights Act (UK) (1998)
Presumption of liberty (re: detention, arrest, etc.)	√ (Clause 2.a & c)	√ (Clause 3.a & c)	√ (Article 20.1)	√ (Clause 9)	√ (Article 18)	√ (Clause 22)	√ (Article 4)
Right to interpreter where necessary	√ (Clause 2.g)	× (only generic fair hearing)	√ (Article 25.1.d)	√ (Clause 14)	√ (Article 26.h)	√ (Clause 25.g)	√ (Article 5.3.e)
Right to silence	√ (Clause 2.d)	×	√ (Article 21.b)	√ (Clause 11.c)	√ (Article 26.i)	√ (Clause 23.4)	×
No retrospective punishment	×	√ (Clause 3.g & h)	√ (Article 27.1)	√ (Clause 11.g)	√ (Article 27)	√ (Clause 26)	√ (Article 7)
Prompt trial	×	×	√ (Article 20.6 & Article 22)	√ (Clause 11.b)	×	√ (Clause 25.b)	√ (Article 6.1)
Right to facilities for defence	×	×	√ (Article 25.1.b)	×	√ (Article 26.d)	√ (Clause 24.f)	√ (Article 6.3.c)
Right to cross-examine witnesses	×	×	√ (Article 25.1.c)	× (but right to fair hearing (Clause 11.d))	√ (Article 26.f)	√ (Clause 25.f)	√ (Article 5.3.d)
Right to lesser penalty	×	×	√ (Article 27.2)	√ (Clause 11.i)	√ (Article 27)	√ (Clause 25.g)	×

Prohibition of slavery/forced labour	×	×	√ (Article 31)	×	√ (Article 19)	×	√ (Article 4)
No unreasonable search or seizure	×	×	√ (Article 19)	√ (Clause 8)	×	√ (Clause 21)	×
Trial by jury	×	×	×	√ (Clause 11.f)	√ (Article 24)	√ (Clause 24.e)	×
No double jeopardy	×	×	×	√ (Clause 11.h)	√ (Article 29)	×	√ (Article 7)
Right to bail	×	×	√ (Article 20.7–9)	√ (Clause 11.e)	√ (Article 22)	×	×
Civil rights							
Freedom of assembly	√ (Clause 1.e)	√ (Clause 2.f)	√ (Article 13)	√ (Clause 2.c)	√ (Article 10)	√ (Clause 16)	√ (Article 11)
Freedom of association	√ (Clause 1.e)	√ (Clause 2.f)	√ (Article 14)	√ (Clause 2.d)	√ (Article 11)	√ (Clause 17)	√ (Article 11)
Freedom of religion (thought and conscience)	√ (religion only) (Clause 1.c)	√ (Clause 2.d)	√ (Article 10)	√ (Clause 2.a & b)	√ (Articles 8–9)	√ (Clause 13)	√ (Article 9)
Freedom of expression	√ (Clause 1.d & f)	√ (Clause 2.e)	√ (Article 11)	√ (Clause 2.b)	√ (Article 7)	√ (Clause 14)	√ (Article 10)
Right to free elections	×	×	√ (Article 15)	√/1 (Clauses 3–5)	√ (Article 6) (incl. access to public employment)	√ (Clause 12)	√ (Protocol 1, Article 3)

(continued)

	Canadian Bill of Rights Act (1960)	New Zealand Bill of Rights Bill (1963)	Australian Bill of Rights Bill (1973)	Canadian Charter of Rights and Freedoms (1982)	Australian Bill of Rights Bill (1985)	New Zealand Bill of Rights Act (1990)	Human Rights Act (UK) (1998)
Freedom of movement	× (but prohibition on 'exile' (Clause 2.a))	× (but prohibition on 'exile' (Clause 3.a))	√ (Article 16 & 17)	√ (Clause 6)	√ (Article 15, 16 & 17)	√ (Clause 18)	×
Right to marry	×	×	√ (Article 18)	×	√ (Article 13)	×	√ (Article 12)
Respect for privacy and family life	×	×	√ (Article 19)	×	√ (Article 12 & 13)	×	√ (Article 8)
No medical/ scientific experimentation without consent	×	×	√ (Article 32) (medical only)	×	√ (Article 31)	√ (Clause 10)	×
Right to refuse medical treatment	×	×	×	×	×	√ (Clause 11)	×
Right to natural justice and judicial review	×	×	×	×	×	√ (Clause 27)	×
Non-discrimination and group rights							
Right to equality/ non-discrimination	√/limited (Clause 1.a)	√/limited (Clause 2.b)	√ (Article 8)	√ (Clause 15 & 28)	√ (Article 4)	√ (enumerated grounds only) (Clause 19)	√ (parasitic only) (Article 14)
Multiculturalism/ minority rights	×	×	√ (Article 9 & Article 12.2)	√ (Clause 27)	√ (Article 5)	√ (Clause 20)	×

Aboriginal rights	×	×	×	√ (Clause 35)	×	×
Rights of child	×	×	×	×	√ (Article 14 & 26.j)	×
Language rights	×	×	×	√ (Clauses 16–23)	×	×
Socio-economic rights						
Right to enjoy property	√ (Clause 1.a)	√ (Clause 2.c)	×	×	×	√ (Protocol 1, Article 1)
Right to compensation if property expropriated	× (due process only)	× (in accordance with law only)	×	×	×	Limited (Protocol 1, Article 1)
Right to education	×	×	×	×	×	Limited (Protocol 1, Article 3)

Bill of rights institutionalization: constructing the scores

Bill of rights institutionalization (BORI) measures what impact a bill of rights is designed to have on the legal and political system. It is constructed as a four-point scale from a composite of variables which detail the strength of a bill of rights along its three dimensions, namely:

- its *status*,
- its *rigidity*, and
- its *scope*.

These three subsidiary variables are also constructed on a four-point scale. The overall BORI measure is then derived by averaging these three results. This appendix details the definition of each of these subsidiary variables and how they are coded. BORI scores for all of the Lijphart (1999) democracies (both at the time of adoption of the bill of rights and currently) are provided in Appendix C.

B.1 Constructing the status, rigidity, and scope scores

B.1.1 *Status*

The *status* variable measures the relationship between the bill of rights and other law. Whilst all bills of rights have some kind of overarching position within the legal system, four broad types of status are possible. Many bills of rights are simply supreme against any contrary non-constitutional legal provision. These are coded as 4 along the status dimension. Other bills of rights are also usually supreme against other law but, nevertheless, may have provisions which establish significant exceptions to this general rule. For example, they may include either a 'savings' or 'notwithstanding' clause which prevent courts from examining laws for consistency with the bill of rights if either they were enacted before the bill of rights or they have been specifically exempted by the political branches. These bills of rights are coded as 3 along the status dimension. Even further away from the supremacy pole, courts may be empowered to formally declare legislation incompatible with a bill of rights but this may trigger only a procedural result (e.g. empowering the government to fast-track remedial legislation) as opposed to striking down the law. These are coded as 2 along the status dimension. Finally, at their weakest, a bill of rights may inform the interpretation of other primary laws rather than being able to void manifestly inconsistent provisions. These types of bills of rights are coded as 1 along the status dimension.

B.1.2 *Rigidity*

The *rigidity* variable measures the designed durability of the bill of rights or, in other words, how easily it can be amended or repealed. Based on Lijphart (1999), four types of rigidity are defined. Firstly, a bill of rights maybe either not formally entrenched at all or only a very weak and procedural type of entrenchment may be in place (e.g. a requirement that an absolute majority of parliamentarians alter the law). These are coded 1 along the rigidity dimension. Next, amendment of the bill of rights may require a significant supra-majority but clearly less than a two-thirds majority. These bills of rights are coded 2 along the rigidity dimension. Further along this dimension, amendment of many bills of rights is based on the idea that the supporters of change must outnumber opponents at least two to one. This two-thirds majority requirement is coded 3 along the rigidity dimension. Finally, in a few cases, amendment of a bill of rights may require a majority of greater than two-thirds. These instruments are coded 4 along the rigidity dimension.

B.1.3 *Scope*

The *scope* variable measures the range of rights which a bill of rights protects. It varies from 1 (minimal rights protection) through 4 (comprehensive rights protection). It is derived from a composite of three 1-point scales measuring different types of rights. Each bill of rights can score a maximum of 1 point each for civil and political rights, for social and economic rights, and for environmental and minority rights. From these three measures, an overall score is derived. Finally, where the substantive content of a bill of rights is entirely derived from rights which a state is already bound to respect through an international human rights mechanism, this result is discounted (or, in Lijphart's language, 'demoted' (1999, p. 213)) by 0.25.

B.1.3.1 *Civil and political rights*
Ten broad categories of rights are considered. If any of the rights included in these categories are mentioned, then this category is considered to be part of the bill of rights.

1. Equality: general equality right.
2. Non-discrimination: non-discrimination provision on the grounds of race, sex, religion, and political opinion.
3. Physical integrity: right to life (coded as such when death penalty is abolished), the prohibition of torture (only coded when this is an absolute prohibition).
4. Liberty: the freedom of movement, the right not to be expelled, the prohibition of arbitrary arrests, and detention.
5. Privacy: privacy of home, of communications, of data, and of family life.
6. Conscience: freedom of religion, conscience, or belief.
7. Expression: freedom of expression and press freedom.
8. Associative rights: the right to assembly and the right to association.

9. Democratic rights: the right to vote/elections and the right to form political parties.
10. Core procedural rights: habeas corpus, right to counsel, right to present a defence, a presumption of innocence, public trial, and prohibition of *ex post facto* laws.
11. Further procedural rights: right to an interpreter, right to remain silent, timeliness of the trial, and prohibition of double jeopardy (not to be tried for the same offence twice).

Based on these ten categories, the countries are coded on the following sub-scale for civil and political rights:

0 = No civil and political rights
0.25 = 1 of any of the categories are present
0.50 = 2 or 3 of the categories are present
0.75 = 4 or 5 of the categories are present
1 = 6 or 7 of any of the categories are present
1.25 = 8 or 9 of any of the categories are present
1.5 = 10 of any of the categories are present

B.1.3.2 *Social and economic rights*

Six broad categories of rights are considered within this category. If any of the rights mentioned with the category are present, then that category is considered to be part of the bill of rights.

1. Work: right to work, right to a minimum wage, right to strike, favourable working conditions, and right to rest.
2. Social security: right to social security, right to adequate standard of living, right to food, and right to housing.
3. Health rights: right to health and right to free health care.
4. 'Positive' education rights: right to education and right to free education.
5. 'Negative' education rights: right to freedom of education and right to establish schools.
6. Property: right to property – but only coded when the bill of rights provides that expropriation requires compensation and that it can only be conducted in the public interest.

Based on these six categories, the following sub-scale for social and economic rights is constructed:

0 = No social and economic rights
0.25 = 1 of any of the categories are present
0.50 = 2 of any of the categories are present
0.75 = 3 of any of the categories are present
1 = 4 of any of the categories are present
1.25 = 5 of any of the categories are present
1.5 = 6 of any of the categories are present

B.1.3.3 *Third-generation rights*

Three broad categories of rights are considered within this category. If any of the rights mentioned within the category are present, then that category is considered to be part of the bill of rights.

1. Environmental rights: right to healthy environment, right to receive compensation when environment is damaged, and right to participate in decisions on the environment.
2. Rights for ethnic minorities/indigenous peoples: general protection of minorities, rights for minorities to speak their own language, to keep their own land, to preserve their own culture and traditional ways, to establish own schooling, to be represented in government, and to have some degree of autonomy.
3. Rights for special groups: children's rights, rights for elderly, rights for handicapped, and rights for consumers.

Based on these three categories, the following sub-scale for third-generation rights is constructed:

0 = No third-generation rights
0.50 = 1 of any of the categories are present
1 = 2 or 3 of any of the categories are present

National bill of rights institutionalization in select democracies: variable and sub-variable scores

Country	National bill of rights institutionalization (time of adoption)				National bill of rights institutionalization (current/2006)			
	Overall score	Status	Rigidity	Scope	Overall score	Status	Rigidity	Scope
Australia	0.00	0	0	0	0.00	0	0	0
Austria	3.08	4	3	2.25	3.17	4	3	2.5
Bahamas	2.58	3	3	1.75	2.58	3	3	1.75
Barbados	2.17	3	2	1.5	2.17	3	2	1.5
Belgium	2.83	4	3	1.5	3.58	4	3	3.75
Botswana	2.58	4	2	1.75	2.58	4	2	1.75
Canada	3.00	3	4	2	3.00	3	4	2
Colombia	3.33	4	2	4	3.33	4	2	4
Costa Rica	3.33	4	3	3	3.50	4	3	3.5
Denmark	2.75	4	2	2.25	2.75	4	2	2.25
Finland	3.67	4	3	4	3.67	4	3	4
France	2.42	3	2	2.25	2.58	3	2	2.75
Germany	3.42	4	4	2.25	3.42	4	4	2.25
Greece	3.00	4	2	3	3.33	4	2	4
Iceland	2.75	4	2	2.25	2.75	4	2	2.25
India	3.33	4	3	3	3.25	4	3	2.75
Ireland	2.50	4	2	1.5	2.50	4	2	1.5
Israel	1.08	1	1	1.25	1.08	1	1	1.25
Italy	3.33	4	2	4	3.33	4	2	4
Jamaica	2.50	3	3	1.5	2.92	3	3	2.75
Japan	3.75	4	4	3.25	3.75	4	4	3.25

(continued)

Country	National bill of rights instituttionalization (time of adoption)				National bill of rights instituttionalization (current/2006)			
	Overall score	Status	Rigidity	Scope	Overall score	Status	Rigidity	Scope
Luxembourg	3.00	4	3	2	3.08	4	3	2.25
Malta	3.25	4	3	2.75	3.25	4	3	2.75
Mauritius	3.17	4	3	2.5	3.17	4	3	2.5
The Netherlands	2.17	1	3	2.5	2.17	1	3	2.5
New Zealand	1.17	1	1	1.5	1.17	1	1	1.5
Norway	2.67	4	3	1	3.00	4	3	2
Papua New Guinea	3.17	4	3	2.5	3.17	4	3	2.5
Portugal	3.67	4	3	4	3.67	4	3	4
Spain	3.58	4	3	3.75	3.58	4	3	3.75
Sweden	1.83	1	2	2.5	2.5	3	2	2.5
Switzerland	2.83	1	4	3.5	2.83	1	4	3.5
Trinidad and Tobago	2.58	3	3	1.75	2.58	3	3	1.75
United Kingdom	1.50	2	1	1.5	1.50	2	1	1.5
United States	3.25	4	4	1.75	3.25	4	4	1.75
Venezuela	3.33	4	2	4	3.33	4	2	4

Notes

CHAPTER 2

1. In yet other cases, such sets of justiciable rights have been read into the law through acts of judicial interpretation. Cases of judicial creation of what amounts to a domestic bill of rights may be seen in the *Associations Law* decision (1971) in France (Bell, 1994, pp. 138–9).
2. *Jamaica (Constitution) Order in Council* (1962), Section 26.8.
3. Section 2, *Canadian Bill of Rights Act* (1960) and Section 33, *Canadian Charter of Rights and Freedoms* (1982). In the case of the *Charter*, invocation of the notwithstanding clause expires after a maximum of five years, but may be renewed indefinitely.
4. Section 5, *New Zealand Bill of Rights Act*; Section 3, *Human Rights Act (UK)* (1998).
5. Section 6, *New Zealand Bill of Rights Act*; Section 6.2, *Human Rights Act (UK)* (1998).
6. Section 4, *Human Rights Act (UK)* (1998). Such a declaration may only be issued by the higher courts. In New Zealand, a similar Declaration of Inconsistency provision applies but only where it is judged that the *New Zealand Bill of Rights Act*'s non-discrimination standard (Section 19) has not been met. See *Human Rights Act (NZ)* (1993), Section 92J.
7. Formally, this article also sets out an even more onerous option of calling constitutional conventions at both federal and state levels. The Twenty-first Amendment (1933), which repealed prohibition, is the only constitutional change which has made any use of this provision to date.
8. This section also provides that the amendment may be effected without referendum if the votes secured in Parliament exceed two-thirds in both chambers. This procedure is more onerous than the alternative one which requires no supramajority in either the legislature or the electorate (Lijphart, 1999, p. 221).
9. See South African Constitution, Chapter 2, Bill of Rights.
10. Further information on the BORI scores including sub-variable results for status, rigidity, and scope are provided in Appendix C.
11. In a very few cases, there may be more than one national bill of rights. For example, Canada has both the statutory *Canadian Bill of Rights Act* (1960) and the constitutional *Charter of Rights* (1982). In these cases, the more important bill of rights (i.e. in this case the *Charter*) is given dominancy in the analysis.
12. Such a correlation is put forward by Shapiro (2002).
13. Again, Hubert/White robust standard errors are used.
14. Given the large number of potential categories, it is not feasible to provide meaningful marginal effects within an ordered probit model.

CHAPTER 3

1. Of course, it remains a distinct, albeit related, question whether the practical operation of bills of rights actually does advance the interests of civil libertarians and social equality seekers. For a high-profile and very sceptical analysis, see Rosenberg (2008). For a more equivocal and nuanced analysis which is confined to considering the purely legal impact of just one bill of rights, see Erdos (2009*a*).

2. Kim Lane Scheppele uses the terminology of 'aversive' constitutionalism to refer to situations where constitution makers are negatively influenced not by prior experience of politics in their country, but rather by knowledge of the prior experience of constitutional provisions in other countries. For an outline of this approach, see Scheppele (2003).

3. This is not the only conceptual lens through which the various theories may be usefully analysed. Alongside the demand–supply continuum, two other continua may fruitfully be constructed. The first is a 'power–ideas' continuum focusing on whether actors' preferences are understood to be discrete, fixed, and self-interested or the product of a political culture and subject to change through normative processes such as persuasion and acculturation. The second is a 'right–left' continuum. Theories that understand modern bills of rights to be radical 'socialist' (Bork, 2002, p. 11) projects of the left may be placed at one end of this continuum, while those who see them as supported by conservative, and most particularly, neo-liberal forces (Mandel, 1998; Hirschl, 2004*a*) occupy the other.

4. In the case of both Canada and Australia, this principle was modified early on so as to accommodate the reality of federalism. Despite this, the normative centrality of Parliament has heavily informed legal and political thinking in these countries as well as elsewhere in the Westminster world.

5. Even in soft pressure situations, it is notable that if the target state subsequently alters its behaviour, there need be no change in its underlying preferences. This is because '[W]hen states adopt institutions as part of coercion and competition, the decision to do so is externally induced. Internal preferences of the government do not change. What changes are the external incentives that alter the cost-benefit analysis on whether to adopt [a particular human rights practice or institution]' (Versteeg, 2008, p. 19).

6. This also comports with institutional theory's claim that there is a *prima facie* linkage between federalism–decentralization and mechanisms at the nation-state level which divide power, such as bills of rights. Nevertheless, the PTT disputes what may be seen as an implication of institutional theory, namely, that a political system with, for example, a strong bicameral legislature or strong federal division of power might find it easier to transition to a strong bill of rights. To the contrary, these institutions act as significant background constraint, raising the bar which any constitutional project, including bill of rights institutionalization, must overcome in order to be successful.

7. The understanding that political elites have such distinct interests and priorities has a long pedigree within political science including, in particular, in elite theory. For example, Higley, Deacon, and Smart noted in the late 1970s: 'Elites are conventionally thought to act in the interests of the social classes, religious, regional and other economic and subcultural categories from which they are recruited and to which they belong. A closer analysis of elite motivations suggests, however, that elite interests are more personal and neutral. For one thing, the need to preserve their organizational power base is always a compelling interest' (Higley, Deacon, & Smart, 1979, p. 6).

8. This reflects the crucial assumption of political insurance theory that 'The political interests of the ruling and opposition parties depend on the role they occupy, not ideology or interests [considered separately from this]' (Finkel, 2005, p. 101).

9. On the other hand, if the judiciary remain opposed to the basic thrust of a bill of rights post-enactment, then the practical effect of such a reform will be severely stunted, as the example of the *Canadian Bill of Rights Act* (1960) also amply demonstrates.

CHAPTER 4

1. The following provinces were later admitted to the Canadian confederation: Manitoba (1870), British Columbia (1871), Prince Edward Island (1873), Alberta (1905), Saskatchewan (1905), and Newfoundland (1949).

2. 'These were not natural rights, let alone human rights, but the practical terms of accommodation and compromise that had been negotiated over time in the course of settling British North America' (Patapan, 1997*a*, p. 120).

3. Relatedly, in 1938, *obiter* from several justices on the Supreme Court of Canada put forward an 'implied bill of rights' argument against Alberta's *Accurate News and Information Act*, an Act which sought to compel newspapers in the province to publish the Alberta Government's rebuttal of criticisms previously included in the newspaper. The argument held that, given that the BNA Act entrenched a parliamentary system of government 'working under the influence of public opinion and public discussion' (Chief Justice Duff), it was constitutionally required that there be 'untrammelled publication of the news and political opinions of the political parties contending for ascendency' (Justice Curtin). Although both Duff and Curtin sought to restrict their argument to legislation at the provincial level, its logic clearly pointed to free political discussion being similarly entrenched vis-à-vis the federal parliament as well (Gibson, 1967, p. 497). In any case, the Act was disallowed for being tied to broader plans to implement a 'social credit' system of economic and social exchange in Alberta. This was held to be incompatible with the BNA Act's general division of powers. See *Reference Re: Alberta Statutes* (1938).

4. Two years later the Saskatchewan Government enacted the statutory *Saskatchewan Bill of Rights Act* which incorporated a limited number of public law rights along with detailed anti-discrimination private law provisions. The previous year, the Social Credit Government in Alberta had also enacted a statutory *Act Respecting the*

Rights of Albert Citizens/Alberta Bill of Rights. This Act declared the existence of a number of rights in Alberta but also included a large section setting up social credit economic institutions including the Board of Credit Commissions and the Consolidated Credit Adjustment Fund. The link between this Act and Social Credit's broader socio-economic agenda was further reflected in a provision providing that it would not come into force until the constitutionality of the economic legislation passed by Social Credit had been tested by the Supreme Court (Lambertson, 2005, p. 331). In *Attorney-General for Alberta* (1947), this latter legislation was found incompatible with the BNA Act's division of powers. See *Attorney-General for Alberta v. Attorney-General for Canada* [1947] AC 503.

5. It is also interesting to note that all three of the parliamentarians who spearheaded the demand for a bill of rights had a strong civil liberties background: Alistair Stewart MP had also been involved in the setting up the Civil Liberties Association of Winnipeg (Maclennan, 2003, p. 25), whilst John Diefenbaker MP and Senator Roebuck presided over the inaugural meeting of the Ottawa Civil Liberties Association in May 1946 (*Ibid.*, p. 48).

6. In terms of strict legal effect, the Jewish community was well aware of the decision of the Ontario Supreme Court in *Re: Drummond Wren* (1945). Drawing on both Canada's ratification of the *UN Charter* and Ontario's passage of the *Racial Discrimination Act* (1944) (neither of which explicitly addressed the matter at hand), this decision held that a restrictive covenant against Jews was 'offensive to the public policy of this jurisdiction' and, therefore, unenforceable at law.

7. Similar support was also forthcoming from other minority ethnic associations including the Chinese Community Centres Association of Ontario, the Canadian Polish Congress, and the Negro Citizenship Association (Canada, Parliament, Senate, Special Committee, 1950, p. 34; Canada, Parliament, House of Commons, Special Committee, 1960, p. 169). It is also notable that many of the parliamentarians who supported a national bill of rights in the lead-up to CBORA had strong links to the minority ethnic community. For example, Diefenbaker himself had not only experienced a 'Prairie upbringing among the newly arrived immigrants from Eastern and South Europe' (MacLennan, 2003, p. 12), but also felt he had suffered discrimination as a result of his German name. Similarly, David A. Croll, the only Liberal member of the House of Commons to consistently support a bill of rights during the 1950s (Canada, Parliament, House of Commons, *Debates*, 24 March 1952, pp. 722–6; 7 February 1955, pp. 919–21) was Jewish and appears to have suffered considerable discrimination in his political career as a result of anti-Semitism (Davies, *c.*1992).

8. Ross Lambertson goes as far as to argue that 'in the pre-feminist era, before the 1960s, there were few people actively opposed to patriarchy' (Lambertson, 2005, p. 6). Whilst Lambertson appears to over-state his case, it is notable that even the National Council of Women representatives before the 1950 Senate committee accepted the argument that women, but clearly not men, should give up employment if and when they were raising a family (Canada, Parliament, Senate, Special Committee, 1950, p. 57).

9. At least at this time, there was a broad consensus that inclusion of such rights would be inappropriate in such an instrument. Even Dr Eugene Forsey, Director of Research at the Canadian Congress of Labour argued that '[w]e [the Canadian Congress of Labour] are not asking for the inclusion in the Bill of Rights of such "economic" rights and freedoms as the right to full employment, or freedom from want, or decent housing, or as much education for every child as he can profit by' since this was the function of detailed legislation and economic policy (Canada, Parliament, Senate, Special Committee, 1950, p. 89).

10. The UDHR rights provisions were broadly divided into three categories: general rights (articles 1–2), civil and political rights (articles 3–21), and social and economic (articles 22–27). A right to property was included as article 17.

11. Whilst rights to the 'enjoyment' of property were included (Clause 1 (a), CBORA), these were not noticeably stronger than in the previous proposals.

12. In particular, Professor F. R. Scott, Tommy Douglas, and Alistair Stewart were committed democratic socialists and members of the CCF. Moreover, at an organizational level, the Association of Civil Liberties' campaign for a bill of rights gained the support of a variety of trade unions and labour organizations including the Canadian Labour Congress (Canada, Parliament, Senate, Special Committee, 1950, p. 34; Canada, Parliament, House of Commons, Special Committee, 1960, p. 169). Additionally, the CCF also became the first mainstream political party to commit to a bill of rights (in 1945) and, from the start, advocated a strong constitutionally entrenched model (Canada, Parliament, House of Commons, *Debates*, 10 October 1945, p. 900). Finally, probably for purely instrumental reasons, Communist-infiltrated bodies such as the League for Democratic Rights were also strong supporters of a bill of rights throughout the late 1940s and 1950s (Lambertson, 2005, p. 357; MacLennan, 2003, p. 117).

13. Similarly, the government also rejected the proposal, made by both the CCF and Liberal parties, that left-of-centre social rights, such as a 'right to employment at a fair and equitable remuneration', be included in the bill (Canada, Parliament, House of Commons, *Debates*, 2 August 1960, p. 7429).

14. Manitoba followed in 1960 (Evans Case, 2004, p. 80).

15. 'The measure that I introduce is the first step on the path of Canada to carry out acceptance either of the international declaration of human rights [*sic*] or the principles that actuated that noble document' (Canada, Parliament, House of Commons, *Debates*, 1 July 1960, p. 6465).

16. Thus, Mary Ann Glendon states '[s]hortly after the [non-legally binding] Declaration's adoption, the window of opportunity closed, to remain shut for forty years' (Glendon, 2001, p. xix).

17. This conceptualization of a bill of rights as a threat to francophone interests, therefore, far outweighed attempts by supporters of a bill of rights, such as John Diefenbaker, to appropriate the limited use of constitutionalized rights in the structuring of francophone and anglophone relations as an argument for the constitutional propriety of a general bill of rights. See Canada, Parliament, House of Commons, *Debates*, 7 February 1955, p. 900.

18. This resolution was introduced by George-Emile Laplame, the parliamentary leader of the Québec Liberals and seconded by Antoine Rivard, Attorney General for Québec. In response to certain assurances, Rivard eventually announced that he was not opposed to CBORA. See 'Not Against Bill of Rights', *The Gazette*, 3 March 1960.

19. For example, Diefenbaker stated when introducing a bill of rights proposal in 1955: 'I believe that today our Indians should no longer be in the position of second-class citizens in the country in which they indeed were the first citizens' (Canada, Parliament, House of Commons, *Debates*, 7 February 1955, p. 900).

20. For example, during the 1950 Senate inquiry on a bill of rights, John Lawrie, Secretary of the Indian Association of Alberta and Canadian Organizer of the Legal of Nations Pan-American Indians argued against unilateral moves (whether under a bill of rights or otherwise) to grant status Indians the right to vote or remove the bar on status Indians consuming liquor in licensed premises. Such measures were characterized as 'a contravention of the treaties which expressly deal with this matter' (Canada, Parliament, Senate, Special Committee, 1950, p. 355). In *Drybones* (1970), the Supreme Court of Canada for the first and, as yet, only time used CBORA to disapply express statutory provisions when it found this latter bar (included in the *Indian Act*) to be directly violative of the CBORA right to equal protection.

21. Even Diefenbaker in introducing his bill of rights proposal in 1947 noted that it posed 'difficulties under the British North America Act and the division of power between the dominion and the provinces' (Canada, Parliament, House of Commons, *Debates*, 16 May 1947, p. 3152). Despite this, cultural arguments were sometimes deployed arguing that Canada's constitutionalization of federal–provincial relations implied the legitimacy of similarly constitutionalizing human rights. See, for example, comments before the 1950 Senate inquiry of Professor F. R. Scott (Canada, Parliament, Senate, Special Committee, p. 19), Dr Eugene Forsey of the Canadian Congress of Labour (*Ibid.*, p. 79) and Archdeacon Hepburn of the Church of England in Canada (*Ibid.*, p. 249).

22. For example, both Justices Rand and Estey had received university-based legal education at Harvard University (Bushnell, 1992, p. 317).

23. For example, Mrs Sugarman of the National Council of Women of Canada stated to the 1950 Senate committee: 'I am very familiar with the United States because I have worked there for a time with another group who originated the National Council of Jewish Women in the United States. Although we have our own charter in Canada, we have a strong affiliation with them. I know the United States, and I find that when the humblest citizen speaks of his rights there is a rise in his voice . . . there is a ring of sincerity in Americans when they speak of their bill of rights: they all have something in common: and I feel that it is one of the most constructive things about Americans of which I am conscious' (Canada, Parliament, Senate, Special Committee, 1950, p. 63).

24. The organizations were as follows: Association of Civil Liberties (Canada, Parliament, Senate, Special Committee, 1950, p. 45), National Council of Jewish

Women of Canada (*Ibid.*, pp. 61–3), Canadian Congress of Labour (*Ibid.*, p. 86), Canadian Association for Adult Education (expressing views in personal capacity) (*Ibid.*, pp. 139–40), Canadian Civil Liberties Union (Vancouver Branch) (*Ibid.*, p. 163), Canadian Committee for a Bill of Rights (*Ibid.*, p. 207), Magazine Publishers Association of Canada (*Ibid.*, p. 326), and the Periodical Press Association (*Ibid.*, p. 351).

25. Much of the analysis offered was extremely eulogistic. For example, Irving Hilmel of the Association of Civil Liberties stated '[T]he [US] Bill of Rights has been one the greatest single forces in uniting the American people and in the development of democracy and respect for human rights in that country' (Canada, Parliament, Senate, Special Committee, 1950, p. 45).

26. Prior to the Second World War there were some 23,000 persons of Japanese descent in Canada, almost all of whom lived in British Columbia (Lambertson, 2005, p. 108). In the wake of Pearl Harbour, these individuals were removed from this province and dispersed, with restrictions on further movement, throughout Canada. After the war, the Liberal Government announced a policy of deporting these individuals to Japan and passed Orders-in-Council to this effect. Throughout 1946 and 1947 a large number were 'voluntarily' deported or repatriated, including some Canadian citizens (*Ibid.*, p. 140). In 1947, however, the government abandoned this policy and repealed the core elements of the Orders-in-Council, although the requirement for persons of Japanese origin to obtain a permit in order to change his or her place of residence remained for a time (Bushnell, 1992, p. 273). By this stage, however, only 1,000 Japanese Canadians were still on the involuntary deportation list (Lambertson, 2005, p. 140).

27. Preferably this would be achieved through agreement with the provinces. However, failing that, and building on the Supreme Court's 'implied bill of rights' jurisprudence, the courts would be asked to confirm the federal Parliament's authority to amend the constitution unilaterally in such cases. Thus Diefenbaker stated: 'We now have in parliament the power to amend our constitution on federal matters without resort either to the consent of the provinces or to submission to the imperial parliament and a constitutional amendment could be passed if the courts should decide that fundamental freedoms are within the competence of parliament' (Canada, Parliament, House of Commons, *Debates*, 24 March 1952, p. 720). Diefenbaker's overriding concern was to adopt as comprehensive a bill of rights as legally possible: '[H]aving determined as a result of this submission to the highest court of all what can be embodied in a bill of rights without invading provincial jurisdiction, we should enact such a bill of rights' (Canada, Parliament, House of Commons, *Debates*, 7 February 1955, p. 902).

28. 'I believe, sir, that freedom needs an anchor, and that anchor is the power of the courts to protect freedoms of the individual under law. I ask for a charter that will guarantee the rights of individuals and minorities' (Diefenbaker at Canada, Parliament, House of Commons, *Debates*, 24 March 1952, p. 721).

29. 'I suggest that a standing committee should be set up as a watchdog to watch encroachments on freedom and invasions of freedom anywhere in our dominion'

(Diefenbaker at Canada, Parliament, House of Commons, *Debates*, 24 March 1952, p. 721).

30. Formally, Diefenbaker remained publicly committed to the long-term aim both of a constitutionally entrenched bill of rights binding at both the provincial and federal levels of government (Canada, Parliament, House of Commons, *Debates*, 2 August 1960, p. 7417) and also to the setting up of a Parliamentary Committee on Human Rights (Canada, Parliament, House of Commons, *Debates*, 4 August 1960, p. 7550).

31. See, for example, comments of Hazen Argen, leader of the Co-operative Commonwealth Federation (Canada, Parliament, House of Commons, *Debates*, 4 July 1960, p. 5668).

32. Between 1958 and 1960, the Premiers of Ontario, Saskatchewan, Québec, and New Brunswick all publicly indicated that they might support enactment of a comprehensive national bill of rights (Belliveau, 1992, pp. 102, 110–111; 'Frost urges Conference on Overall Bill of Rights', *Ottawa Journal*, 9 September 1958). Additionally, representatives of the CCF and Liberal Party indicated that the Premiers of Alberta and New Brunswick were also interested (Canada, Parliament, House of Commons, Special Committee, 1960, pp. 544–6, 567). Some of this support, however, was probably only ephemeral and designed to embarrass the Diefenbaker Government. It is notable that when, subsequent to enactment of CBORA, a series of federal–provincial conferences were held on constitutional reform later in 1960, only Saskatchewan continued to advocate a comprehensive national bill of rights (Belliveau, 1992, p. 113).

33. Fulton to Diefenbaker, 7 March 1960, Diefenbaker Papers, vol. 17 of Restricted Sub Series, file 413.1 Conf., pp. 286472–4, quoted in Belliveau, 1992, p. 104. In contrast, a system of enhancing consideration of human rights within the executive itself was established; under Section 3, the Minister of Justice was placed under a legal obligation to vet all regulations and bills for consistency with the standards set out in CBORA.

34. This focus on protecting core 'process' rights clearly chimes with later influential constitutional theories including, most notably, that of John Hart Ely (1980). An interesting critique of such an understanding of bills of rights is provided by Tribe (1980).

CHAPTER 5

1. Some theorists, however, reject this understanding. For example, Joel Bakan argues that the *Charter* has not managed to systematically effect issues of justice within Canadian society. This, he argues, is because '[t]he *Charter's* potentially radical and liberatory principles of equality, freedom and democracy are administered by a fundamentally conservative institution – the legal system – and operate in social conditions that routinely undermine their realisation' (Bakan, c.1997, p. 3).

2. Key cases which epitomize the narrow interpretation of CBORA include *Gonzales* (1962) (upholding the criminalization of possession of liquor only for status Indian against equal protection challenge) and *Robertson & Rosetanni* (1963) (upholding the federal *Lord's Day Act* against freedom of religion challenge). In the early 1970s, there was some sign of a change in judicial attitude. In particular, *Drybones* (1970) overruled *Gonzales* (1962) and a number of new criminal due process protections were found within CBORA (see e.g. *Brownridge* (1971), *Lepper* (1974), and *Reale* (1975)). The general rules of standing were also significantly relaxed (Epp, 1996, p. 776). Nevertheless, the extent of the change was limited. For example, in *Lavell* (1973), the Supreme Court returned to a non-substantive understanding of equal protection upholding *Indian Act* provisions which discriminated against Indian women as regards property and marriage. Similarly, in *Miller* (1977), the court unanimously declared that the death penalty for murder did not violate the human rights standards within CBORA.

3. Thus, human rights lawyer, Walter Tarnopolsky argued in 1968: 'Perhaps the strongest argument for entrenching a Bill of Rights is the impotence of the present one' (Tarnopolsky, 1968, p. 247).

4. The same year, the federal Parliament enacted the *Official Language Act* (1969). This act gave statutory force to the status of English and French as the official languages of federal Canada. It also granted rights to use either French or English in federal legislative and judicial proceedings and, where there was significant demand, to be provided with federal government services in either language. Both this Act and the cognate constitutional proposals closely followed the final recommendations of the Royal Commission on Bilingualism and Biculturalism (1967), a body which had been set up in 1963.

5. The dissent related principally to the alleged failure of the Victoria Accord to divide jurisdictional power in Québec's favour rather than opposition *per se* to the proposed entrenchment of limited political and linguistic rights (Chrétien, 1990, p. 286).

6. In the interim, statutory bills of rights had been adopted at the sub-national level in Alberta (*Alberta Bill of Rights Act* (1972)) and Québec (*Charter of Rights and Freedoms* (1975)).

7. An amendment to the *British North America* (BNA) *Act* passed in 1949 had granted the Canadian Parliament the power to affect any constitutional change which did not trench on provincial rights and privileges. The government's *Constitutional Reform Bill* (introduced in June 1978) proposed using this power not only to implement the *Charter of Rights* within the federal sphere but also to replace the Senate with a House of Federation. This latter proposal encountered vigorous legal criticism and, in response, the government agreed to suspend passage of the bill and refer the issue on reference to the Supreme Court of Canada. In December 1979, the court finally ruled that the Canadian Parliament did not have the ability to affect such a reform of the upper house through its 1949 powers. See *Reference re: Legislative Authority of Parliament to Alter or Replace the Senate* (1979).

8. See, for example, 'Little Success at Ministers' Conference on Changing Constitution', *Globe and Mail*, 7 February 1979.

9. Thus, the Clark Government's charter of rights drafts excluded all mention of non-discrimination/equality rights and also, interestingly, property rights. See Federal Government, *Draft Charter of Rights* (17 October 1979) (reproduced in Bayefsky, 1989, pp. 574–8) and Federal Government, *Draft Charter of Rights* (5 November 1979) (reproduced in Bayefsky, 1989, pp. 588–92). Reflecting its relatively decentralist vision, the Clark Government also promised not to intervene in the forthcoming Québec sovereignty referendum (Morton, 2001, p. 327).

10. Alberta, British Columbia, Manitoba, Prince Edward Island, and Québec. Saskatchewan also opposed many elements of the constitutional reform package but did not join in the legal action.

11. *Reference Re Amendment of the Constitution of Canada (Nos 1, 2, and 3)* (1981).

12. Unrelated to the *Charter*, this accord also agreed that the new amending formula should be that favoured by the majority of provinces (called the 'Gang of Eight') as opposed to that put forward by the federal government. Additionally, it was agreed that the constitution should include provisions for the extension of provincial powers over natural resources. For the complete text, see Bayefsky (1989, pp. 904–5).

13. Ultimately, only twenty-four MPs (seventeen Conservatives, five Liberals, and two NDPs) voted (for a variety of reasons) against the resolution; 246 MPs voted in favour (McWhinney, 1982, p. 112).

14. The only amendments voted on during these British proceedings took place in the House of Commons and related, firstly, to an attempt to remove the limitation of 'existing' from the aboriginal rights provisions (Great Britain, Parliament, House of Commons, *Debates*, 23 February 1981) and, secondly, to include a provision mandating that any future constitutional change affecting the rights of aborigines would have to gain their consent first (*Ibid.*, 3 March 1981). Both amendments were substantially defeated.

15. Most of its provisions came into legal effect immediately. However, owing to Clause 32 (2), application of the *Charter*'s equality provisions was suspended for three years and, therefore, this part of the *Charter* did not come into effect until April 1985.

16. This aim was fundamentally distinct from the project of countering heterogeneous instability by promoting a bill of rights drafted through an ethnic consociational process as witnessed recently in Northern Ireland (Harvey, 2001). To begin with, despite the presence of the terrorist outrages of the Front Libération de Québec (FLQ) in the 1960s and early 1970s, Québec heterogeneity remained far more civil than in the Northern Irish case. More importantly, in contrast to the Northern Irish Good Friday Agreement's aim of promoting social stability at almost all costs, the *Charter* was fundamentally based on the logic of resolving fundamental issues in favour of the federal centre. As Jean Chrétien (1990, p. 285) put it, the question posed was '[w]as Canada to be an extremely decentralized country of two nations or a strong country with two official languages and room

for minority linguistic groups to prosper everywhere in the country?' In pursuing the federalist cause, the architects of the *Charter* were willing to abandon any pretence of ethnic consociationalism by imposing reform on Québec. In doing so, the federal elite arguably broke the fundamental compact which underpinned Canada. Thus, Guy La Forest (*c.*1995, p. 149) argues that '[i]n a way, there has not been a federal government worthy of the name in Quebec since 17 April 1982'.

17. Notably, as Table 5.2 sets out, compared to both its 1969 and 1978 proposals, the government proved willing to drop constitutional entrenchment of a range of parliamentary, court, and government service linguistic rights as they applied to the provinces. In fact, excepting minority education rights, no such rights were constitutionalized except as applied to New Brunswick which had agreed on a voluntary basis to be so bound. Additionally, even in relation to the educational provisions, the *Charter* replaced the fundamental principle of individual choice (which underpinned the 1967 and 1978 proposals) with an unwieldy and complex formula of eligibility which only partially applied to Québec.

18. The linkage between the promotion of national identity and the protection of aboriginal rights is particularly striking. For example, in 1978, the government white paper *A Time for Action* stated explicitly: 'The renewal of the Federation must foster cooperation between Indians, Inuit and other Canadians in order that the descendants of those who first occupied this country can make their contribution, with equal rights and opportunities, to the *strengthening of national unity*, so that they too are recognized as founders of the future Canada' (Canada, Government, Prime Minister, 1978, p. 9 (emphasis added)).

19. For example, as early as 1969, the government linked promotion of a Charter of Rights to the following vision of the role of federal Canadian institutions: 'The Government of Canada must be given sufficient powers in the Constitution to stimulate and expand the economy, and to manage the economy in such a way as to maintain high levels of employment. It must have the power to co-operate with industry and labour so as to maximize the efficiency of the common Canadian market. It must be able to promote growth in all of the sectors and regions of the economy, if disparities in income and in rates of economic growth are to be diminished. It must have the power to redistribute income and to maintain reasonable levels of livelihood for individual Canadians, if the effects of regional disparities on individual citizens are to be minimized' (Canada, Government, 1969, p. 10).

20. It remains unclear even if the federal elite were universally ideologically committed to the continuing vitality of the anglophone community in Québec. For example, towards the end of the process leading to the *Charter* in 1982, the Minister of Justice Jean Chrétien 'publicly predicted without visible sorrow that the Anglophone minority in Quebec would eventually dwindle to an insignificant number' (Stevenson, 1999, p. 256).

21. In approximate numbers, seventy oral briefs were received favouring such an instrument, whilst ten were opposed. See Folder H-31 (Entrenchment of Human Rights), Box 52, Special Joint Committee of the Senate and of the House of

Commons (1970–2)), National Archives of Canada, Ottawa, RG-14, Records of Parliament, Accession Number: 1991-12/59-66. Furthermore, nineteen written briefs were received supporting an entrenched bill of rights, six favouring some form of bill of rights (type left unspecified), two favouring a statutory bill of rights, and two opposed to any codified bill of rights. See Summary Report (9 November 1971), Folder 7, Box 59, Special Joint Committee of the Senate and of the House of Commons (1970–2), National Archives of Canada, Ottawa (RG-14, Records of Parliament, Accession Number: 1991-12/59/66).

22. The committee's final report strongly recommended inclusion of a charter of rights in the constitution. Although similar to the government's 1969 proposals, the committee recommended the following additional rights provisions: (*a*) that citizenship, once acquired, could not be rescinded, (*b*) a right to fair and equitable representation in the House of Commons and in the Provincial Legislatures, and (*c*) an open-textured equal protection clause (as opposed to close-textured anti-discrimination provision previously proposed). Finally, the committee proposed including within a new preamble recognition of Canada as a multicultural society and the national objective of promoting 'economic, social and cultural equality for all Canadians as individuals' and the reduction of 'regional economic disparities'.

23. Question: Much of the opposition to the patriation plan centres on the issue of including a charter of rights and freedoms in the constitution. In your opinion, should a charter be included or not? Sample: 1,032 adults nationwide. Result: 62% yes, 23% don't know, 15% no. Source: 'Most Feel Trudeau Patriation Plan Will Help Unite Country, Poll Says', *Globe and Mail*, 14 May 1981, p. 8.

24. Question: Do you support the general principle of including a charter of rights in the constitution? Sample: 1,960 adults nationwide. Result: 32% strongly agree, 40% somewhat agree, 11% don't know, 1% no answer, 8% somewhat disagree, 8% strongly disagree. Source: 'Poll Shows 72 Per Cent Questioned Favor Rights Charter in Constitution', *Globe and Mail*, 10 November 1981, p. 10.

25. Question: Do you support a bill of rights which would provide individual Canadians with protection against unfair treatment by any level of government in Canada? Sample: 1,900–2,000 adults nationwide. Result: 84% in favour. Source: 'Westerners Favour Rights Bill by 80% Survey Shows', *Winnipeg Free Press*, 22 October 1981, p. 18. Given its claim that a *Charter* would 'provide . . . protection against unfair treatment', the question posed in this survey was clearly loaded in favour of the *Charter*. This result, therefore, should be treated with extreme caution.

26. See Document 43, Bayefsky, 1989, pp. 743–61.

27. The *Charter* was in no sense a direct response to international developments. Therefore, the link to the ICCPR (which came into force in 1977) can and has been exaggerated (see e.g. Weinrib, 2002, p. 495). Notwithstanding this, some of the *Charter*'s specific articles such as that protecting freedom of conscience and religion (as opposed to CBORA's protection of freedom of religion only) and freedom of thought, opinion, and expression (as opposed to CBORA's protection

of freedom of the press) do appear to reflect an engagement with the ICCPR text. Additionally, some early *Charter* drafts incorporated protections, notably relating to arbitrary or unlawful interferences with privacy, which were found within the ICCPR but not included within the final *Charter* (see Canadian Federal Discussion Draft (4 July 1980), Document 37, Bayefsky, 1989, pp. 599–604).

28. Most of these changes were accepted by the government when the Minister of Justice Jean Chrétien appeared before the committee in mid-January 1981. In addition, the committee's final report of 13 February 1981 recommended that non-discrimination on the grounds of physical and mental disability be explicitly protected. This was then also accepted by the government.

29. Canada, Parliament, Special Joint Committee, 1980, Issue 36, p. 14.

30. Although categories such as sexual orientation were not explicitly added, an avenue was thereby provided where such grounds could be read into the text. See comments of Jean Chrétien before Special Joint Committee (Canada, Parliament, Special Joint Committee, 1980, Issue 39, p. 17). It is therefore not correct to argue, as Morton and Knopff do (2000, p. 43), that protection from discrimination on the grounds of sexual orientation was deliberately excluded from the *Charter*.

31. The continued efforts of feminists partly reflected concerns that the addition of specific protection for multiculturalism (Section 27) and also aboriginal rights (Section 35) might undermine gender equality, thus demonstrating some tension between the various groups who sought protection within the *Charter*.

32. This clause was drafted by the Department of Justice and subsequently unanimously adopted by the Canadian House of Commons (Canada, Parliament, House of Commons, Debates, 23 April 1981, pp. 9567–9).

33. Some political rights (e.g. the right to vote) were always to be outside the notwithstanding clause. In addition, feminists managed to ensure that Section 28 was similarly excluded (Canada, Parliament, House of Commons, *Debates*, 23, November 1981, p. 13140). In fact, the notwithstanding clause has never had a direct, substantive effect on law outside Québec. Outside that province, it has rarely even been invoked. The weak practical effect of the clause was predicted at the time of the genesis of the *Charter* (Russell, 1983, p. 41; Tarnopolsky, 1983, p. 270).

34. There were some exceptions to the adoption of a discourse of difference. For example, the National Indian Brotherhood did state to the Special Joint Committee: 'Indian peoples have been victims of discriminatory and racist laws. There is no question of our support for human rights codes and bills of rights, which are designed to secure fair and equal treatment in this country. . . . We have known pervasive discrimination in Canada and we would welcome protection from discrimination and racism' (Canada, Parliament, Special Joint Committee, 1980, Issue 18, p. 19).

35. This proposed clause stated: 'The guarantee in this Charter of certain rights and freedoms shall not be construed as denying the existence of any rights or freedoms that exist in Canada, including any rights or freedoms that pertain to the native peoples of Canada' (Section 24) (Bayefsky, 1989, p. 750).

36. 'Alberta wants a definition of native rights', *Globe and Mail*, 19 November 1981, p. 8; 'Native rights would create land problems, Ottawa told', *Globe and Mail*, 19 November 1981.

37. The *Indian Act* instantiated rights which explicitly discriminated against Indian women. Moreover, the National Indian Brotherhood (NIB), the peak organization representing 'status Indians' (i.e. those protected under the *Indian Act*) and all its provincial organizations had successfully intervened in *Lavell* (1973) to stop CBORA's equality provision providing a remedy in such cases. Feminists, including aboriginal feminists such as the Native Women's Association of Canada, hoped that the *Charter* would provide an opportunity to reopen these and related issues.

38. In January 1981, the NIB and other aboriginal groups endorsed these clauses. However, shortly afterwards, the NIB announced its opposition to reform and even launched legal action to attempt to stop it, arguing that the clauses still failed to entrench a right to aboriginal self-government, lacked an explicit enforcement provision, and could be amended in the future against the interests of aboriginal peoples and without gaining their consent (Sanders, 1983).

39. As previously noted in the 5 November accord between the federal government and the provinces (Québec excluded), it was originally suggested that these positive protections be entirely excluded. A strong backlash amongst aboriginal groups and also the public led, however, to a partial re-inclusion of reference to positive aboriginal rights in the final text. The following year, the federal government and Provincial Premiers agreed to a modification which provided, firstly, that 'rights that now exist by way of land claims agreement or may be so acquired' were protected as existing treaty rights and, secondly, that aboriginal and treaty rights were 'guaranteed equally to male and female persons'. See *Constitutional Amendment Proclamation* 1983 (SI/82-102). This amendment also granted aborigines a right to be represented and consulted prior to certain constitutional changes being enacted which might affect their rights and interests (Section 35.1, *Constitution Act* (1982) (as amended)). These new provisions were the product of a First Ministers' Conference called to discuss aboriginal issues which the *Constitution Act* (1982) had mandated had to be called within one year of the coming into force of the new act (see Section 37 (now repealed), *Constitution Act* (1982)).

40. Indeed, Sanders argues that the changes made in 1982 were only positively supported by one aboriginal organization – the Métis Association of Alberta (Sanders, 1983, p. 319).

41. 'Rights Charter Would Bind Provinces as Trudeau Presents Plan; NDP Offers Support, Tories Will Fight Move', *Globe and Mail*, 3 October 1980, p. 1.

42. Whilst four Western NPD MPs broke ranks with the federal party in February 1981, the party as a whole reaffirmed its support in the strongest of terms in the lead-up to the parliamentary debates of 23–24 April 1981. See 'NDP Gives Pledge of its Full Backing on Patriation Bill', *Globe and Mail*, 3 February 1981, p. 1 and 'Four New Democrat MPs Break Ranks on Patriation', *Globe and Mail*, 19 February 1981, p. 1.

43. Pauline Jewitt, NPD Member of New Westminster–Coquitlam stated: 'When the proposal was put before the House of Commons I think we all felt that section 15, the equality of rights section outlawing discrimination on the grounds of race, religion, sex and so on, and its second component, the affirmative action provision encouraging legislatures to take affirmative action for disadvantaged groups, was one of the strongest parts of that charter' (Canada, Parliament, House of Commons, *Debates*, 23 November 1981, p. 13129).

44. In particular, during March and April 1981, the Progressive Conservatives sought, firstly, to filibuster the parliamentary proceedings of the Joint Resolution and then to offer an amendment which would have prevented the *Charter* coming into force unless by 1 July 1983 the initiative had the support of two-thirds (i.e. seven out of ten) of the provincial assemblies representing at least 50% of the population. At the time, the federal government had the support of only two provinces (Ontario and New Brunswick). See 'Fascist Element in Tactics of PCs – Trudeau', *Globe and Mail*, 11 April 1981, p. 1.

45. See, for example, the comments of Jake Epp MP, Progressive Conservatives spokesperson on the Constitution, at Canada, Parliament, House of Commons, *Debates*, 6 October 1980, p. 3306.

46. Almost all of the twenty organizational submissions received by the Hays–Joyal Special Joint Committee opposing the idea of a charter of rights were from conservative/right-wing groups. The only possible exceptions were the Regroupment pour les droit politique du Québec (a Québec sovereignty group) and the Canadian Association of Chiefs of Police. In contrast, only three out of the seventy briefs received in support of a *Charter* were from conservative/right-wing groups and only one of these (Counseil du Patronat du Québec) supported an instrument broadly similar to that instantiated in the *Charter* draft. A clear majority (five out of the eight) Provincial Premiers who opposed the *Charter* were Progressive Conservatives. However, one of the Premiers (Alan Blakeney of Saskatchewan) was a member of the NDP and the two Premiers (Ontario's Bill Davis and New Brunswick's Richard Hatfield) who broadly supported the federal initiative throughout the process were Progressive Conservatives. These facts indicate that, although the left were disproportionately supportive and the right disproportionately distrustful of the *Charter*, this relationship should not be over-essentialized.

47. See, for example, written briefs to Hays–Joyal Committee by Catholic Women's League of Canada and the Knights of Columbus (Council 1007).

48. See, for example, written briefs to Hays–Joyal Committee of Alberta Chamber of Commerce.

49. For example, Ron Stewart, Progressive Conservative MP for Simcoe South stated: 'Are we moving towards a society where there is more concern for the rights of the criminal than for the rights of the innocent? I hope not. I do not want to see a society where the civil liberties of the lawbreaker override the basic rights of the law-abiding citizen' (Canada, Parliament, House of Commons, *Debates*, 30 November 1981, p. 13515).

50. See, for example, the written briefs to the Hays–Joyal Special Joint Committee of Canadians for One Canada, the Dominion Party of Canada, and the National Citizens Coalition.

51. In particular, the Progressive Conservative's parliamentary proposals to include references to 'God' and the 'position of the family' in the limitation clause and to exclude both abortion and the right to life from the purview of the *Charter* were successfully defeated. Nevertheless, in response to a vigorous campaign, the Liberals did agree to add reference to God within a new *Charter* preamble and also to add a clause specifically saving denominational schooling rights from being undercut by any of the *Charter*'s rights provisions (Section 29). See Canada, Parliament, House of Commons, *Journals*, 23 April 1981, pp. 1775–81.

52. The new equalization and regional disparities clause within the *Constitution Act* (Clause 36) did bind the State to provide quality public services and promote equal economic and social opportunities for all Canadians. However, this clause was not framed in the language of rights, nor was it subject to extensive judicial oversight. Interestingly, reflecting an awareness of the difficulties of achieving even a limited constitutional *Charter*, the federal NDP leadership did not press for the entrenchment of broader positive socio-economic provisions (Bob Rae MP, interview with author, 26 May 2009). Nevertheless, the minority of NDP MPs obliquely criticized these absences. For example, Ian Waddell (NDP Member for Vancouver-Kingsway) stated: 'Socialists are concerned with the growth of the human spirit. This charter talks of freedom but we know that no one is really free if unemployed, if poor or unable to send his or her children as far as possible in school' (Canada, Parliament, House of Commons, *Debates*, 26 November 1981, p. 13428).

53. 'In a country where politicians and business have traditionally been in lockstep, both the old and new money have always regarded him [Trudeau] with deep suspicion' (Clarkson & McCall, 1990, p. 9).

54. Both the *Constitution and the People of Canada* (1969) and the *Constitutional Reform: Canadian Charter of Rights and Freedoms* (1978) recommend that, at most, private property should be protected against deprivations not 'in accordance with law' rather than the potentially more onerous 'due process' standards required under CBORA. See Canada, Government, 1969, p. 52; Canada, Government, 1978, p. 7.

55. See, for example, Canada, Parliament, House of Commons, *Debates*, 23 April 1981, pp. 1779–80.

56. See, for example, 'PM's Push for "Cerebral" Rights but Not Property Rights Criticised', *Globe and Mail*, 18 October 1980, p. 3.

57. The Hays–Joyal Special Joint Committee received approximately twice as many (23 vs. 12) briefs from groups urging inclusion of a right to property as they did briefs urging the inclusion of various legal rights (e.g. to jury trial, against self-incrimination) which did come to be included.

58. Specifically, on 23 January 1981, the Hon. Robert P. Kaplan, acting Minister of Justice, stated, in response to questioning by Progressive Conservative MPs sitting

on the Hays–Joyal Committee, that the government was 'prepared to see that provision [on property rights] move forward' (Canada, Parliament, Special Joint Committee, 1980–1, Issue 44, p. 25).

CHAPTER 6

1. According to Section 189 of this Act, these provisions could only be altered by a special majority of 75% of all the members of the House of Representatives or a majority of electors at referendum. Nevertheless, given that Section 189 was not itself entrenched, this stipulation was legally ineffective despite its clear moral force.

2. The petition for a written constitution encompassing a bill of rights had been launched just prior to the 1960 general election. However, the precise wording of the proposed constitution had only been finalized in June 1961. See 'Help this Petition for Our Liberties', *Liberator* (Constitutional Society), September 1960, pp. 1–2 and 'Long Job Ended on Constitution', *Liberator* (Constitutional Society), June 1961, p. 3.

3. 'No Loss If Bill of Rights Is Dropped', *Liberator* (Constitutional Society), October 1962, p. 8.

4. Draft letter to Minister of Justice from Secretary of Justice, 8 April 1963, New Zealand, Government, Attorney General's Department, *Bill of Rights Papers*, Agency: AGCS Record: 18/1/253 Part 1, Archives New Zealand.

5. Letter from Permanent Head of the Prime Minister's Office to Law Draftsman, 30 June 1961, *Ibid.*

6. Letter from Deputy-Director (Administration), Department of Health to Law Draftsman, 27 June 1961, *Ibid.*

7. The new draft, by making its provisions subject to existing *Acts Interpretation Act* (1924), made the bill a mere statute of interpretation. It also included a comprehensive saving clause and further and specifically limited many of the rights in turn. All these provisions made the bill significantly weaker than CBORA. For completeness, however, it may be noted that, in a few places, the bill's scope was broader. For example, Clause 2.c protected an individual's rights to 'own property' as opposed to CBORA which, reflecting federalism concerns, had limited this to a right to 'enjoy property'. Similarly, Clauses 3 (g) and (h) added rights against retrospective punishment which had not been included in CBORA. See New Zealand, Parliament, Constitutional Reform Committee, 1965.

8. Letter from Professor C. C. Aiken to Attorney General Ralph Hanan, 4 July 1961, New Zealand, Government, Attorney General's Department, *Bill of Rights Papers*, Agency: AGCS Record: 18/1/253 Part 1, Archives New Zealand.

9. Letter from Professor I. C. Campbell to Secretary for Justice, 26 June 1961, *Ibid.*

10. Overall, of the ten submissions the committee received on the bill, only two submissions (from the newly established ombudsman and the Constitutional Society) could be considered in any way positive.

11. 'Executive Committee – 11 May 1960', New Zealand Council for Civil Liberties Files, Alexander Turnbull Archives, Wellington.

12. Letter from Secretary of Labour to Minister of Immigration, 12 July 1961, in New Zealand, Government, Attorney General's Department, *Bill of Rights Papers*, Agency: AGCS, Record: 18/1/253 Part 1, Archives New Zealand.

13. Letter from Deputy-Director (Administration), Department of Health to Law Draftsman, 27 June 1961, *Ibid.*

14. This divergence was, in fact, perceptively noted by the High Commissioner of New Zealand to Canada, J. S. Reid, during a communication with the New Zealand Government which took place in 1962. In particular, the High Commissioner stated that the enactment of CBORA was related to 'the proximity of Canada to the United States and the influence of American thinking on this country. The very recognition of the necessity for a Bill of Rights has no doubt been influenced by the fact that, in the United States, legislators, publicists and lawyers constantly apply themselves to the civil rights provisions in the Constitution of the United States, and to many uninformed [*sic*] citizens of Canada a statement that the common law of England, as adopted in Canada, contains all necessary protection of human rights seems less than adequate'. This communication followed the New Zealand Cabinet's request for information from the High Commissioner on CBORA which had been made on 13 February 1962. See Letter from High Commissioner of New Zealand in Ottawa to Secretary of State of External Affairs, 14 March 1962, *Ibid.*

15. 'Society's Aims Taken Notice of in Nationalists' Policy', *Liberator* (Constitutional Society), June 1960, p. 4 (reporting approvingly on the National Party's plans for administrative appeal against departmental decisions).

16. As both the 1962 and 1963 annual reports of the New Zealand Council for Civil Liberties make clear, the Council strongly supported the idea of an ombudsman and indeed advocated for an even stronger system than that enacted. Its 1963 annual report stated:

    Ombudsman: Since the last Annual General Meeting the Parliamentary Commission for Investigations Act [*sic*] has been passed, Sir Guy Powles appointed the first Ombudsman, and his first report published. His powers are not as wide as many people and organizations, including this Committee, think desirable, but there is no doubt that Sir Guy is able to perform a very useful public function within the limits set by the Act. (New Zealand Council for Civil Liberties, 1963, p. 2)

17. See, for example, the commentary provided by Professor C. C. Aikman: '[T]he Ombudsman has an important part to play under a system of parliamentary government – at least in an administration as small as New Zealand's – in resolving conflicts between private right and public interest; and, in particular, in ensuring that the case of the individual is effectively argued before officials' (Aikman, 1964, p. 420).

18. Letter from Minister of Māori Affairs to Attorney General Ralph Hanan, 22 June 1961, in New Zealand, Government, Attorney General's Department, *Bill of Rights Papers*, Agency: AGCS, Record: 18/1/253 Part 1, Archives New Zealand.

19. The preamble to the bill did stress that 'the people of New Zealand uphold principles that acknowledge...the dignity and worth of the human of the human person, whatever his racial origins may be' and that 'the New Zealand nation is founded upon the principle that all its citizens of whatever race are one people'. This apparently reflected an attempt (albeit rather one-sided) to instantiate the principles upon which the Treaty of Waitangi was based.

20. Indeed, at a lecture delivered to mark the twentieth anniversary of the Universal Declaration in 1968, Hon. Ralph Hanan, still Minister of Justice and Attorney General in the National Government, stated that 'the imposition at this stage of any meaningful Bill of Rights on our constitutional and legal system would have deplorable effects' (Hanan, 1968, p. 187). In the place of a bill of rights, this period was marked by bipartisan support for a series of administrative measures designed to ensure better respect for human rights. In 1971, a Race Relations Conciliator was established with a remit to investigate and tackle instances of racial discrimination (*Race Relations Act* (1971)). In 1975, the Waitangi Tribunal was set up and charged, on a non-retrospective basis, with making 'recommendations on claims relating to the practical application of the Treaty and to determine whether certain matters are inconsistent with the principles of the Treaty' (*Treaty of Waitangi Act* (1975)). Finally, in 1977, a Human Rights Commission was established. Although its remit mainly related to policing certain private law anti-discrimination measures, it was also granted broader human rights monitoring functions (*Human Rights Commission Act* (1977)).

21. In *Fitzgerald* (1976), the High Court ruled that this action had indeed amounted to an illegal executive suspension of the law contrary to the *Bill of Rights (UK)* (1688) – an 'imperial' statute that remained in force in New Zealand.

22. *Clutha Development (Clyde Dam) Empowering Act* (1982). Geoffrey Palmer described this as 'the greatest attack made on the rule of law in this country within living memory' (speech to New Zealand Labour Party, Central North Island Regional Conference, 7–8 April 1984 (quoted in Rishworth (1995, p. 10))).

23. Section 11, *Whangerei Refinery Expansion Project Disputes Act* (1984).

24. This decision was publicly criticized by Rt. Hon. Bill Rowling, Leader of the Opposition (Palmer, 2004, p. 201). Similarly, Palmer stated that '[t]he ultimate referee, when the chips are down, should not belong to one of the teams playing the game' (Palmer, 1979, p. 21).

25. For example, the *Economic Stabilization Act* (1948), the *Public Safety Conservation Act* (1932), and the *Primary Products Marketing Act* (1953).

26. See *Combined State Unions* (1982). The successful legal argument was that these regulations unlawfully interfered with overriding primary legislation, namely, the *State Services Conditions of Employment Act* (1977).

27. Other than Palmer, supporters of a bill of rights within the Labour caucus included Jonathan Hunt, Bill Dillon (later Chair of the Justice and Law Reform Committee), and Phillip Wooleston.

28. Address to Public Meeting organized by Canterbury Council on Civil Liberties (28 September 1984), New Zealand Government, Ministry of Justice, *Bill of Rights*

Papers, Archives New Zealand, Agency ABVP, Series 7410, Accession W5196, Record LEG 7-1-3, Box 9, Part 1 (1984).

29. Turning to historical specifics, the formal shift to supporting only a more limited bill of rights resulted from a meeting of the parliamentary Labour caucus held on 2 November 1987. See Memo from Palmer to Caucus Justice Committee (22 March 1987) in New Zealand, Government, Ministry of Justice *Bill of Rights Papers*, Agency ABVP, Series 7410, Accession W5196, Record LEG 7-4-3, Box 14, Part 23 (1985–8), Archives New Zealand. Shortly after this, Palmer publicly backed the idea of introducing the bill of rights as an ordinary statute (Rishworth, 1995, p. 20). When such a bill was introduced into Parliament, the Law and Justice Committee made some further amendments which underscored the limited and interpretative nature of the enactment. In particular, a provision was added explicitly stating that the legal effect of 'other enactments' were not affected by the passage of NZBOR (see Section 4, NZBOR (1990)).

30. It remains a matter of profound jurisprudential debate as to whether – and if so how – it is possible to divide rights into those which are procedural and those which are substantial. See generally, Tribe (1980). The important point from a political science viewpoint is that the framers of NZBOR attempted to do just that and then prioritized those that they considered procedural.

31. Kenneth Keith, the key theorist of NZBOR, links his understanding of bills of rights to John Hart Ely's theory (Ely, 1980). Nevertheless, contrary to Keith, Ely himself saw the courts as playing a critical role in removing barriers to political change for discrete and insular minorities.

32. 'Minutes of Officials Committee on Constitutional Reform (First Meeting) (11 December 1984)' in New Zealand Government, Ministry of Justice, *Bill of Rights Papers*, Agency ABVP, Series 7410, Accession W5196, Box 10, Part 4 (1985–6), Archives New Zealand.

33. Submission 135, New Zealand, Parliament, Justice and Law Reform Committee (1985–6).

34. Submission 243, *Ibid.* McBride's support for the 1985 white paper proposals reflected a departure from his previous recent opposition to such a bill of rights (see McBride (1979)).

35. Submission 136, New Zealand, Parliament, Justice and Law Reform Committee (1985–6).

36. Additionally, once the bill of rights proposal was watered down into a statutory form, support was also forthcoming from the Canterbury Council for Civil Liberties, an important civil liberties body which traditionally represents civil libertarian opinion within the whole of the southern half of the country. See Submission 28W, New Zealand, Parliament, Justice and Law Reform Committee (1985–6).

37. Those representing both (non-Māori) ethnic and religious minorities and the physically and/or mentally disabled were almost universally supportive. In contrast, feminist groups were clearly split with four submissions received in opposition and only two in favour (one of those being from an internal Labour Party women's group). See New Zealand, Parliament, Justice and Law Reform Committee, 1989–90.

38. Within both the 1985–6 parliamentary committee proceedings and the latter proceedings in 1989, there was significant civil society pressure to expand the anti-discrimination provisions even beyond this. At this time, however, these efforts were not successful.

39. For evidence of pressure on the government to enact such changes, see comments of Richard Northey MP, Chairperson of Labour Party Caucus Justice Committee in the margins of the report from 1987 Ministry of Justice paper on bill of rights in New Zealand, Government, Ministry of Justice, *Bill of Rights Papers*, Agency ABVP, Series 7410, Accession W5196, Record LEG 7-4-3, Box 12, Part 18, Archives New Zealand.

40. The additional grounds were disability, employment status, family status, political opinion, age, 'the presence in the body of organisms capable of causing disease' (notably, HIV), and sexual orientation. The first six of these categories were added with the virtually unanimous support of Parliament, whilst the last was passed with the combined support of the vast majority of Labour MPs and the socially liberal wing of the National Party. See 'Hardly a Murmur as Rights Bill Passed', *New Zealand Herald*, 19 July 1993. In response to continued ambiguity as to the interface between NZBOR and the *Human Rights Act* (HRA) as this related to public law discrimination, in 2001, the Labour Party enacted the *Human Rights Amendment Act*. This Act gave the Human Rights Review Tribunal and, on appeal, the ordinary courts the power to issue a formal Declaration of Inconsistency if they judged primary legislation to be incompatible with the non-discrimination standard set out in NZBOR. Although not affecting the continued legal validity of the impugned legislation, such a declaration would require the government to bring it to the attention Parliament and provide a report detailing the government's response to it (Section 92K, HRA (1993) (as amended)).

41. The extent of this diversification in migration patterns should not, however, be exaggerated. The great bulk of migrants continued to come from traditional sources, notably the United Kingdom, throughout the 1960s and 1970s. Moreover, it was not until the 1986 migration policy review, which coincided with, rather than had causal effect on, the bill of rights initiative, that 'the traditional emphasis on nationality and culture as criteria for the selection of immigrants' was overturned' (Booking & Rabel, 1995, p. 46).

42. The National Party leadership opposed the bill of rights from the outset. However, at the beginning of the process, at least one National MP (Rt. Hon. Doug Graham) gave 'in principle' support to the idea. See 'Storm Clouds Gathering over Bill of Rights', *New Zealand Herald*, 16 January 1984 (citing opposition of National's Leader Jim McLay but support of Graham for a bill of rights). By the time of NZBOR's enactment in 1990, however, opposition was overwhelming. No National MPs supported passage of NZBOR at third reading and even Doug Graham spoke against it. See New Zealand, Parliament, *Debates*, 21 August 1990, pp. 3760–73.

43. In contrast, the consultation by the Justice and Law Reform Committee in 1989 (albeit conducted on a much smaller scale) indicated much more social support

for a limited statutory instrument. Approximately equal numbers (22 vs. 23 briefs) expressly supported as opposed the revised bill. An even larger number (25 briefs) made constructive amendments regarding its drafting (New Zealand, Parliament, Justice and Law Reform Committee, 1989–90). Also as Paul Rishworth (1995, p. 21) notes '[a] number of those in opposition had failed to understand the significance of the ordinary statute status of the proposed enactment; their opposition was based on what an entrenched bill of rights might do and was discounted'.

44. Approximately, half the parliamentary submissions received in opposition to the white paper were from Christian conservatives who argued that the bill would undermine what they saw as the common law Christian foundations of the New Zealand State. These actors were particularly concerned by the bill's protections relating to freedom of religion, its failure to acknowledge the 'supremacy of God', and its failure to provide clear protection for the human foetus. Additionally, some 18% of opposed submissions were based on a nationalist argument that that the bill threatened the country's sovereignty, identity, and culture in the name of the United Nations or even Soviet Union.

45. See New Zealand, Parliament, Justice and Law Reform Committee, 1985–6 (Submissions 22 and 350W). The Chairman of the NZCCL did support enacting the part of the bill related to the rights for accused persons either as a stand-alone piece of legislation or as an amendment to the *Crimes Act*. See 'Council for Civil Liberties Opposes Bill of Rights', *The Press*, 29 August 1986. Archival evidence indicates that the decision to oppose the white paper was controversial within the organization. See, for example, comments of A. Forseyth (noting support for the white paper within the organization) in Minutes of Meeting, 9 December 1985 (New Zealand Council for Civil Liberties Archive, Alexander Turnbull Library, Wellington).

46. 'Rights Bill Has "Dangers"', *New Zealand Herald*, 8 April 1985.

47. 'Council for Civil Liberties Opposes Bill of Rights', *The Press*, 29 August 1986, p. 4.

48. New Zealand, Parliament, Justice and Law Reform Committee, 1985–6 (Submission 140).

49. Cited in Rishworth (1995, p. 19).

50. See 'A Bill of Rights?', *The Dominion*, 28 April 1986.

51. New Zealand, Parliament, Justice and Law Reform Committee, 1985–6 (Submission 140).

52. In contrast, Canada had attempted to abolish Privy Council appeals in criminal cases in 1875. Although in *Nadan* (1926) this was declared unconstitutional, these appeals were again abolished in 1933 (some fifty years prior to New Zealand) with civil appeals also being abolished by 1949.

53. In particular, in contrast to the European Court of Human Rights, the ICCPR Human Rights Committee was not a court and had no capacity to issue binding judgments.

54. This observation receives backing from heated correspondence in early 1986, after the Law Society had shown its hand, between Geoffrey Palmer and Peter

Clapshaw, the New Zealand Law Society President. See New Zealand, Government Ministry of Justice, *Bill of Rights Papers*, Archives New Zealand, Agency ABVP, Series 7410, Accession W5196, Record LEG 7-1-3, Box 13, Part 20 (1985–90).

55. In fact, Palmer publicly criticized their agenda early on. See 'Government Moving Too Fast Says Mr Palmer', *New Zealand Herald*, 22 April 1985. For similar later comments, see Palmer (1992, p. 179).

56. Memorandum to Department of Justice and Professor Keith from Minister of Justice (24 February 1985). The memorandum later prepared for the cabinet similarly emphasized the deliberate exclusion of economic rights ([Draft] Memorandum for Cabinet [on] the Bill of Rights from Office of the Minister of Justice (prepared 1 March 1985)). Both held in New Zealand, Government, Ministry of Justice, *Bill of Rights Papers*, Archives New Zealand, Agency ABVP, Series 7410, Record LEG 7-1-3, Box 10, Part 7 (1985–6).

57. Hon. George Gair, speech to Lions Club of Napier quoted in full at 'Economic and Social Rights Not Recognized in Draft Bill', *New Zealand Herald*, 12 April 1985, p. 6.

58. In contrast, none of the submissions received in support cited any potential neoliberal benefit from the measure.

59. For example, during the third reading of NZBOR, Graeme Lee, National MP for Coromandel strongly criticized the failure to protect private property and suggested that, similarly to the situation in Eastern Europe, this demonstrated a lack of commitment amongst Labour members to a property-owing democracy (New Zealand, Parliament, *Debates*, 14 August 1990, p. 3471).

60. The inclusion of socio-economic rights was not the only aspect of the Justice and Law Reform Committee's recommendations not to be implemented. The committee also suggested that a dedicated select committee be established to monitor compliance with NZBOR. The government, however, rejected such a committee, preferring to isolate such formal political monitoring within the executive. This was achieved through adopting another suggestion of the committee, namely, that the Attorney General certify whether new bills were or were not compatible with the rights set out in NZBOR (Section 7, NZBOR (1990)).

61. In his submission on the white paper to the Justice and Law Reform Committee, McBride argued: '[M]atters involving economic and social rights should be "left to the political process". Had the proposed Bill attempted to incorporate provisions covering economic and social "rights", I would have come out in opposition to it. The history of the US Supreme Court in this area provides sufficient testimony to convince me of the correctness of my position [a reference to the much-vilified *Lochner*-era jurisprudence in that country]' (New Zealand, Parliament, Justice and Law Reform Committee, 1985–6 (Submission 409)).

62. When interviewed for this research, Palmer stated that he 'resisted totally' the idea of including economic and social rights since he 'didn't think they were capable of judicial management' (Palmer, interview with author, 11 November 2004). The final decision to exclude socio-economic rights was made by the entire Labour caucus and supported by a majority of both the left and the right within it (Northey,

interview with author, 3 November 2006). In fact, a draft bill of rights incorporating socio-economic rights (albeit not in a directly justiciable fashion) had been produced in the Department of Justice, presumably on the off-chance that the vote had gone the other way. See Draft No. 4 (24 July 1989) in New Zealand, Government, Ministry of Justice, *Bill of Rights Papers*, Archives New Zealand, Agency ABVP, Series 7410, Accession W5196, Record LEG 7-1-3, Box 13, Part 19 (1989–90).

63. The proposal was accompanied by a slew of other changes designed to grant Māori interests additional protection. Most particularly, the Waitangi Tribunal was empowered to look into Māori grievances, dating right back to the signing of the Treaty in 1840 (*Treaty of Waitangi Amendment Act* (1985)). The government also began adding reference to the 'principles of the Treaty of Waitangi' in new legislation including the *State-Owned Enterprises Act* (1986), the *Environment Act* (1986), and the *Conservation Act* (1986).

64. 'Unacceptable to Opposition – East', *The Dominion*, 3 April 1985, p. 12.

65. Notable Māori supporters of the Treaty clause included Judge Eddie Durie, Chief Justice of the Māori Land Court and Chair of the Waitangi Tribunal. According to Durie, the clause was 'of crucial importance to Maoridom because it creates new rights previously denied' (International Commission of Jurists (New Zealand Section), 1985, p. 59).

66. [Late] [s]ubmission [on 1985 white paper] by the Department of Maori Affairs to Justice and Law Reform Committee, 1988. Copy held in New Zealand, Government, Ministry of Justice, *Bill of Rights Papers*, Archives New Zealand, Agency ABVP, Series 7410, Accession W5196, Record LEG 7-1-3, Box 14, Part 23 (1985–8).

67. 'Maori Advisers Give Treaty Supremacy', *The Dominion*, 22 September 1987.

68. According to Belich, the Māori proportion of the population increased from around 6% in the 1930s to around 15% in 2000 (Belich, 2001, pp. 466–7).

69. According to Belich, only 26% of Māori were urbanized in 1945. By 1986, this figure had risen to 83% (Belich, 2001, p. 471).

70. For example, as this quote from Apira Mahuika captures nicely, there was a widespread perception that the legislation in 1975 setting up the advisory Waitangi Tribunal had constitutionalized the Treaty in any case: 'Calls from Maori to "Honour the Treaty" went unheeded by the Crown for years, and it was not until 1975 that it became part of New Zealand's constitution' (cited in Coates & McHugh (1998, p. 215)).

71. In this context, it may be of some significance that Māori opinion coalesced against the Treaty clause before *Maori Council* (1987). This case saw the New Zealand Court of Appeal issue a path-breaking, 'pro-Māori', 'partnership'-based understanding of the 'principles of the Treaty of Waitangi' clause which had been included in legislation. The decision had major implications for the New Zealand Government's economic strategy. Interestingly, after this decision, Māori support for including a reference to the Treaty in a bill of rights did increase. In particular, in the 1989–90 consultation, a number of Māori submissions were received advocating some form of inclusion. However, consensus within Māoridom was still not forthcoming and, in any case, by this time the chance to influence debate had probably been lost.

CHAPTER 7

1. 'Courts Prepare for Act that Will Change Lives', *The Times*, 26 October 1998, p. 4.
2. 'Curbing Executive Power', *The Guardian*, 2 October 2000, p. 19.
3. 'Shawcross Advocates Bill of Rights', *The Times*, 14 May 1970, p. 2.
4. File 1/12, Constitutional Reform Centre, *Archive*, British Library of Political and Economic Science Archives, London School of Economics.
5. Members were first asked to choose one out of four national goals which they considered to be the 'most important issue facing Britain'. Two of these were 'materialist': 'maintaining order in the nation' and 'fighting rising prices'. Two were 'postmaterialist': 'giving the people more say in government decisions' and 'protecting freedom of speech'. The vast majority (between 86% and 98%) of members from all levels (National Council to Inactive Local Group Members) chose a 'postmaterialist' national goal. Next, members were asked to pick contemporary political issues which they considered to be the most important facing Britain from a mixture of two clusters of 'materialist' and 'postmaterialist' issues. Once again, a large majority (between 78% and 90%) from all groups of membership preferred the 'postmaterialist' option (Evans, 1995, pp. 123–6).
6. These include, from the Labour benches, Roy Jenkins and Roy Gardiner in the 1970s and Harriet Harman and Bernie Grant in the 1980s and beyond. Both Jenkins and Gardiner were strongly associated with the 'liberal' reforms of the 1960s including easing theatre censorship, liberalizing divorce, decriminalizing suicide, and abolishing capital punishment for murder. Meanwhile, both Harman and Grant had a long history of involvement with social equality movements (women and ethic minority, respectively); Harman was also deeply involved in the work of the National Council for Civil Liberties (NCCL) as its sometime legal officer. Similarly, social liberal figures from the Conservative political benches who have supported bills of rights include Viscount Lambton, David Hunt, and Dominic Grieve. Before his public disgrace and withdrawal from public life, Viscount Lambton was a strong proponent of liberalized laws regarding both obscenity and homosexuality. Meanwhile, David Hunt and Dominic Grieve have been strongly associated with the 'One Nation' wing of the Conservative Party, which tends to be more supportive of social liberal concerns than other factions.
7. 'Programme for 1969', *Freedom First*, April/May 1969, p. 21.
8. More recently, a number of groups have attempted to advance a social democratic economic agenda through a bill of rights. The Labour Party's 1993 policy document also suggested that a British bill of rights could be enacted including social and economic entitlements (Labour Party (Great Britain), 1993, pp. 31–2). Meanwhile, more recently, several groups argued before the Joint Committee on Human Rights (JCHR) that positive social and economic entitlements should be included in a future indigenous British bill of rights (Great Britain, Parliament, Joint Select Committee on Human Rights, 2008, p. 43). These submissions led to the JCHR recommending inclusion of rights to health, education, housing, and an adequate

standard of living, albeit subject to only 'relatively light touch' judicial review (*Ibid.*, p. 55). Meanwhile, the recent government's white paper on rights and responsibilities has mooted that social entitlements (especially as regards health and child well-being) might be included in a new bill of rights but also stressed the need to limit the extent to which these rights would be justiciable (Great Britain, Government, Ministry of Justice, 2009). It remains to be seen if this debate will result in concrete reform.

9. The Constitutional Reform Centre's survey of the parliamentary candidates from the main political parties during the 1987 general election provides one vivid, albeit extreme, example of this. Writing back in opposition to the centre's bill of rights agenda, one Conservative prospective parliamentary candidate stated: 'The only rights I and millions more are interested in are the rights of the indigenous population which have been eroded in favour of the ethnics (especially Asians)[.] Digusted[.]', File 1/16, Constitutional Reform Centre, *Archives*, British Library of Political and Economic Science, London School of Economics.

10. This course of action allowed the bill to pass without resort to the delay (and use of parliamentary time) inherent in completely overruling the House of Lords through resort to the *Parliament Act* (1949). At the same time, political forces representing the press expressed concern that the HRA's protection of private and family life might lead to the development of an inappropriate judicially constructed right of privacy. According to Lord Wakeham, the then Chairman of the Press Complaints Commission (PCC), such a development 'would damage the freedom of the press and badly wound the system of tough and effective self-regulation that we have built up to provide quick remedies without cost for ordinary citizens' (Great Britain, Parliament, House of Lords, *Debates*, 24 November 1997, col. 771). In order to placate these fears, the government acceded to the addition of an interpretative provision, cognate to the one on thought, conscience, and religion, requiring the courts to have particular regard to the importance of 'freedom of expression' in developing their jurisprudence (Section 12, HRA). Wakeham, on behalf of the PCC, 'warmly' welcomed this amendment stating that it 'safeguards the freedom of the press and self regulation' (Quoted in Great Britain, Parliament, House of Commons, Debates, 2 July 1998, col. 559).

11. As late as October 1990, John Wadham, the then Legal Officer at NCCL/Liberty (and later Liberty's Director) wrote both that 'I think I am against Liberty working for a Bill of Rights or incorporation of the ECHR' and 'Judges will be given more power. This will cause problems because they are reactionary and will not use their power progressively. They are also very unlikely to decide cases against the Government where the issue is a significant one'. See 'A Bill of Rights? 8/10/90' in DCL/837, National Council for Civil Liberties, *Archive*, University of Hull Library.

12. The influence of the model was largely mediated through the involvement of Francesca Klug, former Director of the Civil Liberties Trust (the charitable arm of NCCL), as a political adviser to the Labour Government on the framing of what became the HRA.

13. This 'power of declaration' proposal clearly emanated from the policy thinking of Francesca Klug. However, it should be stressed that, unlike NCCL's original proposals, it involved a complete rejection of any concept of formal legal entrenchment.

14. The Human Rights and Equality Commission only came into being on 1 October 2007, following passage of the *Equality Act* (2006). This act merged and expanded the powers of the various anti-discrimination boards which had been established over the years. Additionally, however, the new body was given a broader human rights remit. A human rights commission had been promised within the agreement of the Joint Liberal Democrat–Labour consultative committee in 1997 (reprinted in Cook & Maclennan, 2005, pp. 30–1).

15. This court came into being in August 1959, following the receipt of the eighth declaration of recognition from a State Party to the Convention. See FO 371/146087, Great Britain, Foreign Office, Political Departments, *General Correspondence* (1959), National Archives.

16. For example, Thornton noted in 1989 that '[t]hanks to decisions by the European Court the Government was forced to stop interrogation techniques such as sleep deprivation which had been used in Northern Ireland. Mental patients under compulsory confinement now have more rights and fair procedures in the review of their confinement. Homosexuality for consenting adults has been legalized in Northern Ireland. Prisoners' rights have been extended, for example, the rights of access to a lawyer. The laws of contempt of court, under which *The Sunday Times* was banned from writing about the effects of the drug thalidomide, have been amended' (Thornton, 1989, pp. 91–2).

17. Nevertheless, there were clear limits to the domestic legal use of such transnational material. In particular, as the House of Lords emphasized in *Brind* (1991), the Convention could not be used to limit discretion given to the executive by broad statutory provisions. Nevertheless, in *Smith* (1996), the Court of Appeal did find that, when assessing whether such discretion was *Wednesbury* unreasonable, it was possible to require more justification the more any such discretion interfered with human rights (including certain Convention rights).

18. Whilst a few legal figures including Lord Justice Salmon and Lord Justice Scarman did support a bill of rights in the 1970s, the general attitude amongst the legal profession was very different. For example, the members of the Law Society's Law Reform Committee opposed the idea of enacting a bill of rights, either based on the European Convention or otherwise, before a House of Lords Select Committee on a bill of rights in this period (Great Britain, Parliament, House of Lords, Select Committee on a Bill of Rights, 1977–8, p. 69). In contrast, by the mid-1990s, the Law Society, through a unanimous vote of its Council, had changed its mind (Zander, 1997, p. 39). Additionally, the Bar Council (Klug, 1996, p. vi) and a whole host of the senior judiciary had also voiced support for a bill of rights based on the Convention (Lester, 1995, p. 198). Whilst the development of the ECHR was not the only factor which might explain this shift, it was of significance. The then Lord Chief Justice of England, Lord Bingham's statement (1993,

p. 397) is fairly representative: 'What I simply do not understand is how it can be sensible to entrust the decisions on these questions [concerning human rights] to an international panel of judges in Strasbourg – some of them drawn from societies markedly unlike our own – but not, in first instance, to our own judges here'.

19. In this vein, John Morrison (2001, p. 348) states: '[T]he truth is that after a long string of judgements from the European Court in Strasbourg against the United Kingdom, the new Labour government had little choice but to incorporate the Convention, if only to bring the embarrassing run of government defeats [before that Court] to an end'.

20. As Table 7.2 demonstrates, a number of parliamentary proposals put forward in the late 1960s and 1970s either drew substantive inspiration from the *Canadian Bill of Rights Act* (CBORA 1960) or, as in the case of Emelyn Hooson's efforts, were *sui generis*. Meanwhile, the draft bill of rights drawn up by the National Council for Civil Liberties (NCCL) in the early 1990s drew not only from the *European Convention* but also from a range of other international rights documents including the *International Covenant on Civil and Political Rights* (ICCPR), International Labour Organization instruments and the *American Convention on Human Rights* (Klug, 1991).

21. For example, Klug (1999, p. 247) claims that the HRA was also specifically designed to 'play a crucial role in the modernization and democratisation of the political system' and 'usher in a change of culture which goes far beyond the confines of the courts'. In developing her argument, she emphasizes the wide definition of 'public authority' in the Act, the decision not to directly bind the United Kingdom courts to the jurisprudence of the European Court and the specific assurance that the 'margin of appreciation' doctrine would not apply in a domestic context. It is also clear that the special interpretative provisions included in the HRA on the press and freedom of expression and religious organizations and freedom of thought, conscience, and religion strongly suggest that the HRA framers saw the domestic courts performing a different role under that instrument to the European Court of Human Rights at Strasbourg.

22. Whereas Jackson reports only twenty-three findings of breach up until 1989 and only forty-one breaches in the period 1975 through to 1996, Lester notes that by 2004, some 130 adverse judgments had been issued by the European Court against the United Kingdom. Lester (2004, p. 10) relates this high figure to societal factors including 'the readiness and ability of British lawyers to use the Convention system imaginatively on their clients' behalf, and the publicity given to Convention cases by the British media'.

23. 'Mr Jenkins Calls for British Bill of Rights', *The Times*, 30 September 1979, p. 3.

24. 'Call for Bill of Rights for Scotland', *The Times*, 2 February 1978, p. 8.

25. The Scottish National Party (SNP) evidence submitted to the House of Lords Select Committee on a bill of rights in 1977 supported incorporation of the ECHR and the enactment of an indigenous bill of rights. Additionally, this evidence stated that the SNP was committed to a Scottish Constitution including

an entrenched bill of rights (modelled on the ECHR) which would be amendable only if supported by a two-thirds vote in a new Scottish Parliament and carried in a national referendum within Scotland (Great Britain, Parliament, House of Lords, Select Committee on a Bill of Rights, 1977–8, p. 354).

26. According to Charter 88 documents, Irvine became converted to the idea of a bill of rights whilst working on the Labour Party's policy review in the late 1980s ('Charter 88 and Labour', Box 69, Charter 88, *Archives*, University of Essex Library). According to Stuart Weir, Smith was also committed to a bill of rights prior to the 1990s (Weir, interview with author, 27 June 2005).

27. Due to party policy, the MP had not taken his seat. The ban did explicitly exclude reporting dealing directly with parliamentary proceedings or elections (Thornton, 1989, p. 12).

28. Section 28, *Local Government Act* (1988).

29. As previously noted, the first demand of this new constitutional reform grouping was for a bill of rights. Survey evidence from the mid-1990s demonstrated that those involved in the charter overwhelmingly affiliated politically to either the Labour or Liberal Democrats (Evans, 1995, p. 127) and also displayed unusually high levels of trade union membership (*Ibid.*, p. 10). For further analysis of the rise and fall of Charter 88, see Erdos (2009*b*).

30. Additionally, the lawyers' human rights group, JUSTICE, played an important behind-the-scenes role in developing Charter 88 and Liberty's plans on a bill of rights (Wadham, interview with author, 18 June 2005).

31. Indeed, such was the strength of NCCL's links to the trade union movement that during the 1984–5 miners' strike, and in the face of the persecution of miners and their families who decided to continue working, it announced that there was no right not to take part in an industrial dispute. According to NCCL, this was because such an activity 'undermines the collective rights of others, and cannot be supported as a fundamental freedom' (Gostin, 1988, p. 16).

32. See Labour Party (1989, p. 55). Although the left of the Labour Party was generally particularly opposed to a bill of rights, they were joined by a number of Labour modernizers including Roy Hattersely, Jack Straw, and Tony Blair. See Evans (1995, p. 205) [on Hattersley], 'A Charter of Rights that Has Shown Itself Wrong', *The Times*, 23 October 1989 [op-ed by Jack Straw opposing entrenched bill of rights] and 'Spycatcher Provokes Case For and Against Bill of Rights', *The Times*, 28 September 1987 [reporting on speech by Blair opposing bill of rights].

33. 'Kinnock Promises to Put Britain in First Division', *The Times*, 2 October 1991. The following year, Labour's general election manifesto included a commitment to enacting a 'democratically enforced bill of rights' that, according to Labour's chief spokesperson in the Lords, Lord Cledwyn, would be based on the ECHR (Great Britain, Parliament, House of Lords, *Debates*, 11 March 1992, col. 1337).

34. Paul Boetang, 'Making the Bill of Rights Work' in DCL/1034, National Council for Civil Liberties, *Archive*, University of Hull Library.

35. 'Enshrine These Rights: With No Consultation the Public Didn't Buy into the Human Rights Act. We Can Correct that Now', *The Guardian*, 27 June 2005.

36. Since the *European Communities Act* (1972), the judiciary have been empowered to disapply primary legislation if it is incompatible with European Community/ Union law. This power, which was famously exercised in *Factortame* (1990), goes beyond even that of the HRA. Arguably, however, European law constitutes a more clearly defined and bounded area of policy-making than adjudication under the HRA.

37. 'Let's Shut Our Door to Terror Says Smith', *The Sun*, 11 October 2001. By the 2005 general election, this commitment had morphed into a pledge to 'reform or repeal' the HRA. See 'Human Rights Act Is Just Wrecking Britain', *The Express*, 18 March 2005.

38. For a fuller analysis of recent political debate on a British bill of rights, see Erdos (2010).

39. The manifesto did promise to 'set up an All-Party Commission to chart a course to a written constitution' (Labour Party (Great Britain), 2010, p. 9: 3).

40. 'Cabinet Revolt over Straw's Rights and Responsibilities Plan', *The Guardian*, 4 November 2008.

41. 'Coalition Reconsidering Tory Plan to Scrap Human Rights Act', *The Guardian*, 19 May 2010.

CHAPTER 8

1. Both these proposals were time-limited to a period of five years after the end of hostilities. It was, however, hoped that they would subsequently be made permanent (Patapan, 1997*a*, pp. 272–3).

2. Its report did, however, recommend that, in order to deal with the large anomalies in per capita electoral representation between under-represented urban districts and over-represented rural districts, the constitution should be amended so as 'to provide that each division of a State should return one member of the House of Representatives and that the number of electors enrolled in each division in a State should be as nearly as practicable uniform' (Australia, Parliament, Joint Committee on Constitutional Review, 1959, p. 46). The then Liberal/Country Government of Robert Menzies, being constitutionally conservative and with an electoral base partly within rural constituencies, did not follow up on this proposal.

3. Earlier in September 1973, the Attorney General Lionel Murphy convened a Constitutional Convention in Sydney and *inter alia* proposed to it that a bill of rights be entrenched in the Australian Constitution (Australia, Constitutional Convention, 1973). This proposal faced strong opposition from many of Australian states and, perhaps understandably given the onerous requirements of constitutional amendment under Section 128, did not proceed further.

4. 'Bill of Rights Dead, and Now Buried', *Sydney Morning Herald*, 19 August 1986; Australia, Parliament, Senate, *Debates*, 25 November 1986, p. 2724.

5. In late 1990, however, the government did accede to optional protocol one of the ICCPR, thereby allowing individuals, once they had exhausted their domestic

remedies, to take grievances based on the ICCPR before the UN's Human Rights Committee for a non-binding determination. This decision was officially taken as a result of the recommendation of the Royal Commission into Aboriginal Deaths in Custody. For a full analysis of the origins of this decision, see Hovell (2003*b*).

6. This commission was chaired by the former Commonwealth Solicitor General Sir Maurice Byers and included as members former Liberal Premier of Victoria Sir Rupert Hamer, former Labor Prime Minister Gough Whitlam, and Law Professors Enid Campbell and Leslie Zines. Hon. Mr Justice Toohey, then a judge of the Federal Court of Australia, was a member of the commission until 31 December 1986. However, he resigned from this post, following his elevation to the High Court (Australia's supreme court) (Australia, Constitutional Commission, 1988*a*, p. 33).

7. These initial recommendations emerged out of a request made by Bowen in January 1988 that the commission adopt a number of limited recommendations, viewed as suitable to being put to referendum that same year, and deliver these to him by the first week of May 1988 (see Australia, Constitutional Commission, 1988*a*, p. 46). The commission's final report issued later in 1988 went on to recommend a fully entrenched bill of rights modelled on the Canadian *Charter* (*Ibid.* pp. 435–737). This was not followed up.

8. Specifically, it was proposed that existing constitutional rights relating to jury trial, freedom of religion, and the right not to be expropriated of property except on fair terms be both strengthened and extended to the states (*Constitution Alteration (Rights and Freedoms) Act* 1988). In addition, a new requirement that 'fair and democratic' elections be held at both the state and federal level was also proposed (*Constitution Alteration (Fair Elections) Act* 1988).

9. The other proposals put to referendum were to recognize local government within the constitution (*Constitution Alteration (Local Government)* 1988) and to provide for four-year maximum terms and simultaneous elections for both Houses of the federal Parliament (*Constitution Alteration (Parliamentary Terms) Act* 1988). This latter proposal represented a deviation from the commission's own recommendation that whilst the House of Representatives should be given a four-year maximum term, the Senate should have a double (i.e. eight-year) term. This deviation later became extremely controversial during the lead-up to the referenda. See 'Row Over Referendum Campaign Worsens', *Sydney Morning Herald*, 20 July 1988.

10. 'High Court Backing for Free Speech', *Sydney Morning Herald*, 1 October 1992.

11. Moreover, those decisions which went further (notably *Teoh* (1995), which argued that the requirements of international human rights law could, absent indications to the contrary, ground a legitimate expectation that administrative decision-makers would act consistently with its requirements) engendered widespread political opposition even from members of the Labor Government.

12. In particular, Issac Issacs feared that an 'equal protection' clause would undermine factory legislation in the State of Victoria which discriminated against Chinese immigrants whilst John Forrest feared for the future of a legal rule in Western Australia that no Asiatic or African alien could get a miner's right or go mining on a goldfield (La Nauze, 1972, p. 231).

13. Nevertheless, at this stage, the changes in relation to racial non-discrimination were mainly cosmetic as the ALP's policy on immigration remained substantively unamended (Tavan, 2005, pp. 155–6).

14. See, for example, the letter from Ken Buckley, President of the Council for Civil Liberties in support of the bill of rights in *Sydney Morning Herald*, 29 January 1974.

15. In particular, opposition was forthcoming from the National Episcopal Conference of the Catholic Church, the New South Wales Council of Churches, the Presbyterian Church in New South Wales, the Salvation Army, and the Anglican Dean of Sydney. See 'Bill "Threatens Freedom" – Cleric's Attack', *Sydney Morning Herald*, 26 December 1973; 'Rights Bill "Threat" Support', *Sydney Morning Herald*, 28 December 1973; and 'Bishops Attack Rights Bill, Say Religion at Risk', *Sydney Morning Herald*, 25 January 1974.

16. See 'Police Fear Effects of Rights Bill', *Sydney Morning Herald*, 9 March 1974.

17. Queensland Council for Civil Liberties (Australia, Parliament, Senate, Standing Committee on Constitutional and Legal Affairs, 1985, Submission 51), New South Wales Council for Civil Liberties (*Ibid.*, Submission 126), Victoria Council of Civil Liberties (*Ibid.*, Submission 131), and South Australian Council for Civil Liberties (*Ibid.*, Submission 161). No submissions were received from other state Councils for Civil Liberties, although one organization with no links to these bodies but styling itself the Australian Civil Liberties Union did write in opposition (*Ibid.*, Submission 2). Several other civil liberties/human rights groups penned supportive briefs including the Human Rights Commission (*Ibid.*, Submission 135) and the Free Speech Committee (*Ibid.*, Submission 148).

18. This contrasts with a global average of only 40% support from all submissions ($n = 180$) (Australia, Parliament, Senate, Standing Committee on Law and Justice, 1985).

19. Australian Institute of Multicultural Affairs (Australia, Parliament, Senate, Standing Committee on Constitutional and Legal Affairs, 1985), Joint Ethnic Committee (*Ibid.*, Submission 91), Australians for Racial Equality (*Ibid.*, Submission 157), and the Four Directions Council (an Aboriginal rights group based in the United States) (*Ibid.*, Submission 167).

20. Women's Electoral Lobby, Perth (Australia, Parliament, Senate, Standing Committee on Constitutional and Legal Affairs, 1985, Submission 117). See also the supportive submission from the Abortion Law Repeal Association of Western Australia (*Ibid.*, Submission 90).

21. Gay Women's Action Lobby (Australia, Parliament, Senate, Standing Committee on Constitutional and Legal Affairs, 1985, Submission 74).

22. Unemployed Peoples Embassy, Sydney (Australia, Parliament, Senate, Standing Committee on Constitutional and Legal Affairs, 1985, Submission 27).

23. 'Bill of Rights Badly Marketed', *Sydney Morning Herald*, 19 March 1986. The alleged 'fact' is actually incorrect.
24. 'Rights Bill Fault', *Sydney Morning Herald*, 26 May 1986.
25. 'Democrats Seek Bill of Rights Deal', *Sydney Morning Herald*, 10 March 1986.
26. Sample: 1,900 adults nationwide. Support: 72%. Oppose: 16%. Other: 12%. Source: 'Poll Shows 72 Per Cent Questioned Favour Rights Charter in Constitution', *Globe and Mail*, 10 November 1981.
27. Sample: 1,034 adults nationwide. Support: 72%. Oppose: 11%. Other: 17%. Source: 'Plea for More Referendums as One in Two Endorses PR', *The Times*, 25 April 1991.
28. Question: 'As you may know, a bill of rights sets out certain basic rights and freedoms for citizens. It includes the sorts of guarantees we've been talking about, such as freedom of speech, and religious freedom from discrimination and various legal rights. Generally speaking, are you for or against the idea of a bill of rights for Australia which provides these sorts of guarantees or don't you have an opinion either way?' Sample: 1,522 respondents nationwide. Support: 72%. Oppose: 7%. No opinion: 21%. *Source*: Galligan & McAllister (1997, p. 147).
29. During the recent national consultation, the National Human Rights Consultation Committee commissioned a Colnar Brunton Social Research telephone poll (n=1200) designed to ascertain support for and opposition to 'a specific law that defined the human rights to which all people in Australia were entitled' (Australia, National Human Rights Consultation Committee, 2009, p. 264). This found 57 per cent in support, 14 per cent in opposition, and 30 per cent neutral. By contrast, a March 2009 Nielsen survey (n=1000) commissioned by Amnesty International Australia found 81 per cent supported, 8 per cent opposed, and 11 per cent were neutral towards 'the introduction of a law to protect human rights in Australia (*Ibid*).
30. Even more strikingly, during the recent and much more extensive Australian Human Rights Consultation in 2009, some 87.4 per cent of relevant submissions supported a bill or charter of rights, whilst only 12.6 per cent were opposed (n=33,356) (Australia, National Human Rights Consultation Committee, 2009, p. 264).
31. Macintyre estimates that even in the first decade after the Second World War, Australia acquired one million immigrants (equivalent to approximately 15 % of its 1945 population) of whom some two-thirds were of non-British origin (Macintyre, 1999, p. 199).
32. Ideally, it might be best also to exclude the small number of Canadian immigrants who were born within francophone Canada. The data required for this, however, is not available. In any case, the numbers involved would not be significant since in all cases migrants born in Canada constituted no more than 0.2% of the population. In fact, in Australia and New Zealand by far the largest group excluded as a result of this computation were immigrants born within the United Kingdom and Ireland.
33. On the other hand, the smaller size of the Aboriginal community in Australia (compared especially to New Zealand) and also its poorer institutional cohesion

(compared especially to Canada) does explain why, at least until very recently, no specific status-based rights for Aborigines have been included in the bill of rights initiatives which have been forwarded.

34. Given the generally racially homogenous nature of Northern Ireland, inclusion of this part of the United Kingdom would likely have further reduced this figure.

35. The concrete subject matter in the case concerned the legality of the federal *World Heritage Properties Act* (1983) which sought, against the wishes of the Tasmanian Parliament, to stop the building of a dam across the Franklin River in Tasmania. This would have caused the destruction of virgin rainforest and the flooding of caves with substantial prehistoric Aboriginal heritage. The legislation was officially a part of Australia's implementation of an UNESCO world heritage convention. *Tasmanian Dam* followed on from the decision of *Koowarta* the previous year. This latter decision had upheld the primacy of the federal *Racial Discrimination Act* (1975), itself based on the UN's *International Convention on the Elimination of All Forms of Racial Discrimination* (ICERD), against contrary provisions of the Queensland legislature. However, the swing judge (Justice Stephen) in this case narrowed the *ratio decendidi* in this case by holding that any implementing legislation had to be linked to an international treaty whose subject matter was of genuine 'international concern'.

36. The Solicitor General also advised that, despite these terms being included in the International Covenant on Economic, Social and Cultural Rights, these standards could probably not be imposed on the states through the external affairs power since they lacked 'sufficient specificity' (Australia, National Human Rights Consultation Committee, Appendix E, p. 25).

37. The Solicitor General ultimately rejected this argument. He did, however, state that the prospects of such provisions being held constitutionally valid would be enhanced if the law provided that the Attorney General had to be joined as a party to proceedings in order for a declaration to be made and also if the declaration gave rise to some binding legal right. For example, issuance of a declaration could allow the other parties in the legal proceedings to compel the Attorney General to bring the matter to the attention of Parliament.

38. In particular, former Prime Minister Robert Menzies stated that 'to my mind this matter is potentially the most important threat to the whole Constitution and the whole of our constitutional federal system and to the integrity and powers of the State Parliaments'. See 'External Powers' Threat to States – Menzies on Human Rights', *Sydney Morning Herald*, 15 March 1974.

39. These fears were particularly prompted by the fact that the ICCPR, on which the policy was based, had yet to come into international force (Whitlam, 1985, p. 178). This only occurred in 1977.

40. 'Back to Practical Tasks', *The Australian*, 24 April 2010.

41. In his study of thirty-six democracies, Lijphart places the United Kindam Parliament in 1996 in the category of 'between medium and weak bicameralism' (Lijphart, 1999, p. 212). Lijphart judges fifteen parliaments to have stronger

and twenty-three parliaments to have weaker forms of bicameralism than the United Kingdom Parliament.

42. Although the Canadian Senate is, similarly to Australia's, endowed with virtually coequal powers to the lower house, its real power is reduced by the fact that it is not directly elected and, therefore, lacks strong popular legitimacy. Given this, Lijphart (1999, p. 212) places the Canadian Senate in the category of 'medium-strength' as opposed to 'strong' bicameralism.

43. Significant ordinary legislation and administrative reform at the federal level had been passed including the *Death Penalty Abolition Act (Cth)* (1973), the *Racial Discrimination Act (Cth)* (1975), and the *Human Rights Commission Act (Cth)* (1977). These initiatives were complemented by cognate reforms at the sub-national level prohibiting sex discrimination, decriminalizing homosexuality, and securing Aboriginal land rights (Dunstan, 1981; Evans Case, 2004, p. 169).

44. It is entirely consonant with this analysis that Fraser later became the only senior member of the Liberal Party to endorse the need for a bill of rights. See 'Libs Desert Fraser over Bill of Rights', *Sydney Morning Herald*, 26 August 2000.

45. 'Democrats Seek Bill of Rights Deal', *Sydney Morning Herald*, 10 March 1986; 'Bill of Rights Now a Certainty', *Sydney Morning Herald*, 13 March 1986.

46. 'Bill of Rights Not Worth the Trouble', *Sydney Morning Herald*, 18 August 1986.

47. The elite-entrenching nature of the proposals may ultimately have alienated many postmaterialists, thereby helping ensure its defeat in the referendum of 1999 (Tranter, 2003).

48. 'Howard Warning on Rights Bill', *Sydney Morning Herald*, 9 June 1986.

49. 'Empowering ASIO [Australian Security and Intelligence Organization] in Planned Terrorism Bill Endangers Rights', *Sydney Morning Herald*, 21 June 2002. Additionally, it should be noted that sub-national statutory bills of rights were enacted in the Australian Capital Territory (*Human Rights Act (ACT)* 2003) and the State of Victoria (*Charter of Human Rights and Responsibilities (Vic.)* 2006).

50. The survey was undertaken by Colmar Brunton Social Research and had a random sample size of n=1200 (Australia, National Human Rights Consultation Committee, 2009, p. 384.

51. 'Bill of rights looks dead in the water', *Sydney Morning Herald*, 17 February 2010.

52. Rights push finally put out of its misery', *The Australian*, 23 April 2010.

53. *Ibid.*

CHAPTER 9

1. Middle-range theories 'lie between the minor but necessary working hypotheses that evolve in abundance during day-to-day research and the all-inclusive systematic efforts to develop a unified theory that will explain all the observed uniformities in social behavior, social organization and social change' (Merton, 1967, p. 39).

2. Where a non-transition bill of rights was replacing a previous bill of rights then the extent to which the new instrument represented either an extension of, or

retreat from, BORI would ideally be analysed. In situations where a bill of rights has arisen as a result of judicial as opposed to political decision-making, the political trigger aspect of the PTT will not be relevant.

3. Rubinstein was able to do this since, after the elections of 1992, he became Minister of Justice for a time. See 'Barak to Review IDF Orders on Homosexuals', *Jerusalem Post*, 7 February 1993.

4. The other law, *Basic Law: Freedom of Occupation* was in any case less controversial. Indeed, no MKs formally opposed its final enactment in March 1992 whilst, according to the plenum protocol, twenty-three MKs supported it (Israel, Knesset, *Plenum Protocol*, 3 March 1992).

5. The linkage between this foreign policy outlook and 'left–liberal' postmaterialism has been thoroughly documented by Rynhold (2007).

6. Charlie Bitton, the sole representatives of the left-wing party Black Panthers (formerly part of Hadesh) also voted against *Basic Law: Human Dignity and Liberty* despite having supported it at first reading. Far from reflecting a basic antagonism to the law, however, his final vote was rooted in a strong opposition to the various compromises which had been inserted into the text based on both religious and security considerations. See Israel, Knesset, *Plenum Protocol*, 24 December 1991.

7. For example, during the third reading of *Basic Law: Human Dignity*, Shmuel Halpert, MK for Agudat Yisrael, spoke in opposition to the law arguing that 'the bill before us sets new principles, which are not necessarily compatible with the principles of the Jewish heritage, particularly in the interpretation of the values and their balancing when they conflict'. Meanwhile, Elyakim Haetzni, MK for the right-wing nationalist party Tehiya, expressed fears about judicial review asking rhetorically who would determine and by which parameters what the 'values of the State of Israel', 'Jewish and democratic state', 'worthy purpose', and 'in excessive manner' meant (Israel, Knesset, *Plenum Protocol*, 17 March 1992).

8. *Basic Law: Human Dignity and Liberty* also protects some property rights. However, these are phrased so as to principally protect personal property (Clause 3). Moreover, as a number of MKs who pushed forward the Basic Laws on human rights stressed, the inclusion of property rights combined with the non-inclusion of a range of other rights reflected the fact that these rights were not seen to be in strong conflict with traditional Jewish perspectives and so compromise was possible here with those who generally opposed human rights Basic Laws (Meridor, interview with author, 20 October 2009; Virshubski, interview with author, 25 October 2009).

9. Thus, Ahron Barak, former Chief Justice of Israel, has noted in extra-curial writing that 'The Israel Bill of Rights provides in part that "[t]here shall be no violation of the life, body or dignity of any person as such." This provision, which limits State action, reflects a conception of the State as a threat to the individual. However, another provision states that "[e]very person is entitled to protection of his life, person and dignity." Here, the State is conceived as a force that protects the individual. Thus, for example, in one opinion I derived from this provision

the right to minimum goods and services necessary to maintain a human existence.' (Barak, 2006, pp. 219–20).

10. Although arguably apparent since at least the late 1960s (Woods, 2009), this orientation became particularly prominent during the 1980s. Thus, in *Nevo* (1988), the Supreme Court struck down a collective bargaining agreement which provided compulsory retirement for women five years earlier than men. Meanwhile, in *Universal City Studios* (1988), the court found freedom of expression to enjoy supra-legal status in Israel and used this to strike down the censorship board's attempt to ban the showing of the *Last Temptation of Christ.*

11. For example, during a Constitution, Law and Justice Committee meeting to discuss the *Basic Law: Human Dignity and Liberty,* Yitzhak Levy, an MK from the Mafdal (the national religious party) candidly voiced his concerns: 'the HCJ's [High Court of Justice's] judges are very original judges, very surprising, and very productive. And very unexpected in many cases. And let me tell you the truth, this is what I am afraid of' (Israel, Knesset, Constitution, Law and Justice Committee, *Plennum Protocol,* 5 February 1992). By contrast, a number of MKs with a postmaterialist ideology stressed the important role of the courts. For example, during the first reading of *Basic Law: Human Dignity,* Shulamit Aloni (the leader of Ratz), Moshe Shachal, and Haim Ramon (both Labor MKs), all stressed the necessity and value of judicial review (Israel, Knesset, *Plenum Protocol,* 10 December 1991).

12. On the other hand, detracting somewhat from these results, Israelis displayed a particularly strong sense of national pride and respect for national authority.

13. The collapse of the Oslo Accord (1993) peace process in 2000 led to the post-materialist left 'losing credibility and hence political support in Israel' (Rynhold, 2007, p. 434). Therefore, the trends noted here have been temporarily stunted in the post-2000 period. Despite its importance, it is beyond the scope of the discussion here to investigate the extent of this development or its implications for the future of human rights in Israel.

14. This amendment in employment law was particularly pushed by Mordehai Virshubski of Ratz and Haim Orom of Mapan. See 'Gays Fight for Job Rights', *Jerusalem Post,* 25 June 1990.

15. As Dalton (2004) stresses, a decline in public trust in politics has been a common experience of advanced industrialized democracies which can be related to broader sociological trends. Despite this, the trend in Israel is particularly stark and points to a more specific cause.

16. Along the same lines, in 1991, the threshold for election to the Knesset was raised from 1% to the still extremely low figure of 1.5%. This reform was principally aimed at keeping 'one-person lists' out of the Knesset (Ottolenghi, 2001, p. 117).

17. As stressed by former Ratz MK Mordechai Virshubski, a strong supporter of a bill of rights but opponent of the separate election of the Prime Minister, there was far from complete symmetry between the supporters of constitutional rights and the supporters of direct election (Vershubski, interview with author, 25 October 2009).

18. 'Who Needs a Bill of Rights', *Jerusalem Post*, 24 November 1989.
19. 'Shamir Promises Orthodox to Freeze Human Rights Bill', *Jerusalem Post*, 27 November 1989.
20. For the full text of this proposal, see Sharfman (*c.*1993, pp. 168–71).
21. Notably, a savings clause was included providing that existing laws could not be struck down for incompatibility with the Basic Law but rather could only be interpreted according to its principles. This savings clause was particularly aimed at protecting existing religiously discriminatory legislation and security regulations which were strongly valued by the cultural right. For the same reasons, the proposals also excluded mention of freedom of conscience, freedom of non-religion, the right not to be tortured, and the right not to receive capital punishment.
22. Most notably, in committee, an explicit right to freedom of movement was removed and the purpose clause altered so as to specifically reference Israel not only as a democratic but also a Jewish State. Finally, third reading, a provision entrenching the Basic Law against amendment except by an absolute majority of Knesset members was removed. All these compromises proved extremely controversial amongst postmaterialist rights supporters within the Knesset. Thus, whilst the leader of Ratz, Shulamit Aloni, voted in favour of the Basic Law throughout its legislative passage, she stressed that she was 'not proud of it'. In particular, she stressed her opposition to reference of Israel as a Jewish State ('Jewish and democratic don't go together . . . it's a bluff, it's a lie') and to the absence of an explicit right to equality ('They threw away the basic thing which you have to emphasize in a democratic country') (Aloni, interview with author, 19 October 2009).
23. During the first decades of the twentieth century, this jurisprudence came into increasing conflict with 'Progressive' or social democratic legislative enactments. Most notably, in 1905, the US Supreme Court in *Lochner* struck down a New York law restricting work in bakeries to ten hours a day or sixty hours a week as an unjustified restraint of freedom of contract.
24. Specifically, this provision states:

    Every natural or legal person is entitled to the peaceful enjoyment of his possessions. No one shall be deprived of his possessions except in the public interest and subject to the conditions provided for by law and by the general principles of international law.

    The preceding provisions shall not, however, in any way impair the right of a State to enforce such laws as it deems necessary to control the use of property in accordance with the general interest or to secure the payment of taxes or other contributions or penalties. (Protocol One, Article 1, ECHR)

25. See *Hopkinson v. Police* (2004) 3 NZLR 703 (HC) and *Big M Drug Mart Ltd* (1985) 1 SCR 295. The practical effect of the latter decision was severely limited, however, since the following year the Supreme Court later upheld the *Ontario Retail Business Holiday Act* as compatible with the *Charter* since its restrictions on

Sunday activities were held not to be clearly motivated by an overriding religious concern. See *R v. Edwards Books and Art Ltd* (1985) 2 SCR 713.

26. See *McLean v. Procurator Fiscal Fort William* (2001) 1 WLR 2425.
27. *Anufrijeva v. Southwark LBC* (2003) EWCA Civ 1406, (2004) QB 1124.
28. *Eldridge v. British Columbia (A.G.)* (1997)
29. *Campbell v. MGN Ltd* (2004) UKHL 22, (2004) AC 457.
30. See *R v. Keegstra* (1990) 3 SCR 697 and *R. v. Butler* (1992) 1 SCR 452.
31. Moreover, although postmaterialist rights advocates have continued to emphasize the critical importance of civil and political rights, a trend towards supporting the explicit entrenchment of positive social and economic entitlements is also clearly visible.

Bibliography

Books, Chapters, Reports, and Journal Articles

Aikman, Colin (1964), 'The New Zealand Ombudsman', *Canadian Bar Review* (Vol. 42(3), pp. 399–432).

Akerman, Bruce (1991), *We the People: Foundations*, Cambridge, Massachusetts: Belknap Press.

——(1997), *The Rise of World Constitutionalism*, Virginia Law Review (Vol. 83, pp. 771–97).

Auckland Lesbian and Gay Lawyers (1994), *Out Law: A Legal Guide for Lesbians and Gay Men in New Zealand*, Auckland: Auckland Lesbian and Gay Lawyers.

Australia, Australian Bureau of Statistics (1994), *Estimated Resident Population by Country of Birth, Age and Sex, Preliminary June 1992 and June 1993*, Canberra: Australian Bureau of Statistics.

Australia, Constitutional Commission (1988*a*), *First Report*, Sydney: The Commission.

——(1988*b*), *Final Report*, Sydney: The Commission.

Australia, Government (2010), *The Australian Human Rights Framework* (available at http://www.ag.gov.au/www/agd/rwpattach.nsf/VAP/(3A6790B96C927794AF1031D9395 C5C20)~Human+Rights+Framework.pdf/$file/Human+Rights+Framework.pdf (accessed 28 April 2010)).

Australia, National Human Rights Consultation Committee (2009), *Report* (available at http://www.humanrightsconsultation.gov.au/www/nhrcc/nhrcc.nsf/Page/Report_ NationalHumanRightsConsultationReportDownloads (accessed 7 January 2010)).

Australia, Parliament, House of Representatives (Various), *Parliamentary Debates* (Hansard), Canberra: Commonwealth Government Printer.

Australia, Parliament, Joint Committee on Constitutional Review (1959), *Report*, Canberra: A. J. Arthur, Commonwealth Government Printer.

Australia, Parliament, Senate (Various), *Parliamentary Debates* (Hansard), Canberra: Commonwealth Government Printer.

Australia, Republic Advisory Committee (1993), *An Australian Republic: The Options*, Canberra: AGPS.

Ayres, Philip (1987), *Malcolm Fraser: A Biography*, Richmond, Victoria: Heinemann.

Bailey, Peter (1990), *Human Rights: Australia in an International Context*, Sydney: Butterworths.

Bakan, Joel (*c*.1997), *Just Words: Constitutional Rights and Social Wrongs*, Toronto, Buffalo: University of Toronto Press.

Baker, Keith Michael (1994), 'The Idea of a Declaration of Rights' in Dale Van Kley (ed.), *The French Idea of Freedom: The Old Regime and the Declaration of Rights of 1789*, Stanford, California: Stanford University Press.

Barak, Ahron (2006), *The Judge in a Democracy*, Princeton, New Jersey; Oxford: Princeton University Press.

Barnett, Lloyd G. (1977), *The Constitutional Law of Jamaica*, Oxford: Oxford University Press for the London School of Economics and Political Science.

Barzilai, Gad (1999), 'Courts as Hegemonic Institutions: The Israeli Supreme Court in a Comparative Perspective', *Israeli Affairs* (Vol. 5(2), pp. 15–33).

Baumgartner, Frank R. & Bryan D. Jones (1993), *Agendas and Instability in American Politics*, Chicago, Illinois; London: University of Chicago Press.

Bayefsky, Ann (ed.) (1989), *Canada's Constitution Act, 1982 & Amendments: A Documentary History*, Toronto; London: McGraw-Hill Ryerson.

Beck, Ulrich & Elisabeth Beck-Gernsheim (2001), *Individualization: Institutionalized Individualism and Its Social and Political Consequences*, London: Sage.

Beetham, David (1989), 'Civil Liberties, Thatcherism and Charter 88', *Parliamentary Affairs* (Vol. 42, pp. 273–9).

Belich, James (2001), *Paradise Reforged: A History of New Zealanders from the 1880s to the Year 2000*, Auckland: Penguin.

Bell, John (1994), *French Constitutional Law*, Oxford: Clarendon Press.

Bellamy, Richard (2007), *Political Constitutionalism: A Republican Defence of the Constitutionality of Democracy*, Cambridge: Cambridge University Press.

Belliveau, Robert M. (1992), *Mr. Diefenbaker, Parliamentary Democracy and the Canadian Bill of Rights*, PhD dissertation, University of Saskatchewan (Saskatoon).

Betts, Katherine. (1999), 'The Cosmopolitan Social Agenda and the Referendum on the Republic', *People and Place* (Vol. 7(4), pp. 32–41).

Bingham, Thomas (1993), 'The European Convention on Human Rights: Time to Incorporate', *Public Law* (pp. 390–400).

Bogdanor, Vernon (2001), 'Constitutional Reform' in Anthony Seldon (ed.), *The Blair Effect: The Blair Government 1997–2001*, London: Little Brown.

Booking, Tom & Roberto Rabel (1995), 'Neither British nor Polynesian: A Brief History of New Zealand's Other Immigrants' in Stuart Greif (ed.), *Immigration and National Identity in New Zealand: One People, Two Peoples, Many Peoples?*, Palmerston North, New Zealand: Dunmore Press.

Bork, Robert H. (2002), *Coercing Virtue: The Worldwide Rule of Judges*, Toronto: Vintage Canada.

Brazier, Rodney (1998), *Constitutional Reform*, Oxford; New York: Oxford University Press (2nd edition).

Brennan, Frank (1998), *Legislating Liberty: A Bill of Rights for Australia?*, St Lucia, Queensland: University of Queensland Press.

Bushnell, Ian (1992), *The Captive Court: A Study of the Supreme Court of Canada*, McGill-Queen's University Press.

Cameron, David (2006), 'Balancing Freedom and Security – A Modern British Bill of Rights' in David Cameron (2007), *Social Responsibility*, Northampton: Belmont Press.

Canada, Government (1969), *The Constitution and the People of Canada*, Ottawa: Queen's Printer.

Canada, Government (1978), *Constitutional Reform: Canadian Charter of Rights and Freedoms*, Ottawa: Queen's Printer.

Canada, Government, Prime Minister (1978), *A Time for Action: Toward the Renewal of the Canadian Federation*, Ottawa: Government of Canada.

Canada, Parliament, House of Commons (Various), *Debates* (Hansard), Ottawa: Queen's Printer.

——(23 April 1981), *Journals*, Ottawa: Queen's Printer.

Canada, Parliament, House of Commons, Special Committee on Human Rights and Fundamental Freedoms (1960), *Minutes of Proceedings and Evidence [and Final Report to House]*, Ottawa: Queen's Printer.

Canada, Parliament (1865), *Parliamentary Debates on the Subject of the Confederation of the British North American Provinces, 3rd Session, 8th Provincial Parliament of Canada*, Quebec: Hunter, Rose.

Canada, Parliament, Senate (Various), *Debates* (Hansard), Ottawa: Queen's Printer.

Canada, Parliament, Senate, Special Committee on Human Rights and Fundamental Freedoms (1950), *Proceedings of the Special Committee on Human Rights and Fundamental Freedoms*, Ottawa: Queen's Printer.

Canada, Parliament, Special Joint Committee of the Senate and of the House of Commons on the Constitution of Canada (1980), *Minutes of Proceedings and Evidence of the Special Joint Committee of the Senate and of the House of Commons on the Constitution of Canada*, Ottawa: Queen's Printer.

Canada, Royal Commission on Bilingualism and Biculturalism (1967), *Final Report*, Ottawa: Queen's Printer.

Canada, Statistics Canada (1992), *Census 1991: The Nation: Immigration and Citizenship*, Ottawa: Statistics Canada.

Charlesworth, Hilary (1991), 'Australia's Accession to the First Optional Protocol of the International Covenant on Civil and Political Rights', *Melbourne University Law Review*, (Vol. 18(2), pp. 428–34).

Chrétien, Jean (1990), 'Bringing the Constitution Home' in Thomas S. Axworthy & Pierre Elliot Trudeau (translations into English by Patricia Claxon), *Towards a Just Society: the Trudeau Years*, Markham, Ontario: Viking.

Clarkson, Stephen & Christina McCall (1990), *Trudeau and Our Times*. Volume I: *The Magnificent Obsession*, Toronto: McClelland & Stewart Inc.

Cleveland, Les (*c*.1979), *The Politics of Utopia: New Zealand and Its Government*, Wellington, New Zealand: Methuen.

Coates, Ken & Paul McHugh (eds.) (1998), *Living Relationships – Kokiri Ngatahi: The Treaty of Waitangi in the New Millennium*, Wellington: Victoria University Press.

Collier, Ruth Berins & David Collier (1991), *Shaping the Political Arena*, Princeton, New Jersey: Princeton University.

Congleton, Roger D. (2003), *Improving Democracy Through Constitutional Reform: Some Swedish Lessons*, Boston, Massachusetts; London: Kluwer Academic Publishers.

Conklin, William E. (1989), *Images of a Constitution*, Toronto: University of Toronto Press.

Conservative Party (Great Britain) (1979), *The Conservative Manifesto 1979*, London: Conservative Central Office.

Constitutional Society (1957), *Aims and Objects*, Auckland: Constitutional Society.

——(1961), *Suggested Constitution for New Zealand*, Auckland: Constitutional Society.

Craven, Greg (1999), 'The High Court of Australia: A Study in the Abuse of Power', *University of New South Wales Law Journal*, (Vol. 22(1), pp. 216–42).

Craven, Peter (2003), 'Introduction' in Guy Rundle, *The Opportunist: John Howard and the Triumph of Reaction* (Quarterly Essay No. 3), Melbourne: Black Inc.

Dale, Iain (ed.) (2000), *British Political Party Manifestos, 1900–1997*, London: Routledge/ Politico's Publishing.

Dalton, Russell J. (2004), *Democratic Challenges, Democratic Choices: The Erosion of Political Support in Advanced Industrial Democracies*, Oxford: Oxford University Press.

Darrow, Mac & Philip Alston (2000), 'Bills of Rights in Comparative Perspective' in Philip Alston (ed.), *Promoting Human Rights Through Bills of Rights: Comparative Perspectives*, Oxford: Oxford University Press.

Davies, Alan (ed.) (*c.*1992), *Antisemitism in Canada: History and Interpretation*, Waterloo, Ontario: Wilfred Laurier University Press.

De Smith, Stanley (1961), 'Fundamental Rights in the New Commonwealth', *International & Comparative Law Quarterly* (Vol. 10, pp. 83–102 & 215–37).

Dicey, Albert [1908] (1959), *Introduction to the Study of the Law of the Constitution*, London: Macmillan.

Dunstan, Don (1981), *Felicia: The Political Memoirs of Don Dunstan*, South Melbourne; London: Macmillan.

Durodié, Bill (2007), 'Fear and Terror in a Post-Political Age' *Government and Opposition* (Vol. 42(3), pp. 427–50).

Edelman, Martin (2000), 'The New Israeli Constitution', *Middle Eastern Studies* (Vol. 36(2), pp. 1–27).

Elkind, Jerome B. & Anthony Shaw (1986), *Standard for Justice: A Critical Commentary on the Proposed Bill of Rights for New Zealand*, Auckland, New Zealand: Oxford University Press.

Elkins, David J. & Richard Simeon (1980), *Small Worlds: Provinces and Parties in Canadian Political Life*, Toronto: Methuen.

Elkins, Zachary, Tom Ginsburg, & James Melton (2007), 'The Lifespan of Written Constitutions' (draft manuscript available at http://www.yale.edu/macmillan/ ruleoflaw/papers/Ginsburg-Lifespans-California.pdf (accessed 11 October 2009).

Ellis, Kathryn (2004), 'Promoting Rights or Avoiding Litigation? The Introduction of the Human Rights Act 1998 into Adult Social Care in England', *European Journal of Social Work* (Vol. 7(3), pp. 321–40).

Ely, James W. (1992), *The Guardian of Every Other Right: A Constitutional History of Property Rights*, Oxford: Oxford University Press.

Ely, John Hart (1980), *Democracy and Distrust: A Theory of Judicial Review*, Cambridge, Massachusetts: Harvard University Press.

Epp, Charles (1996), 'Do Bills of Rights Matter? The Canadian Charter of Rights and Freedoms', *American Political Science Review* (Vol. 90(4), pp. 765–79).

Epp, Charles (1998), *The Rights Revolution: Lawyers, Activists, and Supreme Courts in Comparative Perspective*, Chicago, Illinois; London: University of Chicago Press.

Erdos, David (2009*a*), 'Judicial Culture and the Politicolegal Opportunity Structure: Explaining Bill of Rights Legal Impact in New Zealand', *Law and Social Inquiry* (Vol. 34(1), pp. 95–127).

Erdos, David (2009*b*), 'Charter 88 and the Constitutional Reform Movement: A Retrospective', *Parliamentary Affairs* (Vol. 64(4), pp. 537–51).

——(2010), 'Smoke but No Fire? The Politics of a "British" Bill of Rights' *The Political Quarterly* (Vol. 81(2), pp. 188–98).

Evans, Mark (1995), *Charter 88: A Successful Challenge to the British Political Tradition?*, Aldershot, England; Brookfield, Vincent: Dartmouth.

Evans Case, R. (2004), *The Politics and Law of Anglo-American Antidiscrimination Regimes, 1945–1995*, PhD dissertation: University of Austin at Texas.

Ewing, Keith (1994), 'The Bill of Rights Debate: Democracy or Juristocracy in Britain' in Ewing, Keith, Conor Gearty & Bob Hepple (eds), *Human Rights and Labour Law: Essays for Paul O'Higgins*, London: Mansell.

——(1999), 'The Human Rights Act and Parliamentary Democracy', *Modern Law Review* (Vol. 62(1), pp. 79–99).

——& Conor Gearty (1990), *Freedom Under Thatcher: Civil Liberties in Modern Britain*, Oxford: Clarendon Press.

Fazal, M. A., (1974), 'Entrenched Rights and Parliamentary Sovereignty', *Public Law* (pp. 295–315).

Finkel, Jodi (2004), 'Judicial Reform in Argentina in the 1990s: How Electoral Incentives Shape Institutional Change', *Latin American Research Review* (Vol. 39(3), pp. 56–80).

——(2005), 'Judicial Reform as Insurance Policy: Mexico in the 1990s', *Latin American Politics and Society* (Vol. 46(4), pp. 87–113).

Flinders, Matthew (2009), *Democratic Drift: Majoritarian Modification and Democratic Anomie in the United Kingdom*, Oxford: Oxford University Press.

Foley, Conor (1994), *Democracy and Human Rights in the UK*, London: Liberty.

Galligan, Brian (1990*a*), 'Australia's Rejection of a Bill of Rights', *Journal of Commonwealth and Comparative Politics*, (Vol. 28(3), pp. 344–68).

——(1990*b*), 'The 1988 Referendum and Australia's Record of Constitutional Change', *Parliamentary Affairs* (Vol. 43(4), pp. 497–507).

——(1995), *A Federal Republic*, Cambridge: Cambridge University Press.

——& Ian McAllister (1997), 'Citizen and Elite Attitudes Towards an Australian Bill of Rights' in Brian Galligan & Charles Sampford (eds.), *Rethinking Human Rights*, Leichhardt, New South Wales: Federation Press.

Gearty, Conor (2006), *Can Human Rights Survive?*, Cambridge: Cambridge University Press.

Gelber, Katherine (2005), 'High Court Review 2004: Limits on the Judicial Protection of Rights', *Australian Journal of Political Science* (Vol. 40(2), pp. 307–22).

Gibson, Dale (1967), 'Constitutional Amendment and the Implied Bill of Rights', *McGill Law Journal* (Vol. 12, pp. 497–501).

Ginsburg, Tom (2002), 'Economic Analysis and the Design of Constitutional Courts', *Theoretical Inquiries in Law* (Vol. 3(1), Article 3, pp. 1–37).

——(2003), *Judicial Review in New Democracies: Constitutional Courts in Asian Cases*, Cambridge: Cambridge University Press.

Glendon, Mary Ann (2001), *A World Made New: Eleanor Roosevelt and the Universal Declaration of Human Rights*, New York: Random House.

Goldsworthy, Jeffrey (1999), *The Sovereignty of Parliament*, Oxford: Clarendon Press.

Goodman, Ryan & Derek Jinks (2004), 'How to Influence States: Socialization and International Human Rights Law', *Duke Law Journal* (Vol. 54(3), pp. 621–703).

Gostin, Larry (1988), 'Towards Resolving the Conflict' in Larry Gostin (ed.), *Civil Liberties in Conflict*, Routledge: London.

Gottlieb, Avi & Ephraim Yuchtman-Ya'ar (1983), 'Materialism, Post-Materialism, and Public Views on Socio-Economic Policy: The Case of Israel', *Comparative Political Studies* (Vol. 16(3), pp. 307–35).

Great Britain, Government, Ministry of Justice (2007), *The Governance of Britain*, London: Stationary Office.

——(2009), *Rights and Responsibilities: Developing our Constitutional Framework*, London: Stationery Office.

Great Britain, Office of Population Censuses and Surveys (1993), *1991 Census Report for Great Britain* (Part 1), 3 vols. London: HMSO.

Great Britain, Parliament, House of Commons (Various), *House of Commons Debates (Hansard)*, London: Stationery Office.

Great Britain, Parliament, House of Lords (Various), *House of Lords Debates* (Hansard), London: Stationery Office.

Great Britain, Parliament, House of Lords, Select Committee on a Bill of Rights (1977–8), *Minutes of Evidence Taken Before Select Committee*, (Vol. I–II), London: HMSO.

Great Britain, Parliament, Joint Committee on Human Rights (2008), *A Bill of Rights for the UK?*, London: Stationery Office.

Griffith, John. (1977), *The Politics of the Judiciary*, Manchester: Manchester University Press.

——(1981), *Public Rights and Private Interests*, Trivandrum: Academy of Legal Publications.

——(1993), 'The Rights Stuff', *Socialist Register* (Vol. 29, pp. 106–24).

Gustafson, Barry (2000), *His Way: A Biography of Robert Muldoon*, Auckland: Auckland University Press.

——(2007), *Kiwi Keith: A Biography of Keith Holyoake*, Auckland: Auckland University Press.

Hailsham of St Marylebone, Lord (Quentin Hogg MP) (1969), *New Charter: Some Proposals for Constitutional Reform*, London.

Hailsham of St Marylebone, Lord (Quentin Hogg MP) (1976), *Elective Dictatorship*, London: Richard Dimbleby Lecture.

Hanan, Hon. J. Ralph (1968), 'Human Rights: The Prospect' in Kenneth Keith (ed.), *Essays on Human Rights*, Wellington: Sweet & Maxwell (NZ).

Harvey, Colin (2001), 'Contested Constitutionalism: Human Rights and Deliberative Democracy in Northern Ireland' in Tom Campbell, Keith D. Ewing & Adam Tomkins (eds.), *Sceptical Essays on Human Rights*, Oxford: Oxford University Press.

Hausmaninger, Herbert (2000), *The Austrian Legal System*, Wein, Manz; The Hague: Kluwer Law International (2nd edition).

Herbert, Nick (2008), 'Rights Without Responsibilities – a Decade of the Human Rights Act' (Lecture at the British Library, 24 November 2008) (available at http://www.bihr.org.uk/sites/default/files/081124%20Rights%20without%20responsibilities%20FINAL.pdf (accessed 27 August 2009)).

Higley, John, Desley Deacon, & Don Smart (1979), *Elites in Australia*, London: Routledge & Kegan Paul.

Hill, Daniel & E. Marshall Pollock (1969), 'Human Rights Legislation in Ontario', *Race* (Vol. 9, pp. 193–203).

Hirschl, Ran (2000*a*), 'The Political Origins of Judicial Empowerment Through Constitutionalization', *Law and Social Inquiry* (Vol. 25(1), pp. 91–147).

——(2000*b*), 'Looking Sideways, Looking Backwards, Looking Forwards', *University of Richmond Law Review* (Vol. 34(2), pp. 415–41).

——(2000*c*), 'The Struggle for Hegemony', *Stanford Journal of International Law* (Vol. 36(1), pp. 73–118).

——(2004*a*), *Towards Juristocracy: The Origins and Consequences of the New Constitutionalism*, Cambridge, Massachusetts; London: Harvard University Press.

——(2004*b*), 'The Political Origins of the New Constitutionalism', *Indiana Journal of Global Legal Studies* (Vol. 11(1), pp. 71–108).

Hirst, Paul (1989), *After Thatcher*, London: Collins.

Hocking, Jenny (1997), *Lionel Murphy: A Political Biography*, Oakleigh, Melbourne; Cambridge: Cambridge University Press.

Horne, Donald (1965), *The Lucky Country: Australia in the Sixties*, Harmondsworth: Penguin.

Hošek, Cavivia (1983), 'Women and the Constitutional Process' in Keith Banting & Richard Simeon (eds.), *And No One Cheered: Federalism, Democracy and the Constitution Act*, Toronto: Methuen.

Hovell, Devika (2003*a*), 'The Sovereignty Stratagem: Australia's Response to UN Human Rights Treaty Bodies', *Alternative Law Journal* (Vol. 28(6), pp. 297–301).

——(2003*b*), 'Lifting the Executive Veil: Australia's Accession to the First Optional Protocol to the International Covenant on Civil and Political Rights', *Adelaide Law Review* (Vol. 24(2), pp. 187–216).

How, W. Glen (1948), 'The Case for a Canadian Bill of Rights', *Canadian Bar Review* (Vol. 26(5), pp. 759–96).

Huntington, Samuel (1974), 'Postindustrial Politics: How Benign Will It Be?', *Comparative Politics* (Vol. 6(2), pp. 163–91).

——(1991), *The Third Wave: Democratization in the Late Twentieth Century*, Norman: University of Oklahoma Press.

Inglehart, Ronald (1971), 'The Silent Revolution in Europe: Intergenerational Change in Post-Industrial Societies', *American Political Science Review* (Vol. 65(4), pp. 991–1017).

——(1977), *The Silent Revolution: Changing Values and Political Styles Among Western Publics*, Princeton, New Jersey; Guildford: Princeton University Press.

——(1990), *Culture Shift in Advanced Industrial Societies*, Princeton, New Jersey: Princeton University Press.

——& Jacques-René Rabier (1986), 'Political Realignment in Advanced Industrial Society: From Class-Based Politics to Quality-of-Life Politics', *Government & Opposition* (Vol. 21(4), pp. 456–79).

——& Christian Welzel (2005), *Modernization, Cultural Change, and Democracy: The Human Development Sequence*, Cambridge: Cambridge University Press.

International Commission of Jurists (New Zealand Section) (1985), *Transcript of Seminar Held on Bill of Rights on 19th May 1985*, Wellington: International Commission of Jurists (New Zealand Section).

Israel, Knesset (Various), *Plenum Protocols* [in Hebrew], Jerusalem: Knesset.

Jackson, Donald W. (1997), *The United Kingdom Confronts the European Convention on Human Rights*, Gainsville, Florida: University of Florida Press.

Johnson, Carol (2003), 'Heteronormative Citizenship: The Howard Government's Views on Gay and Lesbian Issues', *Australian Journal of Political Science* (Vol. 38(1), pp. 45–62).

Joseph MP, Sir Keith (1975), *Freedom Under the Law*, London: Conservative Political Centre.

Kahn-Freund, O. (1974), 'On the Uses and Misuses of Comparative Law', *Modern Law Review* (Vol. 37(1), pp. 1–27).

Keith Ewing, (1994), 'The Bill of Rights Debate: Democracy or Juristocracy in Britain' in Ewing, Keith, Conor Gearty, & Bod Hepple (eds.), *Human Rights and Labour Law*, London: Mansell.

Keith, Kenneth (1978), 'A Lawyer Looks at Parliament' in Sir John Marshall (ed.), *The Reform of Parliament Papers Presented in Memory of Dr. Alan Robinson*, Wellington, New Zealand: New Zealand Institute of Public Administration.

——(1985), 'A Bill of Rights for New Zealand? Judicial Review Versus Democracy', *New Zealand University Law Review* (Vol. 11, pp. 307–22).

Kelly, Paul (2000), 'John Malcolm Fraser' in Michelle Grattan (ed.) *Australian Prime Ministers*, Sydney: New Holland.

Kelsen, Hans (1942), 'Judicial Review of Legislation: A Comparative Study of the Austrian and the American Constitution', *Journal of Politics* (Vol. 4(2), pp. 183–200).

Kelsey, Jane (1990), *A Question of Honour? Labour and the Treaty*, Wellington, New Zealand: Allen & Unwin.

King, Anthony (2007), *The British Constitution*, Oxford: Oxford University Press.

Kingdon, John W. (2003), *Agendas, Alternatives and Public Policies* (2nd edition) (with a new foreword by James A. Thurber), New York; London: Longman.

Klug, Francesca (1991), *A People's Charter: Liberty's Bill of Rights: A Consultation Document*, London: National Council for Civil Liberties.

Klug, Francesca (1996), 'Foreword' in Anthony Lester, James Cornford, & Ronald Dworkin, *A British Bill of Rights*, London: Institute for Public Policy Research (2nd edition).

Klug, Francesca (1999), 'The Human Rights Act 1998, *Pepper v. Hart* and All That', *Public Law* (pp. 246–73).

——(2000), *Values for a Godless Age: The Story of the UK's New Bill of Rights*, London: Penguin.

La Forest, Guy (*c.*1995), *Trudeau and the End of a Canadian Dream* (trans. Paul Leduc Browne & Michelle Weinroth), Montreal; London: McGill-Queen's University Press.

La Nauze, John Andrew (1972), *The Making of the Australian Constitution*, Carlton: Melbourne University Press.

Labour Party (Great Britain) (1976), *United Kingdom Charter of Human Rights: A Discussion Document for the Labour Movement*, London: Labour Party.

——(1989), *Meet the Challenge, Make the Change: A New Agenda for Britain: Final Report of Labour's Policy Review for the 1990s*, London: Labour Party.

——(1993), *A New Agenda for Democracy: Labour's Proposals for Constitutional Reform*, London: Labour Party.

——(1996), *Bringing Rights Home: Labour's Plans to Incorporate the European Convention on Human Rights into UK Law*, London: Labour Party.

Lambertson, Ross (2005), *Repression and Resistance: Canadian Human Rights Activists 1930–1960*, Toronto; Buffalo: University of Toronto Press.

Lange, David (2005), *My Life*, Auckland: Penguin.

League for Social Reconstruction (Research Committee) (1935), *Social Planning for Canada*, Toronto; Buffalo: University of Toronto Press.

Leane, Geoffrey (2004), 'Enacting Bills of Rights: Canada and the Curious Case of New Zealand's "Thin" Democracy', *Human Rights Quarterly* (Vol. 26(1), pp. 152–88).

Lerner, Hanna (2004), 'Democracy, Constitutionalism, and Identity: The Anomaly of the Israeli Case', *Constellations* (Vol. 11(2), pp. 237–57).

Lester of Herne Hill QC, Lord (Anthony Lester) (1969), *Democracy and Individual Rights* (Fabian Tract 39), London: Fabian Society.

——(1995), 'The Mouse that Roared: The Human Rights Bill 1995', *Public Law* (pp. 198–202).

——(2000), 'Human Rights and the British Constitution' in Jeffrey Jowell & Dawn Oliver (eds.), *The Changing Constitution*, Oxford: Oxford University Press (4th edition).

——(2004), '*History and Context*' in Anthony Lester & David Pannick, *Human Rights Law and Practice*, London: Lexis Nexus.

——& Kate Beattie (2007), 'Human Rights and the British Constitution' in Jeffrey Jowell & Dawn Oliver (eds.), *The Changing Constitution*, Oxford: Oxford University Press (6th edition).

——James Cornford, & Ronald Dworkin (1990), *A British Bill of Rights*, London: Institute for Public Policy Research.

Levine, Steven (1991), 'Bills of Rights in Parliamentary Settings: New Zealand and Israeli Experience', *Parliamentary Affairs* (Vol. 44(3), pp. 337–52).

Lijphart, Arend (1984), *Democracy in Plural Societies*, New Haven, Connecticut; London: Yale University Press.

——(1999), *Patterns of Democracy: Government Forms and Performance in Thirty-Six Countries*, New Haven, Connecticut; London: Yale University Press.

Lochery, Neill (1997), *The Israeli Labour Party: In the Shadow of the Likud*, Reading: Ithaca.

Lower, A. (1967), *My First Seventy-Five Years*, Toronto: Macmillan of Canada.

Lowy, Marina O. (1989), 'Restructuring a Democracy: An analysis of the New Proposed Constitution for Israel', *Cornell International Law Journal* (Vol. 22(1), pp. 115–46).

Lutz, Donald (1995), 'Toward a Theory of Constitutional Amendment' in Sanford Levinson (ed.) *Responding to Imperfection: The Theory and Practice of Constitutional Amendment*, Princeton, New Jersey: Princeton University Press.

McBride, Tim (1979), 'Do We Need a Bill of Rights' in J. Stephen Hoadley (ed.), *Improving New Zealand's Democracy*, Auckland, New Zealand: New Foundation for Peace Studies with assistance of the Commission for the Future and Department of Political Science, University of Auckland.

McClelland, Robert (2003), 'How Is a Bill of Rights Relevant Today?', *Australian Journal of Human Rights* (Vol. 9(1), Article 2).

Macdonald, John (1969), *Bill of Rights*, London: Liberal Publication Department.

McHugh, Hon. Michael (2009), 'A Human Rights Act, the Courts and the Constitution' (presentation given at Australian Human Rights Commission) (available at http://www.hreoc.gov.au/letstalkaboutrights/events/McHugh_2009.html (accessed 2 January 2010)).

Macintyre, Stuart (1999), *A Concise History of Australia*, Cambridge: Cambridge University Press.

MacLennan, Christopher (1998), 'The Diefenbaker Bill of Rights and the Question of a Constitutionally Entrenched Charter, 1960–1971' in Donald Story & R. Bruce Shepard (eds.), *The Diefenbaker Legacy: Law and Society since 1957*, Regina: Great Plains Research Centre.

——(2003), *Towards the Charter: Canadians and the Demand for a National Bill of Rights, 1929–1960*, Montreal: McGill-Queen's University Press.

Maclennan, Robert (2005), 'The 1997 Constitutional Compact – and After' in Robin Cook & Robert Maclennan (eds.), *Looking Back – Looking Forward: The Cook-Maclennan Agreement, Eight Years on*, London: New Politics Network.

McRoberts, Kenneth (1988), *Quebec: Social Change and Political Crisis*, Toronto: McClelland & Stewart.

McWhinney, E. (1982), *Canada and the Constitution 1979–1982*, University of Toronto Press: Toronto.

Madsen, Mikael Rask (2004), 'France, the UK, and the "Boomerang" of the Internationalisation of Human Rights (1945–2000)' in Simon Halliday and Patrick Schmidt, *Human Rights Brought Home: Socio-Legal Perspectives on Human Rights in the National Context*, Oxford; Portland, Oregon: Hart Publishing.

Mandel, Michael (1998), 'A Brief History of the New Constitutionalism, or How We Changed Everything so that Everything Would Remain the Same', *Israel Law Review* (Vol. 32(2), pp. 250–300).

——(1999), 'Democracy and the New Constitutionalism in Israel', Israeli Law Review (Vol. 33(1), pp. 259–321).

Manne, Robert (1999), 'The Whitlam Revolution' in Robert Manne (ed.), *The Australian Century: Political Struggle in the Building of a Nation*, Melbourne, Victoria: Griffin Press.

Marr, David & Marian Wilkinson (2003), *Dark Victory*, Crows Nest, New South Wales: Allen & Unwin.

Marsh, Ian (1990), 'Liberal Priorities, the Lib-Lab Pact and the Requirements for Policy Influence', *Parliamentary Affairs* Vol. 43(3), (pp. 292–321).

Marston, Geoffrey (1993), 'The United Kingdom's Part in the Preparation of the European Convention on Human Rights, 1950', *International and Comparative Law Quarterly* (Vol. 42(4), pp. 796–826).

Marx, Karl [1843] (1978), 'The German Ideology' in Robert C. Tucker (ed.), *The Marx-Engels Reader*, New York: W. W. Norton & Co.

Merton, Robert K. (1967), 'On Sociological Theories of the Middle Range' in Robert K. Merton, *On Theoretical Sociology: Five Essays, Old and New*, New York: The Free Press, pp. 39–72.

Milne, David (1982), *The New Canadian Constitution*, Toronto: James Lorimer.

——(1986), *Tug of War: Ottawa and the Provinces Under Trudeau and Mulroney*, Toronto: James Lorimer.

Minkin, L. (1992), *The Contentious Alliance: Trade Unions and the Labour Party*, Edinburgh: Edinburgh University Press.

Moravcsik, Andrew (2000), 'The Origins of Human Rights Regimes: Democratic Delegation in Postwar Europe', *International Organization* (Vol. 52(2), pp. 217–52).

Morrison, John (2001), *Reforming Britain: New Labour, New Constitution?*, London: Pearson Education.

Morton, Desmond (2001), *A Short History of Canada*, Toronto, Ontario: McClelland & Stewart (5th edition).

Morton, Frederick (1992), 'The Charter Revolution and the Court Party', *Osgoode Hall Law Journal* (Vol. 30(3), pp. 627–52).

——& Rainer Knopff (2000), *The Charter Revolution and the Court Party*, Peterborough, Ontario: Broadview Press.

Murphy QC, Lionel (1974), *Why Australia Needs a Bill of Rights*, Canberra: Australian Government Publishing Service.

Myddelton, David (1994), *The Power to Destroy: A Study of the British Tax System*, London: Society for Individual Freedom.

New Zealand, Council for Civil Liberties (1962), *Annual Report*, Wellington: New Zealand Council for Civil Liberties.

New Zealand, Government (1984), *Human Rights in New Zealand*, Wellington: Ministry of External Relations and Trade.

——(1985), *A Bill of Rights for New Zealand: A White Paper*, Wellington: Government Printer.

New Zealand, Goverment (1987), *White Paper on a Bill of Right: Report of the Department of Justice*, Wellington: Goverment Printer.

New Zealand, National Party (1960), *General Election Policy*, Wellington: National Party.

New Zealand, Human Rights Commission (1986), *A Guide to the Proposed Bill of Rights in Question and Answer Form*, Wellington: Human Rights Commission.

New Zealand, Parliament, Constitutional Reform Committee (1952), *Report*, Wellington: Government Printer.

——(1965), *Evidence Presented to the Constitutional Reform Committee, 1964, on the New Zealand Bill of Rights*, Wellington: Government Printer.

New Zealand, Parliament, Justice and Law Reform Committee (NZ Parliament) (1985–6), *Submissions on 'A Bill of Rights for New Zealand: A White Paper'*, (Vol. 5) Wellington Goverment: Printer.

New Zealand, Parliament, Justice and Law Reform Committee (1988), *Final Report of the Justice and Law Reform (New Zealand Committee on a White Paper on a Bill of Rights for New Zealand)*, Wellington: Government Printer.

New Zealand, Parliament (Various), *New Zealand Parliamentary Debates* (Hansard), Wellington: Government Printer.

New Zealand, Parliament, Public Petitions M to Z Committee (1961), *Report of Public Petitions M to Z Committee 1961 on the Petition of J. Scott-Davidson and Others, Together with Written Submission Made to the Committee*, Wellington: Government Printer.

New Zealand, Statistics New Zealand (1998), *People Born Overseas: 1996 Census of Population and Dwellings*, Wellington: Statistics New Zealand.

Newton, Velma (1988), *Commonwealth Caribbean Legal Systems: A Study of Small Jurisdictions*, Bridgetown, Barbados: Triumph Publications.

Nicol, Danny (2001), *EC Membership and the Judicialization of British Politics*, Oxford: Oxford University Press.

O'Neill, Onora (2002), *A Question of Trust: The BBC Reith Lectures*, Cambridge: Cambridge University Press.

Orange, Claudia (1987), *The Treaty of Waitangi*, Wellington: Bridget Williams Books.

Ottolenghi, Emanuele (2001), 'Why Direct Election Failed in Israel', *Journal of Democracy* (Vol. 12(4), pp. 109–22).

Palmer, Geoffrey (1968), 'A Bill of Rights for New Zealand' in Kenneth James Keith (ed.), *Essays on Human Rights*, Wellington: Victoria University Press.

——(1979), *Unbridled Power?: An Interpretation of New Zealand's Constitution and Government*, Wellington: Oxford University Press.

——(1987), *Unbridled Power: An Interpretation of New Zealand's Constitution and Government*, Auckland: Oxford University Press.

——(1992), *New Zealand's Constitution in Crisis: Reforming Our Political System*, Dunedin: McIndoe.

——(2004), 'Muldoon and the Constitution' in Margaret Clark (ed.), *Muldoon Revisited*, Palmerston North, New Zealand: Dunmore Press.

——& Matthew Palmer (1997), *Bridled Power: New Zealand Government Under MMP*, South Melbourne, Victoria: Oxford University Press.

Parkinson, Charles O. H. (2007), *Bills of Rights and Decolonization: The Emergence of Human Rights Instruments in Britain's Overseas Territories*, Oxford: Oxford University Press.

Patapan, Haig (1997*a*), *The Liberal Politics of Rights: Changing Constitutionalism and the Bill of Rights Debate in Australia and Canada*, PhD dissertation, University of Toronto.

——(1997*b*), 'Competing Visions of Liberalism: Theoretical Underpinnings of the Bill of Rights Debate in Australia', *Melbourne University Law Review* (Vol. 21(2), pp. 497–514).

Pearson, Rt. Hon. Lester (1968), *Federalism for the Future: A Statement of Policy by the Government of Canada*, Ottawa: Government Printer.

Plourde, Michel, Héléne Duval, & Pierre Georgeault (eds.) (*c.*2000), *La Français au Québec: 400 ans d'histoire et de vie* [Saint Laurent, Québec]: Fides.

Power, Michael (1997), *The Audit Society: Rituals of Verification*, Oxford: Oxford University Press.

Ramsay, Janet (2007), 'Policy Activism on a "Wicked Issue": The Building of Australian Feminist Policy on Domestic Violence in the 1970s', *Australian Feminist Studies* (Vol. 22(53), pp. 247–56).

Reid, John Phillip (1986), *Constitutional History of the American Revolution: The Authority of Rights*, Madison, Wisconsin: University of Wisconsin Press.

Rishworth, Paul (1995), 'The Birth and Rebirth of the Bill of Rights', in Grant Hunscroft & Paul Rishworth (eds.), *Rights and Freedoms: The New Zealand Bill of Rights Act 1990 and the Human Rights Act 1993*, Wellington: Brooker's.

Romanov, Roy, John Whyte, & Howard Leeson (1984), *Canada ... Notwithstanding: The Making of Constitution 1976–1982*, Toronto: Carswell/Methuen.

Rosenberg, Gerald (2008), *The Hollow Hope – Can Courts Bring About Social Change?*, Chicago; London: University of Chicago Press (2nd edition).

Royal Commission on Bilingualism and Biculturalism (1967), *Final Report*, Ottawa: Queen's Printer.

Rundle, Gary (2001), *The Opportunist: John Howard and the Triumph of Reaction* (Quarterly Essay No. 3), Melbourne: Black Inc.

Russell, Peter H. (1983), 'The Political Purposes of the Charter', *Canadian Bar Review* (Vol. 61(1), pp. 1–33).

——Rainer Knopff, & Ted Morton (eds.) (1989), *Federalism and the Charter: Leading Constitutional Decisions*, Ottawa: Carleton University Press.

Rynhold, Jonathan (2007), 'Cultural Shift and Foreign Policy Change: Israel and the Making of the Oslo Accords', *Cooperation and Conflict* (Vol. 42(4), pp. 419–40).

Sanders, Douglas E. (1983), 'The Indian Lobby' in Keith Banting & Richard Simeon (eds.), *And No One Cheered: Federalism, Democracy and the Constitution Act*, Toronto: Methuen.

Scarborough, Elinor (1995), 'Materialist-Postmaterialist Value Orientations' in Jan W.Van Deth & Elinor Scarborough, *The Impact of Values*, Oxford: Oxford University Press.

Scarman, Lord Leslie (1974), *English Law – the New Dimension*, London: Stevens.

Schauer, Frederick (2005), 'On the Migration of Constitutional Ideas', *Connecticut Law Review* (Vol. 37, pp. 907–19).

Scheppele, Kim Lane (2000), 'Constitutional Interpretation After Regimes of Horror', Public Law and Legal Theory Research Paper No. 05, University of Pennsylvania Law School.

——(2003), 'Aspirational and Aversive Constitutionalism: The Case for Studying Cross-Constitutional Influence Through Negative Models', *International Journal of Constitutional Law* (Vol. 1(2), pp. 296–324).

Schwartz, Bernard (1977), *The Great Rights of Mankind: A History of the American Bill of Rights*, New York: Oxford University Press.

Scott, Francis (1959), *The Canadian Constitution and Human Rights: Four Lectures*, [Ottawa]: Canadian Broadcasting Corporation.

Scott, Keith (1999), *Gareth Evans*, St Leonards, New South Wales: Allen & Unwin.

Scott, Kenneth John (1962), *The New Zealand Constitution*, Oxford: Oxford University Press.

Scott, Walter (1956), *Civil Liberties in New Zealand*, Wellington: New Zealand Council for Civil Liberties.

Shapiro, Martin (2002), 'The Success of Judicial Review and Democracy' in Martin Shapiro & Alec Stone Sweet, *On Law, Politics and Judicialization*, Oxford: Oxford University Press.

——& Alec Stone Sweet (2002), *On Law, Politics and Judicialization*, Oxford: Oxford University Press.

Sharfman, Dafnah (*c.*1993), *Living Without a Constitution: Civil Rights in Israel*, Armonk, New York; London: M.E. Sharpe.

Simmons, Beth A., Frank Dobbin, & Geoffrey Garrett (2006), 'Introduction: The International Diffusion of Liberalism', *International Organization* (Vol. 60(4), pp. 781–810).

Simon, Rita J. & Jean M. Landis (1990), 'Trends in Public Support for Civil Liberties and Due Process in Israeli Society', *Social Science Quarterly* (Vol. 71(1), pp. 93–104).

Society of Conservative Lawyers (1976), *Another Bill of Rights?*, London: [Society of Conservative Lawyers].

Spencer, Herbert (1982), 'The Man Versus the State [1884]' in Herbert Spencer, *The Man Versus The State with Six Essays on Government, Society and Freedom*, Indianapolis, Indiana: Liberty Fund Inc.

Stevenson, Garth (1999), *Community Besieged: The Anglophone Minority and the Politics of Quebec*, Montreal: McGill-Queen's University Press.

Sturgess, Garry & Philip Chubb (1988), *Judging the World: Law and Politics in the World's Leading Courts*, Sydney; London: Butterworths.

Taggart, Michael (1998), 'Tugging on Superman's Cape: Lessons from Experience with the New Zealand Bill of Rights Act 1990', *Public Law* (pp. 266–87).

Tarnopolsky, Walter S. (1968), 'A Constitutionally Entrenched Charter of Human Rights – Why Now?', *Saskatchewan Law Review* (Vol. 33(4), pp. 247–52).

——(1975), *The Canadian Bill of Rights*, Ottawa: McClelland & Stewart (2nd edition).

Tavan, Gwenda (2005), *The Long, Slow Death of White Australia*, Carlton North, Victoria: Scribe Publications.

Thornton, Peter (1989), *Decade of Decline: Civil Liberties in the Thatcher Years*, London: National Council for Civil Liberties.

Tocqueville, Alexis de [1835/40] (1969), *Democracy in America*, New York: Harper Collins.

Tranter, Bruce (2003), 'The Australian Constitutional Referendum of 1999: Evaluating Explanations of Republican Voting,' *Electoral Studies* (Vol. 22(4), pp. 677–701).

Tribe, Lawrence H. (1980), 'The Puzzling Persistence of Process-Based Constitutional Theories', *Yale Law Journal* (Vol. 89(6), pp. 1063–80).

Trudeau, Pierre [1964] (1996), 'We Need a Bill of Rights' in Pierre Trudeau, *Against the Current – Selected Writings 1939–1996* (ed. Gérard Pelletier) Toronto: McClelland & Stewart.

Tsebelis, George (2002), *Veto Players: How Political Institutions Work*, Princeton, New Jersey: Princeton University Press.

Uhr, J. (2002), 'Explicating the Australian Senate', *Journal of Legislative Studies* (Vol. 8 (3), pp. 3–26).

Van Deth, Jan W. (1995), 'Introduction: The Concept of Values' in Jan W. Van Deth & Elinor Scarborough, *The Impact of Values*, Oxford: Oxford University Press.

——— & Elinor Scarborough (1995), *The Impact of Values*, Oxford: Oxford University Press.

Versteeg, Mila (2008), 'Designed by Diffusion? A Conceptual Framework for the Cross-National Study of Human Rights' (unpublished manuscript on file with author).

Weingast, Barry R. (1997), 'The Political Foundations of Democracy and the Rule of Law', *American Political Science Review* (Vol. 91(2), pp. 245–63).

Weinrib, Lorraine Eisenstat (1999), 'Canada's Constitutional Revolution: From Legislative to Constitutional State', *Israel Law Review* (Vol. 33(1), pp. 13–50).

——— (2001), 'The Activist Constitution' in Paul Howe & Peter H. Russell (eds.), *Judicial Power and Canadian Democracy*, Montreal: McGill-Queen's University Press.

——— (2002), 'Canada's Charter: Comparative Influences, International Stature' in Debra M. McAllister & Adam M. Dodek (eds.), *The Charter at Twenty: Law and Practice*, Toronto: Ontario Bar Association.

Whitlam, Gough (1979), *The Truth of the Matter*, Harmondsworth; New York: Penguin.

——— (1985), *The Whitlam Government, 1972–1975*, Ringwood, Victoria: Viking.

Williams, Cynthia (1986), 'The Changing Nature of Citizen Rights' in Alan Cairns and Cynthia Williams (eds.), *Constitutionalism, Citizenship and Society in Canada*, Toronto: University of Toronto Press.

Williams, George (1999), *Human Rights Under the Australian Constitution*, Melbourne; Oxford: Oxford University Press.

——— (2004), *The Case for an Australian Bill of Rights: Freedom in the War on Terror*, Sydney: University of New South Wales Press.

Woodhouse, Sir Owen (1979), *Government Under the Law* (J. C. Beaglehole Memorial Lecture), Wellington: New Zealand Council for Civil Liberties.

Woods, Patricia J. (2009), 'The Ideological Foundations of Israel's 'Constitutional Revolution'', *Political Research Quarterly* (Vol. 62(4), pp. 811–24).

Woolf, Lord Harry (1995), 'Droit Public – English Style', *Public Law* (pp. 57–71).

Yuchtman-Ya'ar, Ephraim (2002), 'Value Priorities in Israeli Society: An Examination of Inglehart's Theory of Modernization and Cultural Varation', *Comparative Sociology* (Vol. 1(3–4), pp. 347–67).

Zander, Michael (1997), *A Bill of Rights?*, London: Sweet & Maxwell (4th edition).

Zines, Leslie (1991), *Constitutional Change in the Commonwealth*, Cambridge: Cambridge University Press.

Court decisions

Australia

A-G (Victoria) v. Commonwealth (1945) 71 CLR 237 ((First) Pharmaceutical Benefits Case).

Attorney-General (Victoria) ex rel. Black v. Commonwealth (the *DOGS* case) (1981) 146 CLR 559; 33 ALR 321.

Australian Capital Television Pty Ltd v. Commonwealth (1992) 177 CLR 106.

Australian Communist Party v. Commonwealth (1951) 83 CLR 1.

Commonwealth v. Tasmania (the *Tasmanian Dam* case) (1983) 158 CLR 1.

Cunliffe v. Commonwealth (1994) 182 CLR 272.

Federal Council of the British Medical Association in Australia v. Commonwealth (1949) 79 CLR 201 (Second Pharmaceutical Benefits Case).

Koowarta v. Bjelke-Peterson (1982) 153 CLR 168.

Kruger v. Commonwealth (1997) 190 CLR 1.

Lange v. Australian Broadcasting Tribunal (1997) 189 CLR 520.

McGinty v. Western Australia (1996) 186 CLR 140.

Mabo v. Queensland (No. 2) (1992) 175 CLR 1; 107 ALR 1.

Minister of State for Immigration and Ethnic Affairs v. Teoh (1995) 183 CLR 27; 128 ALR 353.

Nationwide News Pty Ltd v. Wills (1992) 177 CLR 1.

Stephens v. Western Australian Newspapers Ltd (1994) 182 CLR 211.

Theophanous v. Herald & Weekly Times Ltd (1994) 182 CLR 104.

Wik Peoples v. Queensland (1996) 187 CLR 1; (1996) 121 ALR 129.

Canada

Reference Re: Alberta Statutes [1938] SCR 100.

Attorney-General for Alberta v. Attorney-General for Canada [1947] AC 503.

Attorney-General of Canada v. Caard (1975) [1976] 1 SCR 170.

Attorney-General of Canada v. Lavell [1973] 38 DLR 3d 481.

Attorney-General of Ontario v. Reale [1975] 2 SCR 624.

Bliss v. Attorney-General of Canada [1979] 1 SCR 183.

Brownridge v. The Queen [1972] SCR 926.

Co-operative Committee on Japanese Canadians v. Attorney-General for Canada [1946] SCR 248; Privy Council [1947] 4 DLR 529.

Cunningham v. Tomey Homma [1903] AC 151.

Curr v. The Queen [1972] SCR 889.

Edridge v. British Columbia (A.G) [1997].

Lepper v. The Queen [1974] SCR 195.

Nadan v. The King [1926] AC 482 (Privy Council).

Quong Wing v. The King [1914] 49 SCR 440.

Re Drummond Wren [1945] 4 DLR 674 (Ontario High Court).

Reference Re Amendment of the Constitution (No. 3) (1981) 120 DLR (3d) 385.

Reference Re Amendment of the Constitution of Canada (No. 1) (1981) 7 Man. R. (2d) 269; 117 DLR (3d) 1 (CA).

Reference Re Amendment of the Constitution of Canada (No. 2) (1981) 118 DLR (3d) 1 (Nfld. CA).

Reference Re Amendment of the Constitution of Canada, (Nos 1, 2, and 3) [1981] 1 SCR 753, 125 DLR (3d) 1.

Reference re Legislative Authority of Parliament to Alter or Replace the Senate (1979) 102 DLR (3d) 1.

Reference re: Alberta Information Act [1938] SCR 100.

R. v. Drybones [1970] SCR 282.

R. v. Miller [1977] 2 SCR 680.

R. v. Big M Drug Mart Ltd [1985]

Regina v. Gonzales [1962] 32 DLR (2d) 290.

R. v. Butler [1992]

R. v. Edwards books and Art Ltd [1985]

R. v. Keegsa [1990]

Robertson and Rosetanni v. The Queen [1963] SCR 651.

Saumur v. City of Quebec & Attorney-General of Quebec [1953] SCR 299.

Singh v. Canada (Minister of Immigration and Employment) [1985] 1 SCR 177.

Switzman v. Elbling & Attorney-General of Quebec (the *Padlock* case) [1957] SCR 285.

The Queen v. Burnshine [1974] SCR 693.

England/United Kingdom/Privy Council

Anufrijeva v. Southwark LBC [2003] Campbell v. MGN Ltd [2004].
Dr. Bonham's Case [1610] 8 Co. Rep. 107.

McLean v. Procurator Fiscal Fort William [2001].

Pratt v. Attorney-General [1994] 2 AC 1, [1993] 4 All ER 769.

R v. Ministry of Defence, ex parte Smith [1996] QB 517 (CA).

R v. Secretary of State for the Home Department, ex parte Brind [1991] 1 AC 696 (HL).

R. v. Secretary of State for Transport, ex parte Factortame Ltd [1990] 2 AC 85.

Wednesbury Corporation v. Ministry of Housing and Local Government [1965] 1 WLR 261.

Wilson v. First County Trust [2003] UKHL 40, [2003] 3 WLR 568.

European Court of Human Rights

Dudgeon v. UK (1982) 4 EHRR 149.

East African Asians v. UK (1973) 3 EHRR 76.

Osmond v. UK (1998) 29 EHRR 245.

Sunday Times v. UK (1979–80) 2 EHRR 245.

Sunday Times v. UK (No. 2) (1992) 14 EHRR 229.

Young, James and Webster v. UK (Nos. 7611/76, 7806/77) (1982) 4 EHRR 38.

France

Associations Law Decision One, 71-44 Déclarations de Conformite (DC) (16 July 1971).

Israel

Nevo v. National Labour Court & Others [1988] SC Is 136.
Universal City Studios & Others v. Film & Theatre Censorship Board & Others [1988] SC Is 229.

New Zealand

Combined State Unions v. State Services Co-ordinating Committee [1982] 1 NZLR 742.
Fitzgerald v. Muldoon [1976] 2 NZLR 615.
Hopkinson v. Police [2004] 3 NZLR 703 (HC).
Hoskins v. Runting [2005] 1 NZLR 1 (CA).
Moonen v. Film and Literature Board of Review [2000] 2 NZLR 9 (CA).
Simpson v. Attorney General (*Baigent's* case) [1994] 3 NZLR 667.
Taylor v. New Zealand Poultry Board [1984] 1 NZLR.
Westco Lagan Ltd v. Attorney-General [2001] 1 NZLR 40 (HC).

United Nations Human Rights Committee communication

Toonen v. Australia, UN Doc. CCPR /C/50/D/488/1992 [Mar. 31, 1994].

United States

Lochner v. New York [1905] 198 US 45.
United States v. Carolene Products Company [1938] 304 US 144.

Newspaper articles

The Australian
'Rights Push Finally Put Out of its Misery', *The Australian*, 23 April 2010.
The Dominion (*Wellington, NZ*)
'Unacceptable to Opposition – East', *The Dominion*, 3 April 1985.
'A Bill of Rights?', *The Dominion*, 28 April 1986.
'Maori Advisers Give Treaty Supremacy', *The Dominion*, 22 September 1987.

The Express (*UK*)

'Human Rights Act is Just Wrecking Britain', *The Express*, 18 March 2005.

Globe and Mail (*Canada*)

'Little Success at Ministers' Conference on Changing Constitution', *Globe and Mail*, 7 February 1979.
'Rights Charter would Bind Provinces as Trudeau Presents Plan; NDP offers Support, Tories will Fight Move', *Globe and Mail*, 3 October 1980.
'PM's push for "Cerebral" Rights but Not Property Rights Criticised', *Globe and Mail*, 18 October 1980.

'NDP Gives Pledge of Its Full Backing on Patriation Bill', *Globe and Mail*, 3 February 1981.
'Four New Democrat MPs Break Ranks on Patriation', *Globe and Mail*, 19 February 1981.
'Fascist Element in Tactics of PCs – Trudeau', *Globe and Mail*, 11 April 1981.
'Most Feel Trudeau Patriation Plan Will Help Unite Country, Poll Says', *Globe and Mail*, 14 May 1981.
'Poll Shows 72 Per cent Questioned Favor Rights Charter in Constitution', *Globe and Mail*, 10 November 1981.
'Alberta Wants a Definition of Native Rights', *Globe and Mail*, 19 November 1981.
'Native Rights Would Create Land Problems, Ottawa Told', *Globe and Mail*, 19 November 1981.

The Guardian (*UK*)

'Curbing Executive Power', *The Guardian*, 2 October 2000.
'Enshrine These Rights: With No Consultation the Public Didn't Buy into the Human Rights Act. We Can Correct that Now', *The Guardian*, 27 June 2005.
'Cabinet Revolt over Straw's Rights and Responsibilities Plan', *The Guardian*, 4 November 2008.
'Coalition Reconsidering Tory Plan to Scrap Human Rights Act', *The Guardian*, 19 May 2010.

Jerusalem Post

'Who Needs a Bill of Rights', *Jerusalem Post*, 24 November 1989.
'Shamir Promises Orthodox to Freeze Human Rights Bill', *The Jerusalem Post*, 27 November 1989.
'Gays Fight for Job Rights', *Jerusalem Post*, 25 June 1990.
'Barak to Review IDF Orders on Homosexuals', *Jerusalem Post*, 7 February 1993.

Liberator (*NZ*)

'Society's Aims Taken Notice of in Nationalists' Policy', *Liberator* (Constitutional Society), June 1960.
'Help This Petition for Our Liberties', *Liberator* (Constitutional Society), September 1960.
'Long Job Ended on Constitution', *Liberator* (Constitutional Society), June 1961.
'No Loss If Bill of Rights Is Dropped', *Liberator* (Constitutional Society), October 1962.

The Gazette (*Montreal*)

'Not Against Bill of Rights', *The Gazette*, 3 March 1960.

New Zealand Herald

'Storm Clouds Gathering over Bill of Rights', *New Zealand Herald*, 16 January 1984.
'Rights Bill Has 'Dangers'', *New Zealand Herald*, 8 April 1985.

'Economic and Social Rights Not Recognized in Draft Bill', *New Zealand Herald*, 12 April 1985.
'Government Moving Too Fast Says Mr Palmer', *New Zealand Herald*, 22 April 1985.
'Hardly a Murmur as Rights Bill Passed', *New Zealand Herald*, 19 July 1993.

Ottawa Journal
'Frost Urges Conference on Overall Bill of Rights', *Ottawa Journal*, 9 September 1958.

The Press (*Christchurch, New Zealand*)
'Council for Civil Liberties Opposes Bill of Rights', *The Press*, 29 August 1986.

The Sun (*United Kingdom*)
'Let's Shut Our Door to Terror Says Smith', *The Sun*, 11 October 2001.

Sydney Morning Herald
'Bill "Threatens Freedom" – Cleric's Attack', *Sydney Morning Herald*, 26 December 1973.
'Rights Bill "Threat" Support', *Sydney Morning Herald*, 28 December 1973.
'Bishops Attack Rights Bill, Say Religion at Risk', *Sydney Morning Herald*, 25 January 1974.
'Letter from Ken Buckley, President of the Council for Civil Liberties', *Sydney Morning Herald*, 29 January 1974.
'Police Fear Effects of Rights Bill', *Sydney Morning Herald*, 9 March 1974.
"External Powers' Threat to States – Menzies on Human Rights', *Sydney Morning Herald*, 15 March 1974.
'Democrats Seek Bill of Rights Deal', *Sydney Morning Herald*, 10 March 1986.
'Bill of Rights Now a Certainty', *Sydney Morning Herald*, 13 March 1986.
'Bill of Rights Badly Marketed', *Sydney Morning Herald*, 19 March 1986.
'Rights Bill Fault', *Sydney Morning Herald*, 26 May 1986.
'Howard Warning on Rights Bill', *Sydney Morning Herald*, 9 June 1986.
'Bill of Rights Not Worth the Trouble', *Sydney Morning Herald*, 18 August 1986.
'Bill of Rights Dead, and Now Buried', *Sydney Morning Herald*, 19 August 1986.
'Row Over Referendum Campaign Worsens', *Sydney Morning Herald*, 20 July 1988.
'High Court Backing For Free Speech', *Sydney Morning Herald*, 1 October 1992.
'Libs Desert Fraser Over Bill of Rights', *Sydney Morning Herald*, 26 August 2000.
'Empowering AS10 in Planned Terrorism Bill Endangers Rights', *Sydney Morning Herald*, 21 June 2002.
'Bill of Rights looks Dead in the Water' *Sydney Morning Herald*, 17 February 2010.

The Times (*London*)
'Shawcross Advocates Bill of Rights', *The Times*, 14 May 1970.
'Call for Bill of Rights for Scotland', *The Times*, 2 February 1978.

'Mr Jenkins Calls for British Bill of Rights', *The Times*, 30 September 1979.
'Spycatcher Provokes Case For and Against Bill of Rights', *The Times*, 28 September 1987.
'A Charter of Rights that Has Shown Itself Wrong', *The Times*, 23 October 1989.
'Plea for More Referendums as One in Two Endorses PR', *The Times*, 25 April 1991.
'Kinnock Promises to Put Britain in First Division', *The Times*, 2 October 1991.
'Courts Prepare for Act that Will Change Lives', *The Times*, 26 October 1998.

Winnipeg Free Press

'Westerners Favour Rights Bill by 80% Survey Shows', *Winnipeg Free Press*, 22 October 1981.

Archival Material

Australia

Australia, Parliament, Senate, Standing Committee on Constitutional and Legal Affairs (1985), *Submissions on a Bill of Rights for Australia*, Parliamentary Library, Canberra.

Canada

Canada, Parliament, House of Commons, Special Committee on Human Rights (1960), RG 14: Records of Parliament, Accession Number: 1987–1988/146, National Archives of Canada, Ottawa.
Canada, Parliament, Special Joint Committee of the Senate and of the House of Commons on the Constitution of Canada (1980–1) [Hays-Joyal Committee], RG 14: Records of Parliament, Accession Number: 1990–91/119/59-73, National Archives of Canada, Ottawa.
Canada, Parliament, Special Joint Committee of the Senate and of the House of Commons on the Constitution of Canada (1970–2) [Molgat-Maguigon Committee], RG 14: Records of Parliament, Accession Number: 1991–92/59-66, National Archives of Canada, Ottawa.

Israel

Israel, Knesset, Constitution, Law and Justice Committee (1992), *Protocols* [in Hebrew], Knesset Archives, Jerusalem.

New Zealand

New Zealand, Government, Attorney-General's Department (1960–4), *Bill of Rights Papers*, Agency: AGCS, Record: 18/1/253 Part 1, Archives New Zealand, Wellington.
New Zealand, Government, Department of Justice (1984–90), *Bill of Rights Papers*, Agency: ABVP, Series: 7410, Archives New Zealand, Wellington.
New Zealand, Parliament, Justice and Law Reform Committee (1989–90), Submissions on the New Zealand Bill of Rights Bill: as received by the Justice and

Law Reform Select Committee of the House of Representatives of New Zealand, 1989-90, Parliamentary Library, Wellington.

New Zealand Council for Civil Liberties (Various), *Archive*, Alexander Turnbull Library, National Archive of New Zealand, Wellington.

United Kingdom

Charter 88 (Various), *Archive*, University of Essex Library.

Constitutional Reform Centre (Various), *Archive*, British Library of Political and Economic Science Library, London School of Economics.

Great Britain, Foreign Office, Political Departments (1959), *General Correspondence* (FO 371/146087), National Archives, Kew.

National Council for Civil Liberties (Various), *Archive*, University of Hull Library.

Interviews

Aloni, Shulamit, 19 October 2009.
Grieve MP, Dominic, 7 March 2007.
Howe, Brian, 8 February 2005.
Hunt, Rt. Hon. Jonathan, 21 June 2005.
Lester of Herne Hill QC, Lord, 18 May 2005.
Mahameed, Hashem, 9 November 2009.
Mason, Sir Anthony, 12 January 2005.
Meridor, Dan, 20 October 2009.
Northey, Richard, 3 November 2006.
Palmer, Sir Geoffrey, 16 November 2004.
Rae MP, Bob, 26 May 2009.
Romanov, Roy, 18 April 2005.
Rubinstein, Amnon, 19 October 2009.
Tate, Michael, 11 May 2005.
Vershubski, Mordechai, 25 October 2009.
Wadham, John, 18 June 2005.
Weir, Stuart, 27 June 2005.
Wilson MP, Hon. Margaret, 11 November 2004.

Index